UNIVERSITY OF
GLOUCESTERSHIRE

at Cheltenham and Gloucester

THE OFFICIAL DICTIONARY OF PURCHASING AND SUPPLY

Terminology for Buyers and Suppliers

H K COMPTON   ·   D A JESSOP

Published by Liverpool Business Publishing
an imprint of
Liverpool Academic Press

© H. K. Compton and D. A. Jessop 1995, 2001

This version first published in Great Britain by Liverpool Business Publishing.

A CIP catalogue record for this book is available from the British Library.

ISBN 1 903500 01 X (Paperback)
ISBN 1 903500 02 8 (Hardback)

Typeset by PACE Image & Print, Birkenhead.
Printed and bound by Athenaeum Press Ltd., Gateshead, Tyne & Wear.

Introduction

ORGANIZATION AND PRESENTATION OF TERMS

So far as the variety of sources and disciplines permit, we have drafted our text in line with **BS 3669**, *The Selection, Formation and Definition of Technical Terms.* The sequence of words has thus been kept as consistent as possible so that, as with commodity coding and other data organization, the primary word is used as the head word, followed by any qualifying adjective, phrase, etc. We have included within the dictionary an A-Z of orders and contracts. Users should look within this section for definitions of approaches to ordering, types of contract and related topics.

Where the explanation or definition of a term includes another term, itself defined in our dictionary, we have presented that term in capitals thus:

> **contango.** (com) Premium paid by a buyer of FUTURES to the seller for the buyer's postponement of delivery from the date due to a later one. Sometimes referred to as FORWARDATION.

Sources

British Standards Institution (BSI), by whose permission material has been reproduced and from whom copies of the relevant standards may be obtained at:

The British Standards Institution,
Linford Wood,
Milton Keynes,
MK 14 6LE.

A message from the British Standards Institution

Quality starts with standards. Standards lay down the criteria for products, processes and systems, to ensure that they will do the job properly. They influence every aspect of production, from design to after-sales service. They apply from the time a product is conceived, through design, development and manufacture, to testing for fitness for purpose and durability.

The benefits of standards include: easier design and manufacture through the provision of standard components more efficient, cost effective and easily maintained production systems; greater consumer and customer confidence in products and in the companies that manufacture them.

These benefits are strongly endorsed by the British Standards Society, the UK association for standards users which is administered by the BSI, and exists to promote the application of standards throughout industry and the public sector.

BSI recommend for general reference the following standards:

BS 4778: Part 1: (ISO 8402), *Quality Vocabulary* - international terms.
BS 5532: (ISO 3534), *Statistical Terminology* - a glossary of terms relating to probability and general terms relating to statistics.
BS 5750: (ISO 9000/EN29000, ISO90004/EN 29004) *Quality Systems.*
CEN/CENELEC *Internal Regulations, Part 2* – common rules for standard work.
ISO/IEC *Guide 2* – general terms and their definitions concerning standardisation and related activities.

We have omitted the dates and numbers of standards referred to in the text. This has been done deliberately because of the frequency of change. Readers should check wit · the BSI Standards Catalogue that they are working with the latest editions. The relevant 'EN' and other numbers will be found in the above catalogue.

Chartered Institute of Management Accountants, to which body thanks are expressed for permission to quote from their terminology. Much is particularly appropriate for those engaged in buying and selling, and those dealing with value and price/cost related problems. A major source book in this connection is their publication *CIMA Management Accounting – Official Terminology.*

International Chamber of Commerce (ICC UK), which asked us to include its incoterms: this has been achieved in outline only. The full text and notes will be found in their publication 'Incoterms 2000'. Incoterms are grouped under the heading 'INCOTERMS'. Readers requiring authentic translations are directed to ICC publication no. 417, *Key Words in International Trade,* which gives French, German, Spanish and Italian.

Chartered Institute of Purchasing and Supply. We are indebted to the CIPS which was instrumental in providing the impetus for this work, which is intended to complement the Institute's education scheme.

Simpler Trade Procedures Board (*SITPRO*). We are grateful for their permission and for their kindly checking and aligning our entries which bear the initials SITPRO.

ACKNOWLEDGEMENT

Our thanks are given to Ian Longdin who kindly supplied entries covering relevant legislation, and acted as legal editor for the book.

DISCLAIMER

Although every effort has been made to authenticate, simplify and harmonize every entry we are sure that there will be gaps and gaffes and we welcome suggestions for the next edition. We apologise to anyone whose favourite term has been omitted, and refer readers to our 'exclusion clause', which we have adopted from the Chartered Institute of Management Accountants:

'No responsibility for loss occasioned to any person acting or refraining from action as a result of any material in this publication can be accepted by the authors or tbe publisher.'

Foreword

It is a privilege to contribute this Foreword to the *Official Dictionary of Purchasing and Supply* which originally appeared as the *Dictionary of Purchasing and Supply Management*. This new and greatly expanded publication has three strengths.

Firstly, it is a dictionary of *purchasing and supply*. In 1755 Samuel Johnson defined a dictionary as 'a book explaining the words of any language alphabetically'. The present dictionary with entries from ABC analysis to Z chart does that, but it does more. Word meanings and usage often derive from their context. By placing a word or expression firmly in the area of purchasing and supply the compilers enable users to see the exact meaning of a word or term without having to infer it from a variety of possible meanings or the context in which the word is used.

Secondly, it is an *official* dictionary. As such it will be a point of reference for all users of purchasing terminology whether academics, students or purchasing professionals.

Thirdly, like its predecessor, it is an invaluable aid to both busy writers and purchasing practitioners. In many instances the dictionary not only defines words but also provides a short but clear explanation of their application.

Dr. Johnson made a further observation about dictionaries: 'Dictionaries are like watches. The worst is better than none and the best cannot be expected to be quite true.' Since Johnson's time both watches and dictionaries have improved. The present dictionary is excellent and if there are any definitions that are "not quite true" I have not yet found them. I look forward to using the dictionary myself and I warmly commend it to everyone concerned with purchasing, logistics and related fields.

Kenneth Lysons
July 2001

Preface

Words are coins with which people trade ideas and communicate their needs for goods and services. Unless the words used are clear and correct the ideas, goods and services are also unlikely to be correct. The cynic who has worked in 'purchasing' or 'sales' for many years will doubtless observe that even accurate information will not always secure the correct response.

People throughout industry and trade are continuous communicators and those engaged in purchasing and supply and sales are 'primary communicators'. Those in 'purchasing' must understand and transmit the needs of the people for whom they make purchases to the suppliers. Similarly, those in 'sales' must understand the messages from the purchasing officers of their customers and translate these rapidly and accurately into instructions to their warehouse or production plant.

In preparing this dictionary it has been necessary to renew, update and harmonize definitions in a field which is changing continuously and rapidly. This has led to our spending considerable time rooting out the new jargon which clings to the growing network of communications both at home and internationally. An example of this is provided by e-commerce, which is now practised to some degree by most organizations, yet was in its infancy at the time the previous edition was published.

It would be foolish to pretend that those engaged in purchasing and supply use a range of language peculiar to their own area. Purchasing and supply is a wide-ranging field which touches business at many points and it therefore shares a terminology with sales and other areas. This in itself is a common cause of misunderstanding. The terminology included in this volume is much wider in scope than the title would suggest, and we hope it will contribute to the total communication network of those involved in industry and trade.

H K Compton
D A Jessop
2001

Abbreviations

Abbreviations are employed in this dictionary for three reasons.

1. To indicate the context in which the term defined, and the definition given, are employed.

These abbreviations are:

adm	administration
com	commerce
econ	economics
env	environment
EU	European Union
fin mkt	financial markets
HS	Health and Safety
IT	information technology
mar	marine
log	logistics
stats	statistics

2. To acknowledge the source or basis of a definition.

These are:

BS	British Standard (a relevant British Standard)
CIMA	Chartered Institute of Management Accountants
SITPRO	Simplification of Trade Procedures documentation

3. To indicate whether the term defined is a noun or a verb

These are:

n	noun
v	verb

A

ABC analysis. The application of PARETO'S PRINCIPLE to the analysis of supply data. If items in a store are arranged in descending order of usage-value and the cumulative number of items are plotted against the cumulative usage-value the result would be expected to show a curve of the general form associated with Pareto's Principle. In practice, typical observations are as follows: 'A'. 10% of items account for 70% total usage value; 'B'. 20% of items account for 20% total usage value; 'C'. 70% of items account for 10% total usage value and the rule is often abbreviated to the '80:20' Rule.

abrogate (law) Legal term for abolish, annul, cancel, repeal.

abrogation. A term used in marine insurance to signify that the insured party has abandoned the subject matter of the claim to the insurer to treat as a 'total loss'.

absolute advantage. (econ) The situation in which an enterprise (or State) can produce a product or substance at lower cost than others for the identical item.

absorption costing. (CIMA) Method of costing designed to ensure that total costs, fixed and variable, (direct and overhead) are recovered in the price of goods, etc.

accelerator. (econ) A change in demand for consumer goods which results in a comparatively large change in demand for capital plant supplying the goods.

acceptable quality level. *See* QUALITY, ACCEPTABLE LEVEL.

acceptance limits. *See* QUALITY CONTROL, of ACCEPTANCE LIMITS.

acceptance of goods. The buyer is deemed to have accepted goods when the buyer has had a reasonable opportunity of examining them and intimates acceptance, or does any act in relation to them which is inconsistent with the ownership of the seller. Sale of Goods Act 1979, Sale and Supply of Goods Act 1994).

acceptance of offer. *See* CONTRACT, ACCEPTANCE OF OFFER.

acceptance sampling. *See* QUALITY CONTROL, ACCEPTANCE SAMPLING.

acceptance. (SITPRO) The signing by a drawee of a usance (time or term) of a BILL OF EXCHANGE [DRAFT], which then binds him to pay the bill when due (at maturity).

acceptance. Agreement to meet an obligation. An essential element of a valid contract.

accepting bank. (SITPRO) A bank specifically nominated in a letter of credit as that on which a bill of exchange is to be drawn at a specified time.

access time. The time taken to obtain information from a computer memory store and its presentation to the user in legible and intelligible form. The term was devised for INFORMATION TECHNOLOGY but has implications for manually operated clerical memory/record systems.

accommodate/accommodation. (log) To provide space for something, e.g. storage space in a store, vacant numbers in a coding system. (adm) Adjustment to allow for different or new circumstances, e.g. during negotiations. (fin) A loan from a bank, or in some cases from a purchaser to a supplier for a contract upon which the supplier has a cash flow shortage in starting the contract.

accommodation bill. A bill of exchange signed by one person to 'accommodate' another. The person signing becomes the guarantor.

accommodation stock. *See* STOCK, ACCOMMODATION.

account, unit of in EU. *See* EUROPEAN CURRENCY UNIT.

account. (n) (CIMA) A structured record of monetary transactions such as purchasing transactions with suppliers, and internal transactions such as stores accounts of stock values, receipts, issues, returns, etc.

accounting stock. See STOCK, ACCOUNTING STOCK.

accounting, replacement cost accounting. *See* COST, REPLACEMENT COST, ACCOUNTING.

accounting. 1. the classification and recording of actual transactions in monetary terms. 2. the presentation and interpretation of the results of those transactions in order to assess performance over a period and the financial position at a given date. 3. the projection in monetary terms of future activities arising from alternative planned courses of action.

accreditation, test laboratories, certification of inspection bodies. (EU) The accreditation formally recognises the competence of the above by a process of expert technical assessment against agreed criteria. This involves regular surveillance and periodic assessment.

accretion. Increase in value of goods, with the passage of time, e.g. wines, timber,

cheeses; as opposed to DEPRECIATION.

accuracy. *See* QUALITY CONTROL, ACCURACY.

acid test ratio. Current liabilities divided by current assets (less stock).

acknowledgement* of contract/order. (*Note 'acknowledgment' alternative spelling). Act of recognition of receipt of a communication between parties. Usual context is 'acknowledgement of order'.

acquisition costs. *See* COSTS, ACQUISITION COSTS.

act of God. 'An extraordinary circumstance which could not have been foreseen and which could not have been guarded against.' *Pandorf v Hamilton 1886. See also* FORCE MAJEURE.

activity based costing. An accounting method in which variable and all overhead related expenses are specifically assigned to a business activity, rather than a section or department.

activity chart. One which presents in diagrammatic format the operational activities of operatives/machines, plant, etc. It may display working times, outputs, flow of supplies, etc.

activity sampling. A technique used in work measurement on such activities as fork lift truck operation, order picking, storekeeping, and so on.

ad idem. (law) Of the same mind. Agreement between parties on essential matters. An essential element of a valid contract.

ad valorem. According to value, i.e. not according to weight or other measure. A method commonly applied for computing freight and customs duty, etc.

added value. *See* VALUE ADDED.

addendum. Something such as a clause later added to a document.

adjuster. A person appointed to adjust a claim. For example a loss adjuster's role is to fairly minimise the cost of losses to be borne by an insurer.,

adjustment money. Sums paid to a supplier (or credit from him) by a purchaser in respect of a change in contract costs because of a VARIATION ORDER or ESCALATION CLAUSE, etc.

administration. The control and supervision of operations, practices and policies dictated by MANAGEMENT.

advance freight. *See* FREIGHT.

adversarial relationship. A relationship between buyer and seller in which it is felt that there is a fixed pool of benefits to be competed for. Any gain by one party is seen as a loss to the other. Each party seeks benefit at the expense of the other.

advertisement Any form of representation which is made in connection with a trade, business, craft or profession in order to promote the supply or transfer of goods or services.

Advertising Directive. (EU) This Directive aims to protect businesses and public from effects of misleading advertising.

advice note. (BS) A document sent to a customer advising him of impending delivery of supplies called for on his purchase order.

advising bank. (SITPRO) A bank, usually in a beneficiary's country, through which advice of a LETTER OF CREDIT is sent by the ISSUING BANK.

affiliated company. One of a group of two or more enterprises, one of which exercises control or influence over the other(s) by share ownership or other legitimate means.

affirm. To make a solemn statement.

affreightment. The contract for carriage of goods for a price which is called the freight.

against all risks. Term used in marine insurance meaning insured against all generally accepted risks.

agency bills. Bills of exchange drawn on and accepted by the UK branches of foreign banks, usually in London.

agent. A person, e.g. a buyer or salesperson, appointed to represent a firm (his or her principals) and who is 'held out as doing so' by them or who without contradiction claims to be an agent and commits the firm accordingly. Hence the importance of properly appointing someone to act as agent for a company's purchasing. *See also* CAVEAT SUBSCRIPTOR.

agent, commission agent. One who buys and sells goods for which a commission is usually paid on each transaction.

agent, del credere. An agent who, in return for extra commission, guarantees payment for what is sold.

agent, factoring agent. A mercantile agent who handles specific kinds of goods. He sells goods which come into his possession. He may do this with, or without, the consent of the principal for whom he sells on a commission basis.

agent, forwarding agent (also freight forwarder). A firm specialising in making arrangements for goods to be collected from a CONSIGNOR and passing them to a CARRIER for transport to their destination. The freight forwarder administers the documentation, etc. It is important to establish whether he accepts liability for the actual transit.

agent, manufacturer's agent. Differs from a SELLING AGENT in that s/he is usually restricted to a limited geographical area, may have sole agency and/or handle several manufacturers' lines; usually s/he has little freedom to negotiate or control product design **or** be involved in credit collection and risk.

agent, mercantile. One having in the customary course of his business (as such an agent) authority to: 1. sell, 2. consign for the purpose of sale, or 3. buy goods for such sale, or 4. raise money on the security of goods, Sale of Goods Act 1979.

agent, selling. Agent who takes on the marketing responsibilities for (usually) small firms, leaving the enterprise free to concentrate on production. Some agents carry the risks of credit loss and may negotiate or fix prices. *See also* AGENT, MANUFACTURERS'.

agent, shipping. One specialising in imports and exports of goods by sea and who deals with documentation, insurance, customs, cargo space, etc. May be connected with a shipping company.

aggregation. (EU) In order to determine whether the value of orders of a given kind reaches a THRESHOLD under the relevant directive, a buyer must combine, i.e. aggregate, the value of the orders.

aggregation period. (EU) The period over which a buying organization must aggregate requirements, taking thresholds into account.

agio. 1. The difference between nominal and actual values of a currency, and also the charge payable for conversion of the less valuable currency to the more valuable one. 2. An amount added to the sales price by whichever party accepts a COUNTER-PURCHASE to cover additional costs of disposing of the counter-purchase. 3. Charge for changing one currency for another.

agreement. A manifestation of mutual consent between two or more enterprises or persons. An 'agreement' is binding if it is legally enforceable. This will depend upon the provisions of the applicable law in the matter. An agreement may be either explicit or implicit, depending upon whether it is communicated in words spoken or written by the parties or by their actions. 'Agreement' is an essential component of a valid contract and may be made by any means whatever provided the parties communicate.

agreement, service level. An agreement between a SERVICE provider and a CUSTOMER quantifying the minimum acceptable service to the customer.

Agrément Board, The. *See* BRITISH BOARD OF AGRÉMENT.

air cushion vehicle. (log) A vehicle which rides on a cushion of air. The downward pressure of the air raises the vehicle for travel.

air rights. The effective use of otherwise vacant storage space, by the employment of elevated storage facilities such as high stacks, high racking, etc, handled by suitable equipment. The latter may be automated or semi-automated.

air waybill. *See* WAYBILL.

aisle. (log) The space reserved in a stores or distribution centre for the free passage of personnel and handling equipment.

aligned documentation. (SITPRO) *See* DOCUMENTATION, ALIGNED DOCUMENTATION

all-in contract. *See* ORDERS & CONTRACTS A-Z.

all-in price. *See* PRICE.

all-round price. *See* PRICE.

alligation. A method of ascertaining the proportions of substances in a mixture that will produce either a specified price per unit volume (or weight, etc.), or a required specific gravity.

allocated purchases. An item or items purchased and held for a specific task or project and which must not be issued for normal consumption.

allocated stock. *See* STOCK CONTROL, 'PRE-ALLOCATED' STOCK and STOCK, RESERVED STOCK.

allocation. 1. The sharing out between enterprises of available or potential production, products, services, sales, purchases, suppliers, customers, territories or markets, (illegal in many free enterprise economies). 2. The reservation of material for a specific purpose.

allocation of on-cost. The appointment of indirect expenses (on-costs) to the departments, jobs or contracts in which they occur.

allocation store. *See* STORE, ALLOCATION STORE.

alpha test. (IT) A preliminary test of an experimental PRODUCT or PROTOTYPE, etc. particularly computer software. Such a test is usually done in the enterprise which developed it before applying the BETA TEST. Organizations should be particularly careful to ensure that all information technology programs (e.g. for stock control and provisioning) be subject to rigorous ALPHA and BETA TEST.

alpha-numeric codes. *See* CODES, ALPHA-NUMERIC CODES.

ambient. (log) The temperature, humidity and other factors which prevail in a building, stockyard, vehicle etc. without special provision such as cooling or air conditioning.

amendment order. *See* ORDERS and CONTRACTS.

amphibious. (log) A vehicle or other equipment able to traverse both land and water.

analysis, cost benefit. *See* COST BENEFIT ANALYSIS.

analyst. *See* PURCHASING ANALYST.

appraisal chart. One designed to display the acceptability (or not) of the results of a QUALITY CONTROL, inspection/test, etc., or the performance of suppliers.

appraise. (v) To judge the quality of something, or to give an expert opinion on the value or cost. e.g. carry out a value ANALYSIS. Appraisal (n) The result of such action. *See also* ENQUIRY and INQUIRY.

appreciation. (econ) The increase in value of an asset. *See* ACCRETION.

approved list. 1. List of APPROVED SUPPLIERS. *See also* VENDOR RATING. 2. List of approved supplies (may be recommended or mandatory). 3. May incorporate or be supplemented by a

BLACK LIST of non-approved supplies/ suppliers.

approved supplier. A vendor who meets a client organization's standards, and who may be dealt with without further investigations

apron. *See* HARD STANDING.

arbitrage. An expert operation, usually carried out by banks, etc., for taking advantage of different rates at different centres at a given moment. Operation in two centres is known as 'simple arbitrage', and in more than two centres as 'compound' or 'indirect arbitrage'.

arbitration. The referral of a dispute to one or more impartial persons with formal or informal agreement to accept the decisions arrived at. (refer also to International Chamber of Commerce and CIPS).

Arbitration Act 1996. Act to restate and improve the law relating to arbitration pursuant to an arbitration agreement. It also makes provision relating to arbitration and arbitration awards. Amendments generally aimed at improving procedures to make them more flexible and suited to the needs of the dispute involved. Reduced the grounds of appeal to the courts.

arbitration clause. A clause introduced into contract setting out CONDITIONS which shall be resolved by ARBITRA-TION.

arisings. A general term for SCRAP or WASTE resulting from a manufacturing process.

arm's length. Commercial transactions in accordance with the market, and disregarding any connection such as common ownership of the companies involved, or any form of special relationship. *See also* RELATIONSHIPS: TRANSACTIONAL. (law) 'Conduct of negotiations in a strictly formal manner' (L B Curzon).

arrangement. (n) An understanding or agreement in less formal and specific terms than those involved in a firm contract, e.g. in a 'Forward Supply Arrangement'. *See* ORDERS & CONTRACTS. Note: Arrangements can become binding contracts if the parties 'communicate in some way so that each has intentionally aroused in the other an expectation that he will act in a certain manner' (Justice Cross, 1962).

arrest. The detention of a vessel temporarily, by Port Authorities.

as is. A sales agreement where the buyer takes the goods without warranty, etc.

as seen. Term of sale by which the purchaser has accepted full personal responsibility for condition of the goods and/or its suitability for purpose.

ascertained goods. *See* GOODS, ASCERTAINED GOODS.

assay. The accurate examination, weighing, chemical (or other) analysis of a thing, particularly ores and precious metals.

assembly. (BS) A combination of parts and possibly raw materials put together to make up a composite article.

assets. (CIMA) Anything of value, owned by an enterprise and which could be used to raise cash to pay debts. *See also* BOOK VALUE, CURRENT ASSETS and FIXED ASSETS.

assets, current assets. Cash or other assets (as listed below or short term investments) held for conversion into cash in the normal course of trading, e.g. STOCK, RAW MATERIALS, BOUGHT OUT STOCKS, WORK IN PROGRESS, FINISHED GOODS.

assets, fixed. Any asset acquired for retention as an entity for the purpose of providing goods or services, and not for resale in the normal course of trading.

assets, fungible. Those which are moveable, may be perishable goods, and which can be measured by quantity, weight, volume, etc. e.g. grains, wines etc.

assets, intangible. Those which are not physical and usually difficult to evaluate, e.g. patents, copyright, designs.

assets, real. Assets in the form of buildings and fixed plant.

assign. (law) To transfer property from one party to another by assignment. The assignor is the person who transfers, the assignee the person to whom it is transferred.

assigned/assignment of stock. See STOCK, PRE-ALLOCATED and RESERVED STOCK.

assignment. (law) Something that has been assigned, a mission or task, the transfer to another of a right, interest or title to property.

assignment of contract. The transfer of property or a right; the passing of a contract to a third party.

at sight. A term sometimes written on bills of exchange. The amount must be paid immediately it is asked for, without any such allowance as that known as DAYS OF GRACE.

atmosphere, explosive atmosphere. (law) The ambient condition in which volatile substances with low FLASH POINTS may easily ignite or even explode. Apart from segregations and other precautions in stores attention is needed to localized electrical equipment.

attachment. (law) The enforcement of a direction to pay money - the seizure of property and the placing of it under public control.

attestation. (EU) Procedure to show that the essential requirements for Health and Safety, etc. have been satisfied in respect of MACHINERY* supplied. The manufacturer or their authorized representative established in the European Union must draw up and keep available a 'technical construction file' as Annex D of the'Machinery Directive'. (*See annex to EU Directive for exceptions.)

attractive goods. Goods which although not necessarily of high INTRINSIC VALUE- may be subject to petty theft and/or pilferage if not housed in a SECURE STORE.

attribute. (n) (BS) A characteristic that is appraised in terms of whether it meets or does not meet a given requirement (e.g. 'go' or 'no go' as determined by the use of a 'go: no-go' gauge).

auction. A sale of goods or property prospective buyers bid in which for the goods, the bidder of the highest price securing them. See also MARKET, COMMODITY MARKET, AUCTION AT.

auction, Dutch. An auction where the AUCTIONEER begins by offering the lot for sale at a price selected by the auctioneer. If no bids are received successively lower prices are offered until a BID is made. The first bidder is the buyer of the lot.

auctioneer. one who conducts an AUCTION.

audit. (CIMA) A systematic examination of books, accounts, activities, records, etc. by a qualified person to check they are accurate and properly kept, Also can be applied to examination of procedures to ascertain they have been carried out correctly. *See* STOCK AUDIT.

audit, management audit. A systematic, objective, independent appraisal of the standards, efficiency and techniques of management. It aims to identify existing and potential weaknesses within an organization and to recommend ways to rectify the weaknesses.

authority. The right to use power. This should be clearly defined, understood and accepted by all those over whom it is exercised. (Excessive use of this power tends to lead to authoritarianizm, block lines of communication upwards as well as downwards, inhibit initiative by subordinates and their job satisfaction). *See also* RESPONSIBILITY and 'DEPARTMENTALISM'.

automated purchasing. Orders prepared and communicated direct by on-line computers linked between purchasers and suppliers. Applicable in highly stable, large user, enterprises, e.g. mass production, continuous process industries, supermarkets and large service industries, etc. Also known as 'paperless purchasing'.

automation. Intensive mechanisation with or without the use of robots comprising the co-ordinated automatic control of processes and machine systems, and the automatic transport, testing and treatment of materials and products throughout a sequence of operations depending upon FEEDBACK without human intervention.

AVCO. (abb) Average cost. Term used for average valuation of stock.

average. 1. A term commonly used as a synonym for the mathematical term MEAN. 2. As used in the context of marine insurance the term 'mean' refers to the loss or damage to a vessel or its cargo, or to both cargo and vessel. (der. from Spanish 'averia' meaning damage/break down, etc., old Italian 'avaria' and ultimately from Arabic 'awar' meaning damage/blemish.) *See also* AVERAGE, GENERAL AVERAGE and AVERAGE, PARTICULAR AVERAGE.

average adjuster (or average stater). A person who makes adjustments in marine insurance claims, etc.

average bond. Bond given to the owner or captain of a ship by a consignee pledging to pay their share of average of any loss.

average clause. The clause in a marine insurance policy which deals with several liabilities connected with the AVERAGE.

average cost. *See* COST, AVERAGE COST.

average price. *See* PRICE, AVERAGE PRICE.

average, customs average. Average TARE taken by customs for a number of containers all containing the same kind of goods, for duty purposes.

average, general. A term in marine insurance signifying that loss or damage to a ship or cargo will be borne proportionally by all parties to the venture and their underwriters.

average, particular. A marine insurance

term meaning the loss of a particular thing which must be borne by its owner alone, or his insurers, i.e. it is not shared amongst the other participants in the venture, for which *see* GENERAL AVERAGE.

avoirdupois System of weights based on the pound (16 ounces).

B

back order, production. (BS) An order against stock which cannot be met until a replenishment quantity is received.

back order, purchasing. That portion of an order which a supplier cannot deliver on schedule and which he enters for shipment at a later date. A former practice which has now been largely abandoned.

back order, stores. The order document prepared by stores for an item currently out of stock which will be supplied when new supplies are available.

backfreight. *See* FREIGHT.

backhander. *See* BRIBE

backhaul. The return journey of a truck or other vehicle. Attempts will often be made to find a load to defray the total cost of the round trip. The term is sometimes used for 'return load' which implies that the haulier has a load back from the destination to which the outgoing load was delivered.

backwardation. (com) The difference between the spot price and futures price at a particular date for the same commodity. See also FORWARDATION.

bad debt. A debt owed by a person or organization which has gone out of business or is unable to pay for some reason.

bad faith. A deliberate attempt to deceive and avoid the honouring of an agreement, e.g. the offer of a delivery which the supplier knows to be beyond his capability. *See also* GOOD FAITH.

bailee. The person, such as a warehouseman, a carrier, to whom goods are temporarily entrusted. He is fully responsible for their safe custody while in his possession.

bailment. The temporary handing over of goods to another for custody.

bailor. The person who hands over goods temporarily into the custody of another, without transfer of ownership.

balance, credit/debit balance. A credit balance is where positive values exceed negative ones, i.e. gains exceed losses, credits exceed debits. A debit balance is the converse of a 'credit balance', i.e. a loss.

balanced ordering. Ordering for assembled products in which all materials and parts are ordered in product sets modified only as necessary for spares supply and for addition of a scrap allowance.

bale. A parcel (usually large) of goods compressed and bound securely with (cordage, plastics or steel) bands.

ballast. Heavy, dense materials such as iron or crushed stone used to provide stability to a vessel or other vehicle. A vessel 'in ballast' is not carrying any cargo.

bankruptcy. (CIMA) Bankruptcy occurs when a 'bankrupt' not only makes it clear he is INSOLVENT but also that he does not expect to pay his debts in full, and an adjudication order has been made by a court for this reason.

bar coding. *See* CODES AND CODIFICATION, BAR CODING.

bar diagram, bar chart. (BS) A graphical representation of the FREQUENCY DISTRIBUTION of a DISCRETE VARIATE. Straight line bars, proportional to the absolute (or relative) frequencies of the variates, are drawn perpendicular to an axis on which the values of the variate are represented on a linear scale.

bargain. (n) 1. A contract or agreement concerning sale. 2. Any agreement or stipulation. 3. A purchase on favourable terms. (v) 4. To seek an advantageous outcome to negotiations.

barratry. (mar) The desertion or wilful damage to a ship and/or its cargo.

barter. *See* ORDERS AND CONTRACTS, A-Z.

base stock-control. *See* STOCK CONTROL, BASE STOCK-CONTROL.

basing point price. *See* PRICE, BASING POINT PRICE

basis price. *See* PRICE, BASIS PRICE.

batch. A definite quantity of some product manufactured or produced under conditions which are presumed uniform, and for production control purposes passing as a unit through the same series of operations. *See* LOT.

batch costing. *See* COSTING, BATCH COSTING.

batch frequency. The number of batches of an item produced, planned for production or delivery in a given period of time, e.g. per week, month or PRODUCTION PERIOD, etc.

batch life. The length of time a given batch of supplies can be expected to last at a given rate of production output. *See* STOCK LIFE *and* SHELF LIFE.

batch production. A type of production in which the batch quantities used are greater than one and in which material flow is of the functional type.

batch quantity. *See* QUANTITY, BATCH QUANTITY.

bay. (log) A group or run of bins, shelves or racks. Also a dock, as in 'loading bay'.

beach-head price. (energy) The price of gas when it arrives at the land terminal.

bear. (com) (fin) A speculator who trades in the expectation of a falling market.

benchmarking. A technique used by firms to help them to become successful. The technique involves: (a) establishing what makes the difference in the eyes of their customers between an ordinary supplier and an excellent supplier, (b) setting standards in each of the above things according to the best practice they can find, (c) finding out how the best compromises meet those challenging standards, (d) applying both the experience of others and their own ideas to meet the new standards - and, if possible, exceed them. The goal is to build on the success of others and to improve future performance.

beneficiary. (SITPRO) The party in whose favour a LETTER OF CREDIT is issued.

berth, LO-LO berth. A berth (usually for short sea transits) designed for lift-on lift-off of containers. *See also* BERTH, RO-RO BERTH.

berth, RO-RO berth. A berth designed so that vehicles may roll-on and roll-off ships.

berth, side-loading berth. A berth designed to facilitate loading and unloading vessels with side opening doors in place of the more conventional

11

hatches and rear opening doors. Fork-lifts in place of cranes are needed for this traffic.

best value. The replacement for Compulsory Competitive Tendering as a tool for acquiring goods and services in local government. Implicit in the term is a recognition that value, not simply price should be a key determinant in the buying process.

beta test. (IT) A test upon an experimental or newly developed (or developing) product - such as, for example, a computer program for stock control, provisioning, etc. The beta test should be carried out by an external and independent organization after ALPHA TESTS have been carried out.

bi-modal transport. The utilization of more than one means of transport for shipments, e.g. use of ISO containers or swap from road and rail for a transit.

bid. An offer to buy, as at an auction. An offer to buy or sell at a stated price. Also, an offer made by a seller to a buyer in response to an enquiry, particularly an invitation to TENDER. (fin mkt) The rate at which a dealer will buy currency or borrow funds.

bid bond. *See* BOND, BID BOND.

bill. A seller's statement of money owed, usually for immediate payment, e.g. in a shop or cafe as distinct from a credit sale when an INVOICE is appropriate.

bill of entry. A certified statement by an importer to Customs giving the nature, amount and value of goods.

bill of exchange (draft). (CIMA) An unconditional order in writing addressed by one person to another and signed by the person giving it and requiring the person to whom it is given to pay on demand or at a certain fixed time or date a certain sum of money to the person named on the bill (or to the bearer).

bill of lading. An acknowledgement for the receipt of goods for shipment. It contains terms and conditions of carriage. It is not a negotiable instrument as it gives no special title to the possession of the goods. Article 3(3) of Hamburg Rules on transit documents gives details of contents of standard bill of lading.

bill of lading, clean. A bill of lading is said to be 'clean' if it bears no declaration (usually by the master of the ship) that the goods or their packaging, etc. are defective, in which case it is termed a 'foul' or 'dirty' bill.

bill of lading, combined. One where several consignments are covered on the same bill.

bill of lading, house bill of lading. A certificate issued to the exporter of a small shipment which has been consolidated into a larger load (e.g. a container) which has its own bill of lading for the entire consignment. The certificate does not have the status of a bill of lading but confirms shipment to the small shipment exporter.

bill of lading, short form. (SITPRO). A bill of lading where the carrier's normal detailed conditions shown on the reverse of a 'long form bill of lading' are written into a brief incorporation clause on the front of the form. This form is recognised by the International Chamber of Commerce and supported by the United Nations. It is acceptable for DOCUMENTARY CREDITS, unless the letter of credit specifies otherwise.

bill of materials. A list of all the components, including the quantities required, to produce the required number of units of the end product. Used in MRP. *See also* PARTS LIST *and* BILL OF QUANTITIES.

bill of quantities. A list of numbered items, each of which describes the work to be done in a civil, engineering or building contract.

bill of sale. A way of raising cash by means of a written agreement to transfer ownership of goods to a purchaser while possession (and therefore use) remains with the seller.

bill of sight. If an importer has not received the shipping documents when the ship arrives he may not have sufficient details to pass the required customs entry. Customs will provide him with a 'bill of sight' enabling him to examine the goods in the presence of a Customs officer.   He must then complete the entry as soon as possible (known as 'perfecting the sight') and may take delivery after payment of any duties, if dutiable.

bill of store. 1. An import licence giving permission for the re-import (within a statutory time) of dutiable goods which had been previously exported. 2. A document exempting from duty those goods which had only been imported and stored in transit for early re-shipment.

Bills of Exchange Act 1882. Act which codified the law on bills of exchange, cheques and promissory notes

bin card. (BS) Local stock record, normally simplified and kept close to the parts, e.g. at the bin where the stock is held.

bin, storage bin. Colloquialism for adjustable steel shelving used in stores.

biodegradable The property of a substance which enables it to be broken down by the action of bacteria or other natural processes.

black list. *See* APPROVED LIST.

blank-cheque ordering system. *See* ORDERS & CONTRACTS, CHEQUE ORDERS.

blanket buying. *See* ORDERS, CONTRACTS, BLANKET ORDERS.

blanket orders. *See* ORDERS *and* CONTRACTS, BLANKET ORDERS.

blanket rate. A shipping charging rate per unit hauled that does not vary according to the distance the cargo is shipped.

blending. The mixing of various grades or qualities in such a way as to produce a new desired or specified standard uniform variety or quality.

Blue Book, the. *See* INTERNATIONAL MARITIME DANGEROUS GOODS CODE.

body language. Communication of information by conscious gesture, such as signals by a slinger to a crane driver, or unintentionally such as by posture or eye movement in a meeting or negotiation.

bona fides. Good faith, absence of fraud or deceit.

bond, a bond. A document binding one party to pay a sum to another party, or to perform - or not to perform - some action or deed.

bond (in contracts for supply). In general, a bond is a deed by which a person binds himself to pay a sum of money at a certain time, or under certain conditions.   In contracts, *see* CBI TERMINOLOGY.

13

bond note. A note countersigned by a Customs officer authorising the transfer of goods from one warehouse to another or for export.

bond warrant. Certificate issued by a bonded warehouse official authorizing the person it names to withdraw bonded goods from the warehouse.

bond, advance, progress or repayment. These guarantee that any monies advanced will not be lost through default or poor performance by the seller.

bond, bid/tender. These assure the buyer that the bid is a reasonable one and that the bid is guaranteed by a bank and also that the bidder will not withdraw his bid, or depart from the conditions set out in his tender.

bond, contract / performance / supply. These guarantee that a seller will satisfactorily perform the contract in accordance with all its terms and conditions.

bond, maintenance bond. These guarantee that once the construction has been completed the contractor will fulfill his obligations throughout the maintenance period.

bond, performance. A bond obtained from a supplier so that in the case of default on the contract to which the bond applies, funds will be available from a third party to compensate the buyer for loss. 'Performance bonds' place the onus (generally on the buyer) to prove default by the seller and generally indemnify the principal for any loss he may have incurred, but only up to the value of the bond.

bond, retention bond. These are used by contractors as a means of financing contracts rather than as a guarantee of performance and in lieu of RETENTION MONEY or against early release of retention money, or of monthly progress payments.

bonded goods. *See* GOODS BONDED.

bonded store warehouse. *See* WAREHOUSE/STORE BONDED. *See also* STORE, SECURE STORE.

book value. (CIMA) The recorded value of an asset in a company's books. May be: 1. 'historical cost' = original cost of asset (goods or services), 2. 'net book value' = historical cost or valuation less depreciation, etc.

bottom line. Final line of a financial statement showing profit, loss or outcome.

bottomry. Pledging of a ship and its cargo as security for a loan to enable it to continue on its voyage

bought-in (supplies). Term sometimes used for supplies purchased from an outside source. *See* BOUGHT OUT. Both terms have double and ambiguous meanings and the words 'purchased' or 'bought' should be used. *See also* IN-HOUSE.

bought-out (supplies). A term sometimes used for supplies obtained from outside the firm requiring them. The preferred term is 'purchased, goods or supplies'. *See also* IN-HOUSE.

brain storming. (adm) A technique whereby group members throw in ideas and suggestions for later analysis and discussion. e.g. may be employed in VALUE ANALYSIS or (particularly) in VALUE ENGINEERING.

brand, own brand. Goods offered for sale by (usually) a large multiple store as of their own manufacture, although in fact the output of another supplier.

brand loyalty. The (often subjective) wish of users of supplies to restrict their usage to a particular brand in preference to others.

brand name or trade mark. The name (or mark) used by a manufacturer or supplier for a particular make (or commodity) to distinguish his product from others and to promote its sale. A brand name or mark gives no warranty as to suitability for purpose, maker, or other features unless these are incorporated into the name or mark e.g. 'instant cold cure'. *See also* QUALITY, MERCHANTABLE QUALITY.

brand stretching. The extension of a well known brand name to a new product with a view to increasing the acceptability of the new product.

breach of contract. *See* CONTRACT, BREACH OF CONTRACT.

breach of duty. *See* CONTRACT, BREACH OF DUTY IN.

break bulk. (v) To break down a bulk or unitised cargo (or material in bulk) into its component parts or smaller lots.

break-bulk. (n) Break-bulk cargo is general or conventional cargo as distinct from UNITIZED, CONTAINERIZED etc. cargo.

break clause. A clause in a contract enabling the purchaser to foreclose on the contract without redress should he wish to do so. [A condition in some government contracts].

break-even analysis. The technique to establish the point (or points) at which two (or more) functions give the lowest total value - known as the 'break even point'. For straight line functions this point will be where the lines cross. But this will not necessarily apply where one

or both the lines are curved - as is often assumed in the analysis. *See* BREAK-EVEN CHART.

break-even chart. A statistical chart developed from DATA derived from BREAK-EVEN ANALYSIS. A curve is the developed for each of the functions being considered. A further curve may be developed for the sum of the two curves. This curve displays the total of the others and also the combined effects of the functions.

break-even point. The point at which the sum of two (or more) functions - e.g. costs for alternative courses of action (purchases etc.) - are at their lowest total. *See also* BREAK-EVEN CHART.

bribe. A secret and corrupt gift. Can be money or money's worth offered to a person in a position of trust and influence in order to persuade him (or her) to use their power to the advantage of the person (or firm) offering the bribe. See 'IPS Ethical Code', IM'Code of Best Practice for Professional Managers', and ICC Code 'Extortion and Bribery in Business Transactions' also the various 'Corruption Acts' of the UK.

Brisch coding. *See* CODE, BRISCH CODING.

British Board of Agrément. A national authority for the testing and assessment of new building methods and materials. The organization was set up by the Minister of Public Works and Buildings in 1966.

British Institute of Management. *See* INSTITUTE OF MANAGEMENT at Appendix.

British Standards Institution. British body concerned with standards and quality management services. BSI provides services in the areas of product testing, CE marking, global trade inspection,

15

environmental management, information security and provision of technical services to exporters. *See also* KITEMARK.

British Standards Society (BSS). A body administered by the BSI for standards users who wish to join on a personal basis. Aims are, amongst others, to help standards users in their understanding and use of standards.

broker. A firm (or person) who buys and sells for a client on commission called 'brokerage'.

brought on charge. Stock is said to be brought on charge when it is accepted and accounted for in the supply system.

browser. Computer program that allows viewing and navigation on a World Wide Web system

Brussels Tariff Nomenclature (BTN). An internationally agreed system of classification of goods with notes defining tariff headings now adopted by most states.

budget. Financial and/or quantitative statement prepared prior to a defined period of time of the policy to be pursued during that period for the purpose of attaining a given object.

budgetary control. (CIMA) The establishment of budgets relating the responsibilities of executives to the requirements of a policy, and the continuous comparison of actual with budgeted results, either to secure by individual action the objective of that policy or to provide basis for its revision.

budgetary period. The period for which a budget is prepared and used. It may be sub-divided into control periods. In purchasing and supply it can have important implications for control of stocks and intake of supplies.

buffer stock. *See* STOCK, BUFFER STOCK.

bulk buying. The concentration of total demand for a commodity into one purchase; also, buying in large quantities to achieve economics of scale. *See also* ORDERS AND CONTRACTS, BULK ORDERS.

bulk cargo. A cargo not in separate bags, bales or other containers, such a cargo is usually all of one commodity such as oil or wheat, etc.

bulking. (v) Turning out the contents of numerous containers of the same commodity and mixing them to achieve a uniform quality/ variety for the whole.

bull. (com & fin) A speculator who trades in expectation of a rising market.

bund wall. (log) A low wall acting as a barrier to impound spilled or overflowing liquids.

Business Process Re-engineering. A means by which an organization can achieve radical changes in performance as measured by cost, cycle time, service and quality, by the application of a variety of tools and techniques that focus on the business as a set of customer oriented core business processes rather than a set of organizational functions. (H J Johansson et al 'Business Process Re-engineering', Wiley, 1993).

business sale (business contract). 'Sale to a person who buys or holds himself out as buying in a course of' business', Paraphrase of Supply of Goods (Implied Terms) Act 1973 now embodied into other Acts.

buy. To acquire by paying money. *See also* PURCHASING and PROCUREMENT.

buy out/bought out. 'Buy-in', 'buying-in', 'buy-out', 'buying out : are terms frequently used (indiscriminately) for SUPPLIES (goods, materials and services) obtained from a source outside the enterprise which requires them. The terms are all tautologisms, and lack the precision required for purchasing and supply. Recommended terms are 'purchased' or 'bought'.

buy, sell and lease back. *See* ORDERS & CONTRACTS, BUY, SELL & LEASE BACK.

buy-back. A transaction in which the seller agrees to purchase goods or services from the buyer up to an agreed percentage of his deliveries to the buyer.

buyer. An official appointed to buy supplies and services sometimes styled as a purchasing officer. Notes: 1. legal definition: 'A person who buys or agrees to buy goods'. 2. under the Supply of Goods and Services Act 1983 the legal terms for the parties to contracts are: for the 'seller' read 'transferor' and for the buyer read 'transferee'.

buyer, lead buyer. A buyer who undertakes principal responsibility for a defined group of goods or services on behalf of a range of different operating locations.

buyer's market. *See* MARKET, BUYER'S MARKET.

buying, maverick. Buying undertaken outside an organization's properly approved purchasing policy and procedures.

by-product. (CIMA) A product which is recovered incidentally from the material used in the manufacture of recognised main products. Such by-product may have either a net realisable value or a usable value. A value may be relatively low in comparison with the saleable value of the main products. In the contexts of ENVIRONMENTAL CONTROL and HEALTH AND SAFETY, etc. it is not unknown for pollutants, waste and scrap to be converted into viable and sometimes valuable by-products.

C

cabotage. 1. Restriction of the use of coastal waters and air space by a country for its own domestic use. 2. Agreement between airlines that where passengers or goods are loaded and discharged within the territories of one State, including colonies and protectorates, they shall be carried by the airline of that State. Cabotage Community rules. Adopted by HMG.UK. 1.1.1993.

call for competition. (EU) The requirement that all contracts or series of contracts above the appropriate threshold must , with few exceptions, be advertised in OJEC.

call-off. (BS) Specific request for delivery(ies) from time to time. *See* ORDERS & CONTRACTS, CALL OFF ORDERS.

call-off arrangement. *See* FRAMEWORK AGREEMENT.

cancel (v), **cancellation** (n). To nullify the legal effects of a document, such as a purchase order or contract. Cancellation can not usually be undertaken unilaterally.

cancellation order. *See* ORDERS & CONTRACTS, CANCELLATION ORDER.

cannibalisation. The use of servicable components from one machine on another.

capability study. A study in which machines and processes are measured and analysed to show whether they are capable of the full required output.

capacity per ton-mile (tonne-kilometre). The capacity of a vehicle multiplied by the distance travelled. Used for costing a transport operation.

capital commitment. (CIMA) Future capital expenditure in respect of which contracts have been made. Important in the financial management of purchasing and supply in relation to CASH FLOW.

capital equipment. *See* GOODS, CAPITAL GOODS.

capital goods. *See* GOODS, CAPITAL GOODS.

capital sanction (financial sanction). A procedure usually in documentary form whereby expenditure on major projects and other large commitments are subject to scrutiny and approval by top and principal functional managers.

capitalized, over-, under-capitalised. (CIMA) Terms used to describe a surplus or deficiency of capital in relation to the current level of activity of a business. [Important to financial management in purchasing].

carcinogenic. (HS) Appertaining to substances which which if inhaled, ingested or penetrate the skin may induce cancer in the individual or may increase the risk of it. *See also* PRO-ACTIVE.

carcinogens. Substances liable to cause cancer.

card, purchasing. A charge card (not a credit card) used by an organization's staff for buying low-cost goods and services.

care, 'duty of care'. This term, which has many applications to business contracts, is best defined by the following example. 'You must take REASON-ABLE care to avoid acts or omissions which you can reasonably foresee would be likely to injure your neighbour...i.e. the person or persons closely and directly affected by any act that ought reasonably have been in contemplation...when directing the mind to the acts or omissions which are called in question'. Judge Lord Atkin in *Donaghue v Stevenson 1932.*

cargo. Goods and materials loaded for transport.

cargo manifest. A document listing all the cargo on a ship, truck or aircraft. Gives identification marks, names of CONSIGNEE and CONSIGNOR of each item.

carnet. A customs document providing certain limited facilities for movement of goods, etc., temporarily waiving certain formalities.

carnet du passage. International shipping document of simple form used by Customs at frontier points for international through traffic to certify that the traffic has passed through their control in good order. The carnet must travel with the goods.

carousel. Storage equipment which brings its material to the picker; may turn on a vertical or horizontal axis.

carriage. 1. A vehicle which carries goods. 2. The act of conveying goods. 3. Cost of conveying goods, more accurately the 'freightage'.

carriage (or freight paid to). *See* FREIGHT, CARRIAGE PAID.

carriage forward. An arrangement whereby carriage is paid by recipient.

Carriage of Goods by Sea Act 1992. Act which replaced the Bills of Lading Act 1855 with new provisions relating to bills of lading and a number of other shipping documents

carrier. Any person by whom or in whose name a contract has been made for carriage by road, rail, sea or air - or a combination of these. *See also* CARRIER, COMMON CARRIER.

carrier, common carrier. A person who for hire or reward undertakes as his particular business to carry goods for anyone who hires him.

carrier's lien. *See* LIEN, CARPIER's LIEN.

carrier's risk - *See* RISK, CARRIER'S.

cartel. An arrangement whereby organisation agree with each other to sell their products at prices higher than they would achieve under free competition with one another. Any agreement between enterprises, or concerted decisions of associations of enterprises; practices between enterprises which have the purpose or effect of preventing, restraining or distorting competition. Applies to all aspects of business including sales, production and purchasing. Usually in breach of national or European Community laws. Common types of cartel are 'price fixing' and 'market sharing'.

case. (BS) A close boarded timber container to completely protect goods from the elements. *See also* CRATE.

case marks. Markings on cases which enable them to be identified during transit to their destination. *See also* SHIPPING MARKS.

case numbers. Numbers which are unique to each case in a consignment. Usually the number of each case is followed by the total in the consignment, thus 3/24 is the third case in a consignment of 24 cases.

case register book. *See* PACKAGE REGISTER.

cash against documents. Terms in a contract under which the captain of a ship will not (on arrival in port), hand over the **BILL OF LADING** and **DOCUMENTS OF TITLE,** or the goods, until the covering draft from the consignor has been paid. *See* PAYMENTS AGAINST DOCUMENTS.

cash and carry. *See* ORDERS & CONTRACTS A-Z.

cash flow. The movement of cash into ('positive flow') and out of ('negative flow') in an enterprise. The difference is 'net-cash flow'. *See* DISCOUNTED CASH FLOW.

cash on delivery (COD). *See* ORDERS & CONTRACTS A-Z.

cash with order (CWO). *See* ORDERS & CONTRACTS A-Z.

cash, prompt. *See* PRICE, TIME RELATED PRICE.

cash, spot. *See* PAYMENT, SPOT CASH PAYMENT.

catalogue (stores commodity catalogue). A classified list of supplies which are normally carried in stock - may also include some 'exceptional' and 'difficult' items. Gives COMMODITY CODE for each item. May give: specification reference, location, user department, FORWARD SUPPLY ARRANGEMENTS, UNITS OF ISSUE, and so on.

catalogue library. The filing place for suppliers' catalogues and price lists, etc. Usually it is (or should be) situated in the purchasing department with full availability to all other departments.

catalogue number. See CODE, COMMODITY CODE.

catalogue, commodity. A list of all the commodities normally used in an enterprise. It usually incorporates, or is integrated with a STORES CATALOGUE but may well include non-stock items such as infrequently used but vital plant spares, etc. It should as far as practicable be based upon the firm's vocabulary of supplies. (Note: Many organizations adopt their own title for this record.)

catalogue, sales. A classified list of goods or services for marketing with brief or detailed specifications, illustrations, identifying code or list numbers *See also* PRICE LIST.

catastrophic maintenance management. A reactive approach to maintenance management that, basically, waits until plant or machinery fails, at which time repair is affected.

caveat emptor. 'Let the buyer look after himself' or 'let the buyer be on his guard'. It reflects the tendency of the law to protect the possessor of property against more powerful parties.

caveat subscriptor. 'Let the person who signs be on his guard'. A warning to all who sign purchase orders or other supplies documents.

caveat venditor. 'Let the seller look after himself', or 'let the seller be on his guard'.

CE mark. (EU) Signifies that the product to which the mark is affixed conform with the relevant EU regulations.

CEN/CENELEC, Central Secretariat. The administrative headquarters of the joint European Standards Institution formed by CEN and CENELEC, located in Brussels. [CEN = Comité Européen de Normalisation] [CENELEC =Comité Européen de Normalisation Electrotechnique] *See also* EUROPEAN COMMITTEE FOR STANDARDISATION, etc.

census of production. *See* PRODUCTION, CENSUS OF PRODUCTION.

centralization. (adm) The control and exercise of administration of operations, such as purchasing and supply, from a central point as distinct from decentralization of the function to a number of points. e.g. a central office controlling or serving a number of operational units which may be dispersed over a wide area. *See* MANAGEMENT.

centrally planned economy. *See* ECONOMY, CENTRALLY PLANNED ECONOMY.

certificate of adequacy, application for. (EU) An application for a 'certificate of adequacy' must be accompanied by the design and manufacturing schedule. A United Kingdom 'approved body' must, if satisfied that the schedule contains all the required information and that the subject of the certificate manufactured in accordance with the schedule would conform with the relevant national standard, issue the CERTIFICATE OF ADEQUACY.

certificate of adequacy, the certificate. (EU) A statement by an impartial CERTIFICATION BODY that a product, process or service conforms with a specified standard or similar document. Certification bodies certify either companies' QUALITY SYSTEMS or their products [and services]. This generally involves ASSESSMENT and regular surveillance and often draws on results of testing and inspection.

certificate of conformity. *See* QUALITY CONTROL-CERTIFICATE OF CONFORMITY.

certificate of damage. (mar) An inspection document prepared by a dock survey officer concerning goods found damaged on receipt at the dock. The document is needed by the importer to recover insurance.

certificate of inspection. *See* QUALITY CONTROL, INSPECTION, CERTIFICATE OF *also* RELEASE NOTE.

certificate of origin. A statement required by customs to indicate to their officers the country of origin of goods.

certificate of survey. *See* CERTIFICATE OF DAMAGE.

certification. The outcome of a process by an impartial CERTIFICATION BODY that a product, process or service conforms or complies with a specification, standard or similar document.

certification, characteristic. (stats) (BS) A property which helps to differentiate between ITEMS in a given POPULATION of DATA. The differentiation may be: 1. quantitive-(variables) e.g. varying quantities of supplies, 2. qualitative, (attributes), e.g. properties of various supplies.

Chaebol. Large South Korean industrial conglomerate (Samsung and Daewoo for example) characterized by central decision making and an authoritarian management style.

charge. A sum demanded for (principally) a service or supply (e.g. energy, water, etc.) as distinct from that demanded for goods; also, for an additional facility, or a premium above the price of goods (or service) e.g. a 'charge' or 'surcharge' for 'express delivery'.

charges forward. A term used when the purchaser is to pay freightage and any other charges on receipt of the consignment. *See also* CARRIAGE FORWARD AT EX WORKS.

charter. An arrangement by which a shipowner hires out a ship to a consignor on a single written agreement known as a charter party. The charter may be either 1. a voyage charter or 2. a time charter.

Chartered Institute of Management Accountants (CIMA) Influential British Professional Body. Provided definitions for several of the terms in this dictionary

Chartered Institute of Purchasing and Supply (CIPS). British professional body concerned with all aspects of purchasing and supply. Offers qualifications in the field, and provides many specialist and technical services for its members.

chattel. Moveable property such as furniture, stocks of materials, machinery.

check digit. *See* CODES AND CODING.

check lists. Questions in list form to remind, enquire or act upon matters which require attention.

check, internal check. Procedures designed to provide assurance that all transactions and other accounting information which should be recorded, have in fact been recorded. *See also* STOCK CHECK.

checking. 1. comparisons of figures or words between a copy and an original or other document. 2. count of actual quantities received with supplier's advice note. 3. to check the condition of something (e.g. packages received at GOODS INTAKE to see if undamaged). *See also* EXAMINATION and INSPECTION.

Cheques Act 1957. Act which amended the law relating to cheques and a number of other instruments

chose in action. (law) Goods or property which, while not at pesent in a person's possession, could be so possessed by legal means.

chronic effects. Health conditions which develop slowly, or are of long duration, or in an H&S context are PROACTIVE i.e. effect may appear long after exposure to the agent(s) which caused it, e.g. asbestosis. May also result from prolonged or frequent exposure.

claim. (CIMA) An assertion of a right; a demand for something due; a right or just title to something; the basis for a demand.

class (statistical class). In the case of quantitative characteristics, 'class' is each of the consecutive intervals into which the total of all the intervals (e.g. the RANGE) is divided.

class, supplies, class of supplies. A range of similar items forming a section within a group.

classification. (CIMA) The arrangement of items (e.g. items of supplies, stock, etc) into logical groups having regard to their nature (subjective classification) or the purpose to be fulfilled.

clearance. An indication that goods have been passed as in compliance with some regulation, duty or other condition.

clearance certificate. A customs certificate authorising a vessel to leave port having paid all necessary dues and duties and observed all formalities.

clearance inwards. A certificate known as a clearing bill or JERQUE note given by the customs house officials after searching a ship on its arrival at port and satisfying themselves that all duties have been paid or that all goods on which duties can be levied are under seal awaiting payment.

clearance outwards. Before a ship proceeds to sea a list must be handed in to the customs authorities of the goods making up the cargo, and permission must be granted before she can leave port. Note: with the adoption of Community Rules, those for import and export clearance are waived in respect of intra-community traffic.

clearance, negative clearance. (EU) An individual examination granted by the Commission in respect of an article of Community enactments. (May be needed for some special purchasing contract which otherwise may be in breach of e.g. Community requirements on competition).

clearing and switch buying. A bilateral trade agreement whereby two governments agree to exchange a given value of specified goods over a specified period.

clerk of works. A client's representative at site on construction, civil engineering works, etc, under instructions of the architect or engineer. He is responsible for execution of the contract in quantity and quality, also to keep records of work done, particularly work which is later hidden, such as foundations.

climate change levy. (energy) A tax aimed at reducing the output of pollutant gases which takes the form of a flat rate addition to the cost of energy.

closed height. The height of a fork lift truck with the mast fully lowered.

clothing, personal protective. *See* PROTEC-TIVE EQUIPMENT.

co-makership. Jargon employed where buyer and seller organizations cooperate closely on the development, manufacture or supply of a product.

cocooning. The practice of heavily coating or wrapping items for long-term storage.

code, accommodation of codes. Indicates the number of items a code is able to define.

code, alpha-numeric. Those in which a combination of letters and numerals are combined to give greater 'hospitality' or provide a mnemonic. *See* CODES, MNEMONIC CODE.

code, alphabetic. Those based on a combination or sequence of letters of the alphabet.

code, bar code. A bar code comprises an array of parallel lines (bars) and spaces between the lines. The bars and spaces of varying widths are arranged in such a manner as to represent a sequence of numerals or other characters. These are read automatically by a bar code reader, or 'scanner' which translates the bars and gaps into data.

code, binary. The numerical system of coding used in computers and similar equipment whereby the numerals '0' and '1' denote (or cause) the absence or presence of' an electrical impulse in given time or sequence.

code, Brisch coding. A method of coding adopted by Brisch and partners for identifying and classifying stock. A significant system usually classifying by blocks of digits describing the goods.

code, check digit. A check digit is a symbol which is included within a code and whose value is based mathematically upon other characters in the code. It is used to provide a mathematical check upon the accuracy of reading or transcription of the code.

code, classification by identity. A number of digits (the 'hospitality' of the code) are used to define the article either by kind or by function, e.g. (kind) 'Batteries/6 volts/ dry/for bells' or (function) 'Bells/ batteries for/6 volts/dry'.

code, colours. Combinations of colours (often bands or dots) providing codified identities for items (particularly those which are too small to accept other forms of coding).

code, commodity code. A code identifying a commodity and unique to that commodity. Usually, such codes are related to the physical or other descriptive attributes of the commodity. (Complications may arise where enduse or function are combined with description).

code, European Article Numbering System (EAN). A coding system widely adopted by retailers for stock items. The code is compatible with BAR CODING.

code, European country codes. The ISO code adopted to identify goods, transits etc within the European Community: for example BE - Belgium: DE - Germany:

code, ideograms (or ideographs). Symbols used to convey ideas or concepts.

code, key. The number of digits or other positions in the hospitality of a code which are taken to define a particular feature, e.g. at least two positions are usually needed to define measurements such as diameter.

code, location. A code for location of stock in stores or stockyard. The code should define the floor layout and the elevation of the rack or bin into which supplies are to be stowed and retrieved. The location code can be used to program the automated stowage and retrieval of supplies by automated handling equipment.

code, mnemonic. Codes which are designed to trigger memory recall and/or the recognition of the item.

code, NATO. The code used by North Atlantic Treaty Organisation based upon USA Federal Classification.

code, pictograms. Representation of a feature or hazard such as hazard codes by a picture of the hazard.

code, product block. A code where blocks of numerals are allocated, e.g. for raw materials and components of an end-product, such as, an electric motor.
e.g. field windings 1000 to 1100
        bearings   1101 to 1199
        shafts   1200 to 1250
        (and so on . . .)

code, random. A code issued without regard to sequence or classification.

code, sequential. Codes which are allocated to items in sequence as they arise without reference to classification except that codes allocated will relate to time sequence and may therefore indicate batches of product or supplies etc., e.g. wallpapers, etc.

code, significant. A code where the individual characters have a special meaning, e.g. product block code.

code, universal product code (UPC). A coding system widely employed for use in conjunction with bar coding

codes and codification. A system of symbols for identification of items, e.g. for supplies, commodities, equipment, spares, cost-centres, accounts and so on. whereby each item is given a complete and unique identification symbol which cannot be confused with another and can be recorded, retrieved and recognised throughout the enterprise, and also by its customers where appropriate (kinds of code and their characteristics are listed below).

coding, harmonized for commodities. (EU) The system of commodity coding used by the Community and accepted worldwide for trading in place of the (previously used) Brussels nomenclature and codification. The extension in use of the coded data facilitates the transfer of information by Electronic Data Interchange methods.

coemption. Buying up the whole supply of a commodity, 'cornering the market'.

cohesion, social cohesion. (EU) 'Commitment by the Community to help the less well-off regions to achieve the average level of Community development. A cohesion Fund will contribute to this goal.' 'Cohesion' may help to create the 'level playing field' when purchasing and selling from and to the 'less well-off' regions. cf. Article 2 of Maastricht.

collusion. The action in agreement or concert with others either in a clandestine manner or for an illegal end or by illegal means or by some or all of these.

combined bill of lading. *See* BILL OF LADING, COMBINED.

combined transport operator. 'One who undertakes responsibility for an entire (usually) containerised consignment over its entire journey'.

'combo' ships. Vessels, usually a combination of BREAK-BULK conventional between deck - and container ships. They are particularly used in feeder services between ports.

comfort letter. (EU) A document provided by the Commission upon appeal by a person against an article of the Community. e.g. a letter stating that in the opinion of the Commission an agreement (i.e. a purchase contract) does not infringe article 85 of 'Competition Law'.

commerce, electronic. The trading in goods or services using electronic means.

Commercial Agents (Community Directive) Regulations 1993. Regulations which define 'commercial agent' and govern the relationship between such agents and their principal, including rights and obligations, remuneration, and conclusion and termination of the agency contract

commission. Amount paid for services rendered, usually a percentage, e.g. commission on sales paid to a sales representative.

Commission of the European Union. (EU) The Community body which makes 'PROPOSALS' for legislation. The COUNCIL of the EUROPEAN UNION which discusses, adopts or amends. The Commission executes Council decisions and supervises day to day running of policies. (See COUNCIL (EU)).

commissioning. (BS) The advancement of an installation from the stage of static completion to full working order to specified requirements.

commitment, inadvertent commitment. The creation or modification of a contractual commitment through the AGENT of an enterprise making an unguarded verbal or written comment which could be reasonably constructed as an intention to create or modify a binding commitment.

committed stock. *See* STOCK, PREALLOCATED STOCK *and* STOCK. RESERVED STOCK.

commodities. Goods which are the subject of trade and commerce as below: 1. 'consumer goods'- those which have already reached the domestic market, 2. 'economic' commodities; an element of wealth: an economic good; articles of utility which are not in unlimited supply, 3. primary commodities = RAW MATERIALS, 4. 'PRODUCER GOODS', 5. secondary commodities = manufactured goods, 6. sensitive commodities. *See* COMMODITIES, SENSITIVE COMMODITIES.

commodity agreements, multi-lateral agreements. Multi-lateral arrangements between consumer and producer nations to stabilize supplies and prices of individual commodities.

commodity catalogue. *See* CATALOGUE COMMODITY CATALOGUE.

commodity code. *See* CODE.

commodity exchange. *See* MARKETS.

commodity market. *See* MARKETS.

commodity numbers. Numbers assigned to commodities for their identification and use in commodity coding, etc. United Nations commodity numbers, for example, must be stated when shipping dangerous goods. The numbers displayed in a label (such as a 'Hazchem' label) alert and inform fire, ambulance and other rescue services the steps needed to prepare for any associated hazards.

commodity, 'sensitive commodity'. A commodity the price of which in the market is sensitive to economic and market conditions such as supply and demand, shortage, the exchange rate and many other international and national factors.

commodity, 'soft' commodity. Term used on the COMMODITY EXCHANGE referring, in general, to agricultural products and their derivatives - cocoa, fishmeal, sugar, for example.

commodity/commodities, 'hard'. Term referred to on COMMODITY EXCHANGE, applying to metals.

common carrier. *See* CARRIER, COMMON.

common law. *See* LAW, COMMON LAW.

Common Market. Usually refers to the EUROPEAN UNION (EU) but can also mean any customs union which eliminates all trade barriers within the group and establishes a common external tariff on imports from nonmember countries. Common markets similar to the EU exist in Central America, EFTA, etc.

common user items/supplies. Those items of supply, usually stock items, which are used in more than one department or work-centre of an organization. e.g. furniture, tools, stationery, etc.

communication. The sending and receiving of information, instructions, ideas, intentions and so on by means of language symbols (written* or spoken), electrical or other impulses, between people, and/or (in the case of machines) by FEEDBACK. Communication is particularly important in SUPPLIES administration, and vital in PURCHASING for which absolute accuracy and clarity are essential. Communication is essential for the creation of a valid contract. (*Written communications in contracts can constitute DOCUMENTS OF RECORD).

communication, oral in supplies. This kind of communication, or the conduct of the parties, can bind both seller and buyer in a contract. In all important cases, oral communications should be confirmed in writing. *See* SALE OF GOODS ACT 1979.

communication, written in supplies. Although for creation of a valid contract, communication need not be in writing, written communications can, as DOCUMENTS OF RECORD, provide valuable evidence of the INTENTIONS OF PARTIES to create a contract. Usually the latest communication is the governing document - hence the need for careful scrutiny of ACKNOWL-EDGEMENTS from suppliers, of purchase orders.

compact disk – read only memory. Storage medium for data. Can not be 'written' to.

compact disk – re-writable. Data storage device capable of being re-used.

compensation trading ('buyback'). A form of COUNTERTRADE in which the exporter may be required not only to supply plant and instal it, provide the technology and training of the work-force but also to purchase the end-product, i.e. the output of the plant.

compensatory financing. A programme of the International Monetary Fund (IMF) which offers loans to countries suffering temporary shortfalls in income due to temporary falls in prices of commodities.

competition. Competition in business can be described as the effort of one trader to secure financial advantage over others who vie for the same business. In economic theory, competition between buyers for each to secure the best price for himself, while sellers equally compete each to secure the best bargain.

Competition Act 1998. Act replacing earlier legislation on competition law including Restrictive Practices Act 1976, Resale Prices Act 1976, and majority of Competition Act 1980. Replaces it with two prohibitions (Chapter One Prohibition regulating collusion between independent undertakings; Chapter Two Prohibition regulating abuse by a single undertaking of a dominant position). Substantially based on European Union regulation, in particular, Articles 81 & 82 of the European Treaty.

competition rules, community rules. (EU) The rules are those set down in the Treaty of Rome and are aimed at ensuring the equality of treatment of organizations throughout the Union. The rules restrict practices which contravene Section 85(1) of the Treaty of Rome dated 1957. This has been strengthened by later DIRECTIVES of the EUROPEAN UNION.

competition, market. The general 'imperfect' competitive condition encouraged by trade and met with in most environments of purchasing and supply. It requires free market conditions in which a variety of products/services are available to satisfy given needs at competitive quality, prices, deliveries, etc. to numerous buyers - who may themselves be competing for the same supplies and services.

competition, monopolistic. A hypothetical condition as by definition it excludes true competition - until an alternative source, product or service becomes available. (*See also in this section* MONOPOLY, DUOPOLY, OLIGOPOLY AND OLIGOPSONY.)

competition, non-price. Aspects of competitiveness which, unlike relative prices and costs, are not readily quantified. May be effective in results of VALUE ENGINEERING and VALUE ANALYSIS.

competition, perfect. A theoretical condition in the market wherein the following conditions must exist: 1. no single producer, seller or buyer can by his own action affect price, 2. all are free to enter and leave the market, 3. all suppliers offer the same identical product, 4. all products are equally acceptable to the purchasers, 5. there are many buyers and sellers, 6. there is complete freedom from State interference. *See also* MONOPOLY, etc.

complementary demand. *See* DEMAND, COMPLEMENTARY DEMAND.

completion date (of contract). *See* CONTRACT, COMPLETION DATE OF CONTRACT.

compliance. *See* QUALITY CONTROL, COMPLIANCE.

compliance directive. Directive under which aggrieved suppliers may seek redress in the event of an infringement of European supplies or works directives.

complimentary supply. A service or goods supplied without charge.

composites. American term for plastics

compounding. Enables the calculation of value in future of a sum invested today at an agreed rate of interest over a given period, usually 'years'.

compulsory competitive tendering (CCT). Statutory regulation resulting from EU directives. This directs public authorities to submit requirements to competitive tendering. Requirements now subject to BEST VALUE contracting.

computer aided design (CAD). The use of computers, usually associated with graphical display units having high definition. CAD enables designs to be modified, updated and appraised during design.

computer, analogue computer. One which represents numerical quantities by their presentation in graphical/pictorial form, e.g. the face and hands of a clock, a pressure gauge, etc.

computer, digital computer. One which confines its operation to the presentation of data by mathematical symbols (i.e. digits). It can thus store, manipulate or present data such as 'stock levels', 'stock movements', etc. in numerical format.

computerized ordering systems. Systems which rely upon electronic data interchange (EDI) whereby requirements for supplies are notified to a purchasing department direct by on-line computer from the store or other department requiring them.

concurrent engineering. Undertaking design, development and other processes in parallel to reduce TIME TO MARKET.

conditions of contract. *See* CONTRACT CONDITIONS OF.

conditions of contract, implied conditions. *See* CONTRACT, IMPLIED CONDITIONS OF CONTRACT.

conditions of purchase. Details usually printed on purchase order forms (and enquiry forms) indicating the standard TERMS and CONDITIONS which the purchaser wishes to apply to his contracts. If conditions of purchase etc. are printed on the reverse of the form for legal reasons it is essential to call attention to them on the face of the form. *See also* CONTRACT, CONDITIONS OF.

conference (or 'liner conference'). (mar) Two or more shipowners operating on a particular trade route between specified ports and providing regular, scheduled, advertized services at a CONFERENCE FREIGHT RATE.

conference freight-rate. (mar) IM. Uniform rates of freight based upon published tariffs charged by Member Lines of a CONFERENCE.

conformity. See QUALITY CONTROL, CONFORMITY.

consensus ad idem. A meeting of minds in one and the same intention. An essential component along with others for a valid contract.

consequential loss. See LOSS CONSEQUENTIAL.

consideration. Some 'advantage' (money, or money's worth) which under the terms of a contract moves from one party to the other. The giving of mutual advantages by the parties is the essence of the bargain, and is known as consideration. In any transaction where there is no consideration there is no contract. Strictly speaking therefore PROCUREMENT (in UK usage) does not necessarily constitute a contract.

consign. To forward goods from one place or one person to another.

consignee. (SITPRO) Person to whom goods are sent.

consignment. (BS) Goods or products issued or received as one delivery (and intake) and covered by one set of documents. A consignment may consist of one or more LOTS or BATCHES.

consignment (on-consignment) imports. Goods which instead of being imported against definite orders are brought in and transferred to an agent for sale on commission.

consignment note. (CIMA) A haulier's own form of freight contract. It is his receipt for the goods he transports and, by the signature of the purchaser's representative at goods intake, his evidence of delivery in good order. See EXTERNAL GOOD ORDER.

consignment stock. See STOCK, CONSIGNMENT STOCK.

consignor. A person who sends goods to another.

consolidation (distribution, freight). The grouping together of a number of small consignments into a bulk shipment, for the purpose of qualifying for lower freight tariffs.

consortium. An association of contractors or other bodies to carry out a large project. They may issue tenders separately or a single tender, e.g. for a TURN KEY CONTRACT. See ORDERS & CONTRACTS.

consortium buying. The use of a consortium may be made by a group of local (or similar) authorities. Such an arrangement may improve price, delivery, etc. from suppliers, but, in doing so such authorities need to be aware of, and avoid conflict with, EU rules on competition.

constructive total loss. See LOSS, CONSTRUCTIVE TOTAL LOSS.

consular invoice. See INVOICE, CONSULAR.

consumable stock. See STOCK, CONSUMABLE STOCK.

consumables. See SUPPLIES, CONSUMABLE SUPPLIES.

consumer. One who purchases products

and services for domestic use only and not in any way for commercial, industrial or trade purposes.

Consumer Credit Act 1974 Act which created a system, administered by the Director-General of Fair Trading, requiring licences to be obtained by traders concerned with the provision of credit (or the supply of goods on hire or hire- purchase). Also imposed other controls on above traders.

consumer durables. Consumer goods which have a relatively long life, e.g. cars, or a very long life, e.g. houses. cf. non-durables which include consumables such as food, and factory SUPPORTING GOODS e.g. lubricants.

consumer liability. *See* CONSUMER PROTECTION.

consumer protection. The principle enshrined in various enactments for the protection of domestic consumers against the supply of goods and services which are not of merchantable quality or suitable for purpose. Such enactments in UK do not usually protect business sales. However, a business purchaser needs to have regard to any supplies he may purchase which pass into a domestic end-product and sale.

Consumer Protection Act 1987. Act which makes provision relating to the liability of persons (predominantly producers of goods) for damage caused by defective products. Part One concerns personal claims for compensation by consumers. Parts Two - Five amend earlier criminal legislation relating to consumer safety and misleading price indications.

Consumer Protection (Cancellation of Contracts Concluded Away From Business Premises) Regulations 1997, amended 1998. Regulations which protect consumers who buy products or services from cold calling traders. Issues covered by the regulations include rights of cancellation, recovery of money paid by consumer, and return of goods by consumer after cancellation. These regulations have been complemented by the CONSUMER PROTECTION (DISTANCE SELLING) REGULATIONS 2000

Consumer Protection (Distance Selling) Regulations 2000. Regulations which implement the Distance Selling Directive (97/7/EC) intended to give legal protection to consumers who may feel at a disadvantage when buying goods or services in non-fact to face situations, in particular, via the internet, telephone, fax and mail order. Issues covered by the regulations include information provision, rights of cancellation, fraudulent payments and performance.

consumer sale (contract). A contract (not being one of sale by AUCTION or by competitive TENDER) in which one party to the contract deals, and the other party to the contract (the consumer) does not deal or hold himself out as dealing, in the course of business (abb. Unfair Contract Terms Act 1977.25(1) a).

consumption (economic). The destruction of value by use. If consumed during a manufacturing process it is known as 'productive consumption'; if there is no direct or indirect end-product it is known as 'unproductive consumption'.

consumption, in stores. The usage of stock supplied over a given period. Can be classified into 'recurring' and 'non-recurring' consumption.

consumption, history. The recorded recurring and/or non-recurring consumption of stock supplies detailed on stock records.

containerisation. The transfer of goods for shipment from the former BREAK BULK methods to their packaging in unit containers thus making possible safer, cheaper transit. IM'Management Guide No. 6. Distribution'.

containers, freight 'ISO' type. (BS) Containers of the **iso** type are of modular size 8ft x8ft and of lengths 10, 20, 30 and 40 feet. There are numerous types to suit special cargoes, and all are equipped for lifting by the provision of lifting points at each corner.

containers, intermediate bulk (IBC). Containers between approximately 0.5m 3 and 3.Om 3 (usually) of flexible material, suitable for handling by fork truck or crane and for use in process by direct discharge.

contango. (com) Premium paid by a buyer of FUTURES to the seller for the buyer's postponement of delivery from the due date to a later one. Sometimes referred to as FORWARDATION.

contents note. A document attached to a container (crate, case, etc.) listing the number of packages within that container. *See also* PACKING NOTE.

contingency cover. (ins) Insurance taken out by a shipper to cover transit where the customer has arranged his own insurance. The policy covers the shipper (exporter) until the property in the goods has transferred to the customer.

contingent liabilities. (CIMA) Obligations which may arise in respect of past or future events (e.g. the purchaser or supplier has infringed a patent).

continuation clause (mar ins) One covering situations where a ship is still at sea when insurance cover runs out. The insurer agrees to cover risks at *PRO RATA* rate of premium.

continuous inventory. *See* STOCK CONTROL CONTINUOUS *and* INVENTORY.

continuous stock control. *See* STOCK CONTROL, CONTINUOUS.

continuous stock-taking. *See* STOCK-TAKING.

contra-flow. A situation wherein supplies or traffic flow in opposite directions. May result in congestion, wasted movements, etc. Should always be examined in regard to operational efficiency, safety and costs in stores, handling, transportation, etc.

contract. A 'business contract' implies the entry into an unambiguous legal agreement with a company, another party, person (other supplier) to deliver supplies (goods or services) or to do something (e.g. construct a building) on mutually agreed terms. A business contract generally involves: 1. an offer and an unqualified ACCEPTANCE, 2. a CONSENSUS AD IDEV, 3. an intention of the parties to contract, 4. a genuine consent of the parties to the agreement, 5. the capacity of the parties to contract, 6. legality of the objectives of the contract, 7. the possibility of its performance, 8. certainty of the TERMS and CONDITIONS applied, 9. the passing of CONSIDERATION.

contracts and orders, administration of. Definitions in this section refer mainly, only to the formation and administration of contracts (and purchase orders).

contract bonds and guarantees. *See* BONDS.

contract costing. (CIMA) Form of specific order-costing where work is undertaken to purchaser's special requirements and each order is of long duration (compared with those to which JOB COSTING applies), e.g. constructional work.

contract date. (Order date for most purposes). The date when a contract or order enters into effect according to the INTENTIONS OF THE PARTIES.

contract for supply. (law) A contract is made where parties have reached an agreement or when they are deemed to have done so, and the law recognises the rights and obligations arising. Almost all industrial contracts are simple contracts, as distinct from speciality contracts i.e. those made under seal. Three of the essential elements are: 1. AGREEMENT (CONSENSUS AD IDEM), 2. INTENTION, 3. CONSIDERATION. *See also* ORDERS AND CONTRACTS.

contract management. Activities of a buyer during a contract period to ensure that the seller fulfils all his obligations under the contract.

contract note. Written particulars for a sale made in a central exchange, such as a COMMODITY MARKET - particularly on FUTURES.

contract of sale. 'A contract for the sale of goods is a contract in which the contract seller transfers or agrees to transfer the property in goods to a purchaser for a money CONSIDERATION called the PRICE'. Sale of Goods Act 1979 Sect. 2 - (1).

contract period. The period from the agreed date of the start of a contract to the agreed due date for its completion.

contract price adjustment (CPA). *See* PRICE, CONTRACT PRICE ADJUSTMENT, CONTRACT, ESCALATION CLAUSE.

contract, price re-opener clause. *See* PRICE: RE-OPENER CLAUSE.

contract procedures (negotiated). (EU) Negotiating procedures whereby contracting authorities consult suppliers of their choice and negotiate the terms of the contract with one or several of them . [Source P&SM 5/89

p.371 See also TENDERS/ TENDERING.

contract record. A record of progress of a contract, e.g. of DRAW-OFF, ORDERS, schedules, etc. from FORWARD SUPPLY CONTRACTS or FORWARD SUPPLY ARRANGEMENTS. *See* ORDERS & CONTRACTS A-Z.

contract scheduling. A system of ordering and production control associated with the control of large-scale projects where the release of orders is based upon schedules related to the progress of the contract. May be controlled by NETWORK ANALYSIS.

contract, acceptance of offer. In a contract, the agreement of a party that he or she accepts an offer submitted to him and is prepared to enter into a contract. For a contract to be valid the acceptance must be unqualified. A qualified acceptance is equivalent to a counter-offer or an offer, and is not an acceptance.

contract, amendment to. Changes to orders and contracts may be required. Amendment should be by mutual agreement. Good practice is that the amendment, modification or change order should be in writing.

contract, arbitration clause. A contract clause setting out conditions which may be resolved by arbitration in the event of a dispute. Arbitration procedures might also be laid down.

contract, breach of (duty in). Breach of (duty in) a contract results from breach of: 1. any obligation arising out of the express or implied terms of a contract to take reasonable care or exercise reasonable skill in performance of the contract, 2. any common law durt to take reasonable care or exercise reason-able skill.

contract, cancellation of contract. The act of nullifying or invalidating a purchase order, i.e. a CONTRACT. The action may constitute a breach of contract on the part of the buyer, unless the agreement to cancel has been negotiated with the other party.

contract, completion date of contract. The date agreed in a contract for 1. the delivery of supplies, 2. date of arrival of plant on site, 3. its test, 4. its commissioning and certificate of approval by the purchaser, 5. some other date which must be agreed by the parties to the contract. *See* PLANNING *and* PROGRESSING.

contract, conditions, legal conditions, (terminology of). 1. Concurrent condition: one depending upon the performance by the other party to the contract. 2. Precedent condition: one where the contract shall not bind the party until it is fulfilled. 3. Subsequent condition: one which shall bind the party or release them upon the happening of another event, e.g. suspension of contracts on the outbreak of war. 4. Implied condition: one which although not explicit in a contract have been implied by words or actions and seen to be understood and accepted by both parties to the contract. *See also* DEALING, A COURSE OF DEALING.

contract, conditions of contract. Terms which go to the heart of a contract. Traditionally, if a promiser breaks a 'condition' in any respect however slight, the other party may treat himself as discharged from the contract and sue for damages immediately. *See also* WARRANTY.

contract, contracting out. The equivalent of BUYING IN but in this case to place a contract with an outside supplier or service contractor for an operation or supply which the purchaser could otherwise provide from his own facilities IN HOUSE.

contract - cost ceiling controlled. Any contract which has established a limit to the costs entailed in carrying out the contract.

contract, dishonoured contract. One which has suffered breach. (This may be a suitable term to apply when a failure by a supplier to comply with CONDITIONS of a contract such as failure to meet delivery date or quality, etc. appears imminent.)

contracts, 'escape clause'. A clause inserted into a contract by the parties to the agreement. The objectives may be various and may involve a BREAK CLAUSE or the cancellation or renegotiation of the contract under certain defined eventualities agreed in advance between the parties.

contract, escalation clause. A clause which allows price to be adjusted to a predetermined formula which relying on some mutually agreed index or indices published by a third party. Known as a price adjustment clause (cf).

contract, exclusion clause. A clause which one party to a contract (usually the supplier) endeavours to embody into a contract whereby he can escape liabilities or commitments he wishes to avoid. (Note: 'A statement on a purchase order excluding a seller's conditions is no protection to the buyer and does not legally affect the 'counter offer' situation.

contract, fixed time-cycle review ordering. Contracts/orders placed at regular time intervals, after taking account of DUES IN, stock available (i.e. allowing for any ALLOCATED etc. stock) at the time of review. Quantity is ordered sufficient to bring stock to STOCK LEVEL MAXIMUM, or other quantity to meet expected demand for production, process or sales.

contract, forward purchase. Buying in advance of need. May, or may not, involve delivery and inflation of stocks and incur increased STOCK-HOLDING COSTS.

contract, frustration of contract. Any situation where the PERFORMANCE of a contract is prevented from being carried out. Under the 'doctrine of frustration' courts provide for the 'discharge of a contract' if certain types of contingency intervene, such as: 1. the basis or subject of the contract is destroyed; 2. an essential event did not occur; 3. government intervenes; 4. method of performance is impossible, (and others).

contract, futures. (com) A uniform contract subject to the rules of a commodity exchange requiring that a certain quantity of a commodity at an agreed price will be transferred from one person to another at an agreed future date.

contract, implied conditions in contract. Conditions in contract. Conditions which although not explicit in a contract have been implied by words or actions and seen to be understood and accepted by both parties to the contract. *See also* DEALING, A COURSE OF DEALING.

contract, inadvertent. Apart from one made 'inadvertently' this definition can also apply to a contract made by mistake, made prematurely or by a person who is unauthorised but is HOLDING OUT and may commit the enterprise to a binding contract. (Rules of contract are not at the time of writing uniform throughout the European Union. It is important to check that a contractual commitment will not result from the 'innocent exchange of quotations and letters with a continental supplier.)

contract, loyalty contract. (mar) A contract offered by LINER CONFERENCES to shippers who are willing to guarantee to send their cargoes (in a particular trade or area) exclusively by the ships of that particular conference; 'may involve pooling arrangements'.

contract, quasi-contract. A contract which does not embody all the conditions needed for a valid contract. A quasi-contract may become a firm legal contract by the words and actions of the parties.

contract, re-determination clause. A clause in a contract where costs cannot be predetermined, e.g. after production has started the 'unknowns' become 'known' and a final price may then be agreed. In some instances further 'pre-determinations' may be needed.

contract, retention of ownership clause. *See* TITLE, RETENTION OF TITLE.

contract, severable. *See* ORDERS & CONTRACTS A-Z.

contract, terms, conditions, warranties. Terms, in the context of purchasing and supply comprise the substantive components of a contract, and create contractual obligations, the breach of which may lead to action. Broadly speaking, terms are of two kinds - 'conditions' and 'warranties'.

contract - termination. The ending of a contract agreement due to the failure of a party to fulfil the term of the contract or to meet contract conditions.

contract, time the essence. *See* TIME THE ESSENCE.

contract, unenforceable contract. A contract which, though valid in itself, may not be enforceable at law for a valid reason, e.g. an ACT OF GOD or *FORCE MAJEURE* or STATE LEGISLATION.

contract, works. A contract let for the design and/or carrying out of works of a building, construction or civil engineering nature.

contract/order, acknowledgement of (unwritten). The acceptance and acknowledgement of the existence of a valid contract may be established by non-written means, thus: 1. oral communication e.g. telephone, face to face, etc., 2. evidence of intention to contract e.g. starting work, 3. by 'performance' - actual despatch of the goods, 4. by 'acceptance' of goods, e.g. purchaser does something consistent with his ownership of them, 5. instructions by on-line computers, if a course of dealing exists between the parties, e.g. the computer programs trigger ordering instructions automatically when re-order level is reached.

contract/order, acknowledgement of order (written). The acknowledgement between parties that a contract exists. A supplier's written acknowledgement of a purchase order establishes the existence of the contract and will (usually) bind the purchaser - unless he responds and signifies he is not making an unqualified acceptance of the acknowledgement, in which event full and unqualified acceptance must be established by further negotiations before a valid contract can be established.

contractor. A party who agrees to provide supplies or services in accordance with a valid and legal agreed CONTRACT.

Contracts (Applicable Law) Act 1990. Act which makes provision as to the law applicable to contractual obligations in the case of conflict of laws. Gave effect to the Rome Convention (on the law applicable to contractual obligations) 1980, as amended.

Contracts (Rights of Third Parties) Act 1999. Act creating an inroad into the doctrine of privity contract, entitling a third party (a person who was not a party to a contract) to enforce a contractual term where the contract expressly provides that he may (or where a term 'purports' to confer a benefit on him)

contracts, discharge of. The completion of a contract and liquidation. PERFORMANCE must be complete in accordance with the terms and conditions of the contract.

contracts, model orders. Specimen orders held in electronic or other form which can be used as templates for frequently ordered goods or services.

contracts, overseas. Those contracts made between businesses in States of differing sovereignties, financial systems, and commercial and industrial laws. Integration of States (*See* COMMON MARKET *and* EUROPEAN COMMUNITY) involve applications of varying techniques of purchasing and supply. Some examples **are:** premium and discount currencies; use of 'futures' market; 'traded options'; control of payments made in Sterling against foreign exchange commitments: option spreads; rollovers and conversions; ECUs and Euro currencies; currency credits, etc.

contracts, prototype format. An original model or pattern of contract (or purchase order) from which subsequent copies are made. The prototype order procedure lends itself to the use of EDP. The 'model' order may be retained in the computer file and quantity, price, delivery, etc. completed as required and issued to the supplier. *See also* AUTOMATED PURCHASING.

contribution. (CIMA) The difference between sales and VARIABLE COSTS is expressed as 'contribution' and represents the amounts available to meet overhead costs. It is a useful method for measuring the effectiveness of a single product among all the products produced by an enterprise. 'Contribution per unit' is the difference between the selling price of a product or service and its marginal cost. 'Contribution in total' is the difference between the sales value and variable cost. Contribution is a very important aspect of supply economics.

control of substances hazardous to health (COSHH). *See* SUBSTANCES.

controlled substances. (HS) In the context of environmental control (may also have implications for health and safety), a substance which is ozone depleting (e.g. CFCS, halogens, CTC, trichlorethane, etc.)

copyright. (law) The exclusive right to do, and to authorise (or forbid) other persons to do certain acts in relation to that 'work which is copyright' (Copyright Act 1956.) Such rights include the copying of manufacturer's and supplier's INTELLECTUAL PROPERTY, such as drawings, designs, specifications, schedules and other similar materials which often arise in the course of enquiries, negotiations, etc.

Copyright, Designs and Patents Act 1988. Act restating law of copyright with substantial amendments: to confer a design right in original designs (unregistered design right); to make minor amendments to the Registered Designs Act 1949; to make provision for patent agents and trade mark agents; to make minor amendments to patent law.

core business. Those activities and processes of an enterprise that can be provided with significant competitive advantage and which are the key purpose and mission of the enterprise.

cornering the market. The concentration (usually rapid and temporary) of the major part of supply of a commodity into single ownership, e.g. 'cornering the market in cotton'.

corporate appraisal ('SWOT analysis'). A critical appraisal of the Strengths, Weaknesses, Opportunities, and Threats in relation to internal and external factors affecting an enterprise so as to consider its condition prior to setting up a long-term plan. *See* PLANNING, STRATEGIC LONG TERM.

corporate planning. *See* PLANNING, CORPORATE PLANNING.

correlation. (stats) The degree to which (two) variables vary in relation to one another. Correlation is: a. 'positive' when the increase in one is associated with an increase in the other, e.g. throughput of supplies increases with increase in production, b. 'negative' when as one increases the other decreases, e,g. price (should) decrease as order quantities increase, c. 'perfect' when each change in the one is matched by an equal change in the other.

corruption. Any action which involves inducement by means of improper 'consideration'. In the context of purchasing and supply corruption implies dishonesty (especially bribery).

cost. The total sum involved including price plus all sums associated with ownership and use. Note: 'cost' should not be used as a synonym for PRICE or VALUE.

cost accounting. The application of accounting and costing principles, methods and techniques in the ascertainment of costs and the analysis of savings and/or excesses as compared with previous experience or with standards.

cost analysis. A technique used to determine a fair and reasonable selling price of a product. Having carried out the cost estimate, cost analysis studies continue beyond the manufacturing costs and examine administrative costs, MARKETING, selling, distribution, etc., and endeavour to determine the profit the supplier is applying to that particular product. *See also* VALUE ANALYSIS.

cost centre. (CIMA) A location, person or item of equipment (or groups of these) in respect of which costs may be ascertained and related to COST UNITS.

cost control. The practice of comparing the actual cost of an operation (e.g. total cost of, for example, a 'service contract') with the original cost estimate (or budget) in order to ascertain if the cost is as originally planned or budgeted for.

cost effectiveness. The relationship between cost measured in monetary units and effectiveness measured in terms of actual performance. A cost effective supply is one where the effectiveness is equal to or exceeds the BREAK-EVEN POINT of the related costs.

cost of sales. An accounting term indicating what it costs a manufacturing company to produce its output.

cost plus. A pricing method whereby the purchaser agrees to pay the vendor an amount determined by the costs incurred by the vendor to produce the goods or services purchased, and to which oncosts and profit are added at an agreed percentage, or fixed sum, or according to another agreed formula.

cost unit, a cost unit. (CIMA) A quantitative unit of product, i.e. supply or service in relation to which costs are ascertained, e.g. paper, per ream; sand and gravel, per cubic metre, etc.

cost(s), set up cost(s). The component of production/process or other costs which result from preparation work, e.g. setting machines, robots, process controllers, etc. ready for operation.

cost, accrued (charges). Costs or charges which should be known at the inception of a project or contract, but which will not be due until some predetermined date - such as completion or COMMISSIONING of a project or plant.

cost, acquisition (total). The total of all costs in acquiring supplies of goods or services by purchase or by other means, e.g. hire, loan, procurement, etc, from the inception of the demand for them until their safe and satisfactory delivery at the point required, They include all administrative and physical costs from the time of determination of the need until and including final settlement with the supplier.

cost, actual cost ascertainment. (CIMA) A principle whereby costs at COST CENTRES and of COST UNITS are ascertained, which, subject to certain approximations are deemed to represent actual costs. The use of the term 'historical costs' is not recommended in this concept.

cost, administrative, cost general. The sum of those costs of general management and of secretarial, accounting and administrative services which cannot be directly related to production, marketing, research or development functions of an enterprise. For purposes of economic order quantity (EOQ) it is important that supplies costs in administration be taken into account.

cost, allocation of. (CIMA) Distribution of costs to various COST CENTRES, process, services or products in the proportion in which they have been incurred.

cost, anticipated. A cost expected to arise through some contingency which may, or may not, be easily estimated. cf. ESTIMATED COST.

cost, applied. A cost (actual or percentage) added to costs for ESTIMATE (or sometimes for a QUOTATION) to cover a supplier's contingencies, such as uncertainty as to the purchaser's continued demand for the product, or some special non-standard feature which has been specified by the purchaser. This emphasises the need to use STANDARDS wherever they are applicable.

cost, appraisal. *See* COSTS, QUALITY RELATED COSTS.

cost, batch. (CIMA) Costing of similar Items where these are manufactured in batches.

cost, budgeted. One which has provided for in a budgetary controlled system. May affect the purchasing and supply policy in regard to orders and contract control, and also of INVENTORY.

cost, contract costing. *See* CONTRACT COSTING.

cost, controllable (or 'managed cost'). *See* COST, MANAGED COST.

cost, conversion cost. (CIMA) The sum of the production (process) costs of converting materials (including components for assembly or finishing) into finished products, e.g. direct wages, direct expenses and absorbed PRODUCTION OVERHEADS.

cost, delivered at frontier. *See* DELIVERED AT FRONTIER.

cost, design for cost. To design a product within cost constraints to ensure that it will be competitive in the market place, or as a unit of plant will fulfil its proposed objectives.

cost, development. (CIMA) The cost of the process which begins with the implementation of the decision to produce a new or improved product or to employ a new or improved method, and ends with the commencement of formal production of that product or production by that method.

cost, distribution, optimum total distribution costs. The costs resulting from optimum efficiency in distribution costs by selection of storage, handling and transportation of goods from the point of production to the point of consumption at the least 'total expense' (Summation of all expenses rather than dealing with each operation as an isolated and individual expense).

cost, distribution. (CIMA) That portion of marketing cost which is incurred in warehousing saleable products and in delivering products to customers.

cost, establishment. The cost of running a department such as purchasing and supply. In the context of large contracts consideration may be needed to check the validity of the normal method of calculating ACQUISITION COST used in the ECONOMIC ORDER QUANTITY formulae.

cost, estimated. (CIMA) The predetermination of the probable cost of a job, article, or process.

cost, estimation of costs. A technique used to determine the manufacturing cost of a product, embracing raw materials methods, manufacturing times, labour costs and factory overheads.

cost, external failure. *See* COSTS, QUALITY RELATED COSTS.

cost, factory. The total of PRIME COSTS (i.e. 'variable costs' – which depend upon output plus costs of administration) PLUS 'oncosts' (= 'fixed costs') which do not change with every change in output. 'Factory cost' includes production costs of a product up to despatch, excludes all marketing expenses and overheads except those directly attributable to production.

cost, failure cost(s). Costs which are, as a rule, difficult to predict but which need to be estimated when settling the sums to be allowed for in contracts which contain clauses for LIQUIDATED DAMAGES.

cost, fixed. (CIMA) That which accrues in relation to the passage of time and which, within certain output or turnover limits, tends to be unaffected by fluctuations in volume of output or turnover. e.g. rent, rates, insurance and executive salaries.

cost, handling. A significant factor in supplies costs, usually concealed in purchase price, occurring at numerous points throughout the supply cycle. Includes: supplier packing, and loading onto transport; carrier transit and transshipment; purchaser off-loading, unpacking, checking, etc. Costs are assessed per unit weight, weight per unit distance, unit VOLUME per unit distance, or other measures.

cost, handling cost rule. Every time supplies are handled, something is added to their cost but nothing to their value. (The value may be reduced if damage occurs in handling through inefficient packaging or handling.)

cost, holding. *See* STOCK, COSTS OF HOLDING COSTS.

cost, incremental. The cost resulting from raising the rate of production by one unit. *See also* MARGINAL COSTING.

cost, indirect. (BS) Costs associated with a project that cannot be directly allocated to an activity or group of activities.

cost, internal failure. *See* COSTS, QUALITY RELATED COSTS.

cost, life-cycle. (BS) Total costs of an item throughout its life, including acquisition, maintenance and support costs.

cost, managed. (CIMA) One which can be influenced by the person responsible for the COST CENTRE in which the cost occurs, e.g. cost may arise from excess stock due to bad stock control or excessive scrap through the procurement of faulty material.

cost, marginal. (CIMA) The variable cost of one unit of product or service; i.e. a cost which would be avoided if the unit was not produced (purchased) or provided. Note: in this context a unit is usually either a single article or a standard measure such as the litre or kilogram, etc., but may in certain circumstances be an operation, process or part of an organisation. *See also* MARGINAL COSTING *and* BREAK-EVEN POINT.

cost, marketing (and selling). (CIMA) Marketing costs include publicizing and presentation of products to customers in attractive forms and prices with all research, securing orders and (usually) delivery and in some cases after-sales service. Selling costs (to industry) include salesmen (and other staff) engaged in securing orders by visits,

39

quotations and associated promotional activities. These are areas where purchasing may assist in cost reduction and earn a reduced price to the company.

cost, normal. A cost which is normally incurred at a given level of output in the conditions in which that level of output is normally obtained.

cost, operation. Basic costing methods applicable where standardized products or services result from a sequence of repetitive and more or less continuous operations or processes to which costs can be charged before being averaged over the total units or service produced during the period.

cost, opportunity. The value of a benefit sacrificed in favour of an alternative course of action, e.g. increasing stock investment to ensure continuous production may deprive the firm of the cash (and the opportunity) to buy a more efficient production unit.

cost, over-spend. (BS 4335) The amount by which the incurred cost is greater than the budgeted or planned cost.

cost, premium. A method of remuneration which tends to effect economy in labour costs and materials by the payment of a bonus based on the reduction in total cost compared with standard cost.

cost, prevention. See COST,QUALITY RELATED COST.

cost, prime. (CIMA) The total cost of direct materials (supplies), wages and expenses.

cost, replacement cost accounting. A form of CURRENT COST ACCOUNTING in, which assets are valued at the current

cost of replacing them at the time of a review. Of particular application to INVENTORY by which stock is continuously (or at review) revalued at the current replacement price. See PRICE, REPLACEMENT PRICE.

cost, research. The cost of seeking new or improved materials, methods of manufacture or process, etc. or sources of supply.

cost, standard. (CIMA) A predetermined cost calculated in relation to a prescribed set of working conditions, correlating technical specifications and scientific measurement of materials and labour to the prices and wages expected to apply during the period to which the standard cost is intended to relate, with an addition of appropriate share of budgeted overhead. Its main purposes are to provide bases for control through VARIANCE ACCOUNTING, for valuation of stocks and work in-progress, and, in exceptional cases, fixing selling prices.

cost, stock handling. (BS) The total cost involved in handling and moving stock (including for example order picking and transporting EXCESS STOCKS to other locations).

cost, stock holding. (BS) The costs of maintaining stock in stores. This can include: 1. OPPORTUNITY COST on capital value of stock held, 2. insurance costs and provision for deterioration and obsolescence, 3. cost of storage space, warehouse, stockyard, etc., 4. cost of administration and manning the store.

cost, total cost of ownership. See COST, LIFE-CYCLE COST.

cost, underspend. (BS) The amount by which the incurred cost is less than the budgeted or planned costs.

cost, unit. (CIMA) A quantitative unit of product or service in relation to which costs are ascertained. Cost units are basic for VALUE ANALYSIS and VALUE ENGINEERING, and the comparison of QUOTATIONS, ESTIMATES, TENDERS and PRICES.

cost, use in (more generally 'cost in use'). The cost of ownership of an asset such as a building or unit of plant including interest on capital outlay, costs of operation including repairs, maintenance, depreciation, etc.

cost, variable. (CIMA) A cost which, in the aggregate, tends to vary in direct proportion to changes in volume of output or TURNOVER. Supplies attract VARIABLE or FIXED COSTS according to whether they are embodied in the actual END PRODUCT or are SUPPORTING GOODS or equipment used for production, handling, transport and so on.

cost-benefit analysis. The evaluation of the social and economic worths of a proposed project, or a purchase. *See also* VALUE ANALYSIS.

costs, average (or mean). The figure which represents the average (mean) of a number of different costs and may be derived from the 'simple' or 'weighted' mean of all the costs involved.

costs, direct. *See* COSTS, MATERIAL COSTS.

costs, disposal. The total costs to the owner of material in disposing of an item of material when it has failed or is no longer required for any reason.

costs, historical. (CIMA) Costs based upon the original cost of acquiring an asset, or of purchasing goods (stocks) and services. *See also* PRICE, FIRST-IN, FIRST-OUT PRICE, REPLACEMENT PRICE *and* CURRENT COST ACCOUNTING.

costs, material (direct). Costs of those materials (and services) which are embodied in the manufacture of an end-product.

costs, order preparation. Costs of preparing an actual purchase order. Such costs include: 1. fixed costs which are unaffected by the number of orders placed during any given period, viz. accommodation, plant (computers, VDU'S, office machinery, etc.), maintenance of same and salaries of senior staff, 2. variable costs which are largely proportional to the number of orders placed in a given period, viz. typing, checking, filing, stationery, postage, records, statistical work and wages of routine staff. These costs are a major factor in acquisition costs which in turn influence the calculations of economic order quantities.

costs, ordering costs total. *See* COSTS, ACQUISITION COSTS, TOTAL.

costs, overhead. CIMA Costs incurred in manufacturing which are INDIRECT COSTS (indirect materials, indirect labour and indirect expenses) and include items such as ADMINISTRATION COSTS, MARKETING COSTS, SERVICING COSTS and so on.

costs, production. (CIMA) Comprise PRIME COST plus absorbed PRODUCTION OVERHEAD. *See also* ABSORPTION COSTING.

costs, running. The total costs to the PLANT owner of the operation, MAINTENANCE and modification of an ITEM of plant. *See also* COSTS USE IN.

costs, quality related. The expenditure incurred in defect prevention and quality appraisal activities plus the losses due to internal and external failure.

costs, salvage. Costs of salvaging SCRAP and WASTE; may involve costs of segregation, sorting, handling, storage, baling, compacting, weighing, etc. *See also* COSTS, DISPOSAL COST.

costs, semi-variable. Costs containing both fixed and variable elements, which are therefore partly affected by fluctuations in the volume of output or turnover or purchases. (An area where purchasing NEGOTIATIONS should look for savings). *See also* COSTS VARIABLE COSTS and COSTS, FIXED COSTS.

costs, shortage. The costs associated with having a shortage of supply or service.

costs, storage. Part of stockholding cost includes: buildings and equipment mobile (handling) and static (storage); security; first aid, fire and safety protection; preservation (e.g. humidity, pest control, etc.); administration; labour; energy; rates; hire; insurance; interest on capital outlay. depreciation of buildings, plant and equipment; deterioration, obsolescence and maintenance of buildings and plant. Costs are best expressed as costs per unit volume of space available for storage, etc. (Excluding actual-stock held for which *see* 'COSTS, STOCK-HOLDING COSTS'.)

Council of The European Union (EU). The decision-making body of the Community. It legislates on the basis of COMMISSION proposals, subject to amendment. It comprises ministers and working groups of officials. Note: Legislative power rests with the Council, but some legislation may be made directly by the Commission in order to implement Council decisions.

counter-offer. *See* OFFER, COUNTER OFFER.

counter-purchase. An aspect of COUNTER-TRADE in which an exporter is requested to purchase goods from the country to which his exports are sold. (Note: The 'counter-purchase' from the customer-country may or may not be products used by the purchaser.)

counter-trade. Methods of trading involving exchange of goods rather than money payment. The methods include: BARTER; BUY-BACK; COMPENSATION TRADING, co-operation (production, development, joint marketing of natural resources); COUNTER-PURCHASE; joint ventures.

counting scales. Weighing scales designed so that a read-out of the quantity of items in the balance is given.

course of dealing. *See* DEALING, COURSE OF DEALING.

coverage analysis. A means of establishing optimum stock-holding levels in relation to capital available by making a quantitative analysis of likely demand over a given period of various stock lines and adjusting stock levels to meet demand and at the same time to optimize capital investment.

covering letter. One which accompanies and explains or amplifies the details or data on the principal document - such as a purchase order. If the covering letter is to form part of the contract, attention must be called to it on the face of the purchase order.

cradle to grave. The full lifetime of a product or substance. Of relevance to LIFE CYCLE COSTING and the ENVIRONMENT.

cranage. Charge for use of cranes at port facilities. *See also* CONTAINER RELATED TERMS at LIFT-ON/LIFTOFF.

crane. A materials handling device for lifting heavy items by suspending them.

crate. (BS) A skeleton package or container of open boarded construction. To be differentiated from a CASE.

credit. The opposite of the transfer of cash. This and other meanings briefly as follow: 1. buying and selling without immediate payment. 2. a period of time allowed by a seller for payment. 3. the right-hand column of accounts, or payments received, etc. 4. a document issued by a seller to a buyer entitling him to credit his account with the seller by the sum stated.

credit note. The converse of an INVOICE and a means whereby one party to a transaction (such as a supplier) may make a settlement with another such (such a buyer) to liquidate an overcharge, pay a rebate, meet the value of goods which have been returned to the supplier, etc.

credit sale. One in which the purchaser either defers payment or may pay by instalments.

credit transfer. A method of payment by which a purchaser (for example) may transfer to the bank account of a supplier the money he owes without the use of a cheque.

credit, acceptance credit. Credit given to a large-scale trader of good standing by a bank or accepting house. The trader draws from this within time and finance limits. If the bill matures within the time limit set and is replaced by another, the arrangement is known as a 'revolving credit'. The provision of an acceptance credit usually involves the trader providing a 'letter of hypothecation' pledging the goods to the bank as security.

credit, documentary letter of credit, assignable credit. This arrangement provides for the payment to be made to the supplier's assigns in the event of liquidation.

credit, documentary letter of credit, confirmed credit. Irrevocable letter of credit to which another bank (usually the ADVISING BANK) has added its undertaking on the instructions of the ISSUING BANK. This is in addition to the irrevocable undertaking of the letter.

credit, documentary letter of credit, divisible credit. A credit in favour of a middleman such as an export agent who may transfer the purchaser's money to a number of suppliers in the overseas country, e.g. who may have provided the goods making division according to what they have supplied.

credit, documentary letter of credit, irrevocable credit. A letter of credit under which the issuing bank gives its irrevocable undertaking that payment will be made if all the terms of the letter of credit are met and the specified documents provided. This type of credit cannot be amended or cancelled without the beneficiary's consent. The date on which payment is due is crucial.

credit, documentary letter of credit, negotiable credit. In the case of a LETTER OF CREDIT, one in which a NEGOTIATING BANK can purchase the BILL OF EXCHANGE from the ADVISING BANK of the supplier.

credit, documentary letter of credit, uniform customs, rules and practice. Standard rules for documentary credit issued by the INTERNATIONAL CHAMBER OF COMMERCE and adopted worldwide. Virtually all letters of credit issued nowadays are subject to these rules.

43

credit, documentary letter of credit. (international trade). A facility arranged by an importer (purchaser) for his bank, by means of a LETTER OF CREDIT to the ADVISING BANK of the exporter, to provide credit to pay the exporter (the supplier) on completion of the contract. *See* BELOW.

credit, factoring of credit. The provision of a financial facility by a supplier through a FACTOR who takes charge of the collection of debts from his customers.

credit, revocable letter of credit. One that can be cancelled or amended without prior notice to the beneficiary and is thus of little value to him.

credit, roll-over credit. Extension of a loan by its renegotiation when the sum credited has been exhausted.

credit, transferable letter of credit. One under which the original beneficiary has the right to instruct his bank (with which the letter of credit is available) to transfer it in whole or in part to a third party who is termed the 'second beneficiary'.

creditors. (CIMA) A person or entity to whom money is owed. See also DEBTOR.

critical path analysis. (CIMA) A form of NETWORK ANALYSIS in which a sequence of operations and their interlinking or subsidiary or conditional operations are set out diagrammatically with times, sequence of operations and target dates leading to the final completion of the project, problem or process. Has wide application for construction and plant projects.

cryogenic. A term applied to low temperature substances, apparatus, and processes.

cryptography. In electronic data interchange, the 'scrambling' of data and messages to prevent reading by unauthorised persons.

cumulative delivery diagram. (BS) A curve or block diagram which shows the cumulative number of final products required for delivery in each time period of a manufacturing programme.

currency, convertible. 'Hard currency' that which may be exchanged for gold or other currencies without restriction. Convertible currencies are based on sound, usually developed and industrialised, economies as well as substantial holdings of international reserve assets (gold, US dollars, pounds sterling and SDRS). Unconvertible or 'soft currencies' are usually only used locally in the countries of issue.

current assets. (CIMA) *See* ASSETS, CURRENT ASSETS.

current cost accounting (CCA). (CIMA) A method of accounting requiring that assets (such as stock) shall be shown in terms of what they are worth to the enterprise at the time of review. Usually expressed in equivalent REPLACEMENT COST at that time.

current liabilities. Those liabilities which must be met within (usually) twelve months of the accounting year ahead.

current purchasing power. (CIMA) A method of accounting by which assets are valued at the current purchasing power of the 'present value' of what was originally spent on the asset.

current ratio. (CIMA) An important accountancy ratio indicating to (for example) a purchasing officer the solvency (or otherwise,) of a supplier.

Formula: $Cr = \dfrac{Ac}{Lc}$

Where: Cr is current ratio
Ac is current assets
Lc is current liabilities
As a general rule a sound supplier has a ratio of at least 2:1 i.e. assets, twice liabilities. *See also* ACID TEST. *Also* CONTRACT, CONDITIONS OF CONTRACT and CONTRACT, TERMS OF CONTRACT.

curvilinear. The line of a graph which is curved. It may be random or display regular CHARACTERISTICS, such as for example an OGIVE, a FREQUENCY CURVE or HISTOGRAM, curve of acquisition costs in the formula for ECONOMIC ORDER QUANTITY. *See also* RECTILINEAR (STAT).

custom of a trade. A term in contracts implied by usage and custom, and/or in writing implying various meanings, practices or restrictions appropriate to that particular trade. *See also* DEALING, A COURSE OF DEALING.

Customer relationship management. The philosophy through which a supplier seeks to gather customer information at every point where they touch and interact within an organization.The aim is to better satisfy their expectations through improved knowledge.

customer. 1. A purchaser. 2. The person receiving the services of another.

customs. A general term, for the DUTIES and TARIFFS imposed by an importing country. Also used for the officials and the office from which the customs officers work.

customs, integrated tariff system (TARIC) (EU) An integrated tariff system of the Union based upon the 'harmonised system of COMMODITY CODING'.

customs, single administrative document ('sad'). A single form introduced within the EU to contain no more than one type of customs declaration on a single form and reduction of data requirements resulting in harmonisation of trade data. *See also* CLEARANCE, INWARDS *and* CLEARANCE, OUTWARDS.

cybernetics. The science of communication and control. Applied cybernetics is relevant to ERGONOMICS and especially to automation, such as computer programs for the control of automated storage handling equipment.

cyberspace. The world of computers, their programs and the data held on them. The INTERNET connects these as a virtual reality world.

cycle stock. *See* STOCK, CYCLE STOCK.

cycle time. (BS) The total time taken to complete the elements of a work cycle.

cycle, planning cycle. *See* PLANNING CYCLE.

cyclical fluctuations. Periodic fluctuations in data which may vary at random, variable or fixed intervals on a time base. Can lead to loss in stock-control where overordering can lead to the build up of stock beyond needs, or stock can become OUT OF PHASE with production.

cyclical stock check. *See* STOCK CHECK, CYCLICAL.

D

damages. Money to be paid in compensation for injury, loss, or failure in respect of, for example, contract.

damages, liquidated. Monetary amounts agreed upon by the parties at the outset of a contract and calculated as recompense if the contract is not fulfilled. *See also* DAMAGES, UNLIQUIDATED *and* PENALTY CLAUSES.

damages, remote. Damages which are too remote from the execution of the contract and which might have been (and should have been) expected to be contemplated by the parties themselves when entering into the contract.

damages, unliquidated damages. Damages which were not assessed and agreed at the outset of a contract but were claimed by the plaintiff on breach by the other party (e.g. the supplier). A court will award what it considers REASONABLE compensation for 'actual loss' provided damages are not too REMOTE. (Note: A court will only award damages for loss which arises out of the breach of the contract itself and/or which could have been expected to have been contemplated by the parties themselves at the outset of the contract).

danger warning level. *See* STOCK CONTROL - LEVELS.

danger zone. (HS) Any zone within and/or around MACHINERY in which an EXPOSED PERSON is subject to a RISK to his health or safety.

Dangerous Goods by Road Agreement (ADR). The European agreement for international carriage of goods by road in the EU. It provides for unhindered transits subject to: technical inspection, certification, packing and labelling, vehicle specification and plating, etc.

data. (stat) A collection of observations, measurements, facts or other information. May be classified and statistically analysed in further stages. *See* BS ISO 3534 'STATISTICS, VOCABULARY AND SYMBOLS' for the full range of terminology covering this area. 'Data' is a plural noun.

data bank, data base. (IT) A collection of structured data which supports the operations of the whole, or of a major area of business such as purchasing and supply. The terms are also used to define a centrally located data file which provides the foundations for a computer-based management information system.

data mining. Term coined for extracting useful information from data which may have been obtained from another source than that which generated it.

days of grace. *See* GRACE, DAYS OF.

dead carriage. *See* FREIGHT, DEAD FREIGHT.

dead freight. *See* FREIGHT, DEAD FREIGHT.

dead stock. *See* STOCK, DEAD.

dead weight. Heavy goods paying freight by weight and not by volume of space occupied and frequently deployed as bottom cargo in a ship to maintain stability.

deadline. A definite date by which an action must be completed. TARGETS may be missed but a deadline, if quoted in a contract, is 'of the essence of the contract'. The contract can be deemed to be 'dead' if the deadline is missed.

deal. (n) A term normally reserved for financial transactions, or the result of 'hard bargaining' in a purchase contract situation.

dealer. A person who deals on his own account, and takes the risks of the market in buying and selling to other people.

dealing, 'a course of dealing'. A contractual situation in which a court may find that because of the long association of a buyer and seller both should by now be 'fully aware' of the terms and conditions of contract and trading applied by each to the other.

debenture. A certificate given by customs to an exporter or importer of goods liable to duty, and entitling him to receive drawback.

debit. 1. To charge for goods or services, etc. showing what is owed, 2. The bookkeeping entry which records a sum due.

debit note. The written document showing the amount by which the recipient's account shall be adjusted, e.g. a purchaser returning goods to a supplier seeking to offset a previous undercharge to his customer.

debtor. (CIMA) A person or entity who owes money.

decentralization. The organization of smaller, usually specialised, management/administrative units to which are DELEGATED AUTHORITY. These may be manned by specialist staff who have functional responsibility. *See also* CENTRALIZATION *and* SYNERGY

decision making unit. A unit comprising a group or persons recognised as, and authorised to make and contribute to the making of decisions, e.g. a Supply Management Team.

decision theory. (stat) The use of mathematical techniques to study alternative courses of action such as those of purchasing policies, stock control levels, etc. The techniques use the statistical characteristics of NORMAL DISTRIBUTION, STANDARD DEVIATION, etc.

decision tree. (CIMA) A means of clarifying and analysing management and practical choices, risks, objectives, gains and information. It can be used with or without monetary or other valuation, and is suitable for computerization. At each stage a 'yes' or 'no' decision leads to a branch from a 'decision point' leading to either an 'outcome' or a 'stop'.

decision, community decision. (EU) A ruling issued by the Community. Community decisions are binding in their entirety on those to whom they are addressed, whether member states, companies or individuals. Decisions imposing financial obligations are enforceable in national courts.

deck cargo. Cargo not placed below deck. Special regulations apply to its transport.

deed. (law) A written signed document under seal in a special form that is used to pass legal title of 'real' property from one person to another, so that the public may know who holds the title to the property.

de die in diem. (law) From day to day.

de facto. As a matter of fact.

defect. *See also* QUALITY CONTROL DEFECT.

defect, latent defect. A hidden defect which could not be revealed by reasonable inspection. The purchaser is protected by the law if the latent defect is revealed later.

de jure. (law) As a matter of right.

de novo. Anew, from the beginning,

del credere agent. *See* AGENT, DEL CREDERE.

delegation. (adm) The process of entrusting AUTHORITY, and sometimes RESPONSIBILITY to others in a way which enables them to make the decisions their superior would otherwise make, as opposed to merely carrying out the superior's detailed instructions. The subordinate is RESPONSIBLE to the superior for the results achieved while the superior in turn is ACCOUNTABLE to his own boss for what the subordinate does. [abb. IM]

delimitation. The share of a market (based on previous sales) allocated to the member of a cartel or trade association.

deliverable state. Goods are in a deliverable state statutorily when they are in such a state that the buyer would, under the contract, be bound to take delivery of them.

delivered ex works (ex factory, mill, plantation, warehouse, etc.). Seller's obligations end when he makes goods available at his premises. He is not responsible for loading the goods unless the contract says so. *See* INCOTERMS.

delivery. 1. The voluntary transfer of possession from one person to another. 2. The act of delivering. 3. The time taken, or required, for the shipment of goods. Note: Recommendation by National Economic Development Council: 'Delivery' should be interpreted by suppliers and purchasers as the date when RECEIPT is required at the location of the purchaser. 'Despatch' should always be interpreted as the date when the goods LEAVE a specified location.

delivery note. A document used when a supplier delivers by his own vehicle. Like a CONSIGNMENT NOTE, its endorsement with the CONSIGNEE'S signature is evidence that the goods have been safely delivered. For local deliveries, the delivery note only may be used without a posted ADVICE NOTE.

delivery order. Instructions given by the owner of goods lodged in a warehouse, dock or wharf, etc. and instructing the person acting as bailee and the person holding the documents of title to hand over the goods defined to a person named on the order.

delivery terms, warehousing. The following terms are used in warehousing and similar trades: 'forward goods', delivery of future goods; 'near goods', those which will be ready in the near future; 'to arrive', goods are in transit and will be delivered as soon as they arrive; 'prompt', goods will be shipped in a few days; 'ready', goods are in stock at the time of receipt of customer's order.

Delphi technique. (adm). A procedure for arriving at a consensus of opinions among a group of experts who are given a detailed questionnaire about a problem. Each member of the group produces written answers. Everyone reads the answers of the other participants. In the light of the other responses ideas may be revised. Eventually a consensus should emerge. The consensus may be used to formulate development or change.

demand. The requirements called for by production or a process. Note: This may not be the same as actual issues or usage.

demand pattern. (BS) A time-based representation of past demands, which may be from a number of sources, and may be analysed into the following elements: 1. trend, the general direction in which demand is changing over a period of time; 2. cyclic, the oscillations about a trend of demand. The period of these cycles may be related to the calendar seasons; 3. random variation, the unpredictable element in the demand pattern.

demand, aggregate demand. (econ) The total demand within a national economy for all goods and services. In purchasing and supply, total demand includes the same economic area within the ambit of the particular purchasing and supply organization under review.

demand, complementary. A feature of most industries where commodities are interdependent with the production processes, e.g. welding rods needed to complete the fabrication of steel tanks.

demand, composite. (econ) Where a commodity can be used for more than one purpose in an enterprise, e.g. lubricants used in a machine shop, transport vehicles, handling equipment, lifts, air conditioning, etc., equivalent to 'common user' demand.

demand, contingency. Allowances in provisioning where usage may be dependent upon contingencies which are predictable (e.g. seasonal) or unpredictable (e.g. storm or tempest, etc.)

demand, dependent. Demand which depends on demand for another item. For example the demand for tyres and wheels in a car assembly operation will depend upon the demand for cars

demand, forecast. A forecast of future orders for a product.

demand, independent. Demand which is unrelated to any other demand, for example demand for a single spare part.

demand, inelastic. (econ) The situation where a large change in price only induces a small change in demand. *See also* SUPPLY: INELASTIC SUPPLY.

demand, statistical demand characteristics. Trends (rising, falling, level), predictable, unpredictable, regular, irregular, exceptional, secular, long term, short term, discrete, etc,

demand, supplementary. Where commodities are required in addition to actual production of final product. Viz. spares for customers; samples for marketing; allowance for rejects, scrap and wastage, pilferage, etc.

demand, supplies demand, characteristics of. A vital aspect of supplies management the analysis of which is essential for the establishment of purchasing and stock-control policies and their administration.

demurrage. A charge made for detaining a vehicle, ship or container beyond a specified time.

denomination of quantity. *See* UNIT OF ISSUE.

departmentalizm. (adm) A flaw in ADMINISTRATION or MANAGEMENT in which a department is found to freeze into an isolated unit. It may build up mutual suspicion and hostility with other parts of an enterprise.

deposit. (n) A sum paid to a supplier: 1. paid (or set aside) as security, 2. as a first instalment of total price, 3. to assist the CASH FLOW of the supplier to set up and/or start work, 4. materials which may be ARISINGS from the processes of production. Frequently referred to in connection with ENVIRONMENTAL CONTROL of POLLUTION, TOXICITY, etc.

depreciation. (CIMA) The measure of 'wearing out', consumption or other loss of value of a FIXED ASSET whether from use, passage of time or OBSOLES-CENCE through technology and (or) market changes.

depreciation, accelerated. Depreciation of plant or equipment at a faster rate than planned or normal for that type of plant or equipment. (This is a factor which may need to be taken into account when purchasing plant and equipment which is to be subjected to frequent OVERLOAD or work in exceptionally arduous conditions.)

depreciation, accumulated. The amount which has been written off the value of plant or equipment at a certain specified date in its useful LIFE CYCLE. (May be a factor for negotiation and investigation when buying or taking over used plant and equipment.)

depreciation, straight line. An agreed value of an asset which is written off over its life cycle by equal amounts each year against profits from the asset.

deregulation. (EU) The reduction of the burden of regulation and the improvement of the business environment. The Deregulation Unit of the Department of Trade and Industry checks that all United Kingdom legislation, whether 'domestic', 'Community' or 'international' (e.g. UN, NATO, etc.) in origin is implemented effectively and not officiously. Contact dti. 'Deregulation Unit'.

derogation. (EU) A term frequently used in relation to DIRECTIVES. A clause, obligation or duty etc. may be set aside in respect of a separate industry or trade.

design change. (BS) A change in the specification of a product which generally results in the issue of an amended drawing but does not normally result in a new product, e.g. the introduction of a different thread form in a particular product, or an alteration in tolerances on a machined part.

despatch. See DELIVERY.

despatch date. the date on which goods leave, or are planned to leave, the supplier.

despatch documents. See ADVICE NOTE, DELIVERY NOTE, CONSIGNMENT NOTE, PACKING NOTE, CONTENTS NOTE, INVOICE.

despatch money. See DISPATCH MONEY.

despatch note. (BS) A document recording that products are available for despatch and authorizing arrangements for delivery.

despatch note, customs despatch note. A Customs document sent with goods that are subject to import duty at the port of destination and issued by customs at the port of shipment. The 'despatch note' must be presented to customs at the port of arrival.

deterministic systems. See under PROBABILISTIC SYSTEMS.

detinue. Action at law to make the possessor of goods deliver them up to the rightful owner.

developed market economy countries (UN). The affluent, highly industrialized countries operating under an economic system in which the private sector plays the major role.

development. (OECD) 'Use of scientific or technical knowledge in order to produce new or substantially improved materials, devices or products, to install new processes, systems or services prior to the commencement of commercial production or commercial applications, or to improve substantially those already produced or installed'.

development cost. *See* COST, DEVELOPMENT COST.

deviation. Statistical deviation refers to the difference between a point (event, etc.) and a fixed value. Usually it relates to deviation of an observed figure from a common MEAN. *See also* STANDARD DEVIATION.

dies non. A day upon which for some reason no business is transacted.

differential cost analysis. A system under which the probable costs of alternative schemes are prepared and compared. BREAK-EVEN ANALYSIS may be used for this.

diminishing returns, rule of, in supplies. An economic rule whereby progressively smaller reductions in price are available as larger quantities are purchased, after a certain level is reached. The rule may be upset in industrial purchasing owing to a number of factors such as, change in production method, or plant, standardisation, etc. See also LEARNING CURVE.

dip rod, measurement by dip rod. A means of measuring quantities of fluid in storage vessels. A dip rod is a 'measuring instrument' and NOT a measure. *See Eric Gnapp v the Petroleum Board 1949.*

direct materials costs. *See* COSTS, DIRECT MATERIALS COSTS *and* MATERIALS, DIRECT MATERIALS.

direct materials usage variance. That portion of direct materials costs variance which is the difference between the standard quantity specified for the production achieved, whether completed or not, and the actual quantity used, both valued at STANDARD PRICES.

directive. (EU) An instruction from the EU to member states to change their laws through the normal processes of parliament. *See also* REGULATION - EU.

dirty bill. *See* BILL OF LADING.

dis-utility. A term sometimes used to express the result of intake of defective, sub-standard (etc.) supplies, or the indications from a VALUE ANALYSIS, COST BENEFIT or other study.

disbursements. payments.

discharge of contract. *See* CONTRACT, DISCHARGE OF CONTRACT'.

discount. An allowance (usually a percentage) on an amount, (usually) a purchase price, sale price, etc.

discount register. A purchasing department record showing discounts, rebates and settlement terms agreed with suppliers. Usually kept as a confidential record. *See also* RECORDS, PURCHASING.

discount, at a discount. Something bought below the nominal value, or depreciated.

discount, banker's discount. The amount charged on the face value of a bill by a banker for discounting it, i.e. for paying money upon it before it is due.

discount, bill of exchange, discounting of. On a BILL OF EXCHANGE the difference between the full amount of the bill and lower amount accepted by a seller - or creditor.

discount, cash (commercial discount). The amount of discount allowed between traders on cash transactions

51

between them, e.g. on CASH AND CARRY. *See also* DISCOUNT, REBATE, PROMPT CASH, ORDERS AND CONTRACTS.

discount, cumulative. MULTIPLE DISCOUNTS which are added together before being applied to a price structure, e.g. two discounts, one for (say) bulk quantity of 10% and also one for special transportation arrangements of (say) 5%. Cumulatively:£100 - 15% = £85 (*But see* DISCOUNTS, SEQUENTIAL DISCOUNTS.)

discount, loyalty. A special discount given by a supplier to a purchaser in return for an agreement to confine purchases in full (or in an agreed proportion of total intake) to that supplier. *See also* REBATE, LOYALTY REBATE.

discount, multiple. The allowance of more than one discount on an account. It is important to agree, when negotiating, whether discounts are SEQUENTIAL or CUMULATIVE.

discount, prompt cash settlement. Special discount allowed on settlement of accounts promptly. (Usually in 7-14 days).

discount, quantity. Discount given by a supplier in consideration of the size of order placed by the purchaser.

discount, resale ('trade discount'). The discount allowed by one business to another which buys in order to re-sell by way of trade. e.g. the discount given by a wholesaler to a retailer.

discount, retrospective. An arrangement whereby the discount allowed in a given period is based on the amount of business done in the previous period. Note: this form of discount may result in a 'windfall' profit (or loss) to either party in the year it is given.

discount, sequential discount. MULTIPLE DISCOUNTS which are applied one after the other in sequence.

discount, settlement. A discount given at settlement of accounts, e.g. PROMPT CASH, to encourage prompt payments of accounts by the purchaser.

discount, sliding scale. A discount which increases with the size of order placed allowed by a supplier to a buyer.

discount, trade. The discount on price allowed by one supplier to another in the same trade. *See* DISCOUNT, RESALE DISCOUNT.

discounted cash flow. Evaluates the future net cash flows generated by a project or plant during its expected LIFECYCLE by DISCOUNTING THEM BACK to their present-day value. The two common methods are: 1. calculation of the YIELD determining the internal rate of return (IRR) as a percentage. 2. calculation of net present value (NPV). In this case a suitable discount rate is chosen and a monetary result is obtained. *See* VALUE.

discounting back. (as distinct from COMPOUNDING) gives the sum of the total gross expected income from the investment in a project, or plant, etc. It estimates the 'time value' of money, that is to say, the vestment today which involves expenditure of capital which is sacrificed from other purposes in the hope of future profit.

discrepancy. Variation or actual difference between a stated fact or claim and the actual. e.g. difference between quantity advised and received, actual price and that quoted, estimated or forecast, etc.

discrimination. A differentiation in which some purchasers are given preference over others.

dispatch money. Payment by way of a bonus for loading or discharging a vessel in less time than that stated on the charter party. Generally based upon a set figure per day.

disposal instructions. The document that describes in detail the method and precautions to be observed in discarding or otherwise disposing of material, plant and equipment when it has failed or is no longer required for any reason.

distrainor. Person who brings an action for distraint.

distraint. The seizure of goods for debt.

distress. In law, the act of distraining goods for debt.

distribution cost. *See* COSTS, DISTRIBUTION COST.

Distribution Resource Planning. A system, based on the same principles as Materials Requirements Planning, whereby the resources and tome needed to achieve distribution objectives can be calculated.

distribution system. An organization of administrative procedures, transport, handling, storage and user facilities through which supplies move from a point of origin to user(s). *See also* LOGISTICS.

distribution time. The period of time between the despatch date from the manufacturer and the delivery date to the customer.

distribution, supplies, distribution of. The process of movement of supplies from location to location by any method of transportation, but usually applied to movement by road or rail.

distributor. A MIDDLEMAN engaged in the distribution of a category of goods, (especially) in a specific territory and of goods made (or supplied by) a particular enterprise. *See also* AGENTS.

diversification. The converse of SPECIAL-ISATION. The action of an enterprise to vary (products, operations, etc.) in order to spread risk, expand sales, etc.

diversity, ethnic. A recognition of the fact that society comprises a number of ethnic groups. In purchasing and supply practical acknowledgemet of this fact means encouraging and promoting trading with businesses owned and/or operated by ethnic minorities.

dock. 1. A space or artificial basin with water (usually) impounded to high tide level for reception of water-born craft. 2. A raised platform of suitable height for the loading and unloading of rail or road vehicles.

dock dues. The tolls levied on vessels entering and leaving port.

dock leveller. (log) Device installed between the platform of a loading-dock (bay) and the floor of vehicles of varying heights.

dock pass. Certificate given by harbour authorities to the ship-master on payment of all dock dues.

dock warrant. A document of title given to the owner of goods stored in a dock warehouse.

docket. Slips, tickets or forms.

document of title. *See* TITLE, DOCUMENT OF TITLE.

documentary credit. *See* CREDIT, DOCUMEN-TARY.

documentation, export/import (aligned). (SITPRO) International trade documentation based upon United

Nations agreed formats and used in the UK and world-wide. Can be produced from a single master document in association with office copiers, duplicators, WORD PROCESSORS and computers, etc.

documents of record. Written documents, such as those concerning a transaction, e.g. purchase orders, and which may be used as legal evidence, in a contract.

domain name. An address in CYBERSPACE where each computer linked to the INTERNET may be contacted.

dotcom. A shorthand expression for an organization which has an INTERNET address.

down time. (BS) The period of time in which a workstation is not available for production due to a functional failure. *See also* WAITING TIME *and* IDLE TIME.

draft. 1. An order by which money is drawn from a bank. 2. The money thus drawn. 3. Bill of exchange or cheque drawn by one bank on another for the transfer of money.

draft, sight draft A draft (bill of exchange) which is payable on demand.

draught. The depth of water needed to float a vessel.

draw-off order. *See* ORDERS, DRAW OFF ORDERS.

drawback. 1. Excise drawback: refunds made when excise duties are returned to the owner of goods on which excise duties have already been paid. 2. 'Customs drawback'; import duties returned to the owner of imported goods which are being re-exported, viz. after treatment, processing or repair, etc.

drawee. The party on whom a bill of exchange (draft) is drawn.

drawer. The party who draws a bill of exchange (a draft).

drawings. Separate presentations of documents under a letter of credit.

driver of machinery. (EU)(HS) An operator responsible for the movement of MACHINERY. The driver may be transported by the machinery or may be on foot, accompanying the machinery, or may be guiding it by remote control (cables, radio, etc.) (EC directive 'mobile machinery & lifting equipment.')

drop shipment (wholesaling). A shipment made direct from supplier to the customer of a wholesaler without passing physically through the hands of the wholesaler.

due care. That standard of conduct exercised by an ordinary reasonable and prudent person.

due date maturity. (SITPRO) The date upon which an accepted usance (time or terms) bill of exchange becomes due for payment under letter of credit arrangements.

dues in. Quantities due to be received against a purchase or production order. In the case of stock *see* STOCK, DUES-IN.

dues out. Quantities due to be issued against known future demands such as production schedules, or the balance of requisitions which have not been met in full and for which a BACK ORDER (STORES) has been raised,

dues, harbour dues. *See* DOCK DUES.

dumping. Selling abroad at prices below the normal value. EU Regulations define this value and set out how it is to be determined usually the price charged for comparable sales in the country of origin.

dumpster. *See* SKIP.

dunnage. Wood or other material in strips or blocks, etc. used to separate cargo or goods so as to raise, it from the ground, provide ventilation, protect it from other goods or from rising damp, and/or to give space for entry of forks of lift trucks, etc.

duopoly. A near-monopoly situation where there are only two suppliers in the market.

Dusts Mobile Machinery and Lifting Equipment Directive. (EU) Where MACHINERY may emit dust or gases, suitable containment precautions must be taken. See also dti MACHINERY SAFETY BOOKLET. *See also* FIRE.

Dutch auction. *See* AUCTION, DUTCH

duty free. Goods on which customs or excise duties are not levied.

duty of care. *See* CARE, DUTY OF.

duty, customs duty. Duty levied on imports either to raise revenue or to protect home industry.

duty, excise duty. Tax on goods manufactured in home country for revenue purposes.

duty, specific duty. Customs duty at a specific rate per unit weight, volume or other measure.

dynamics. The study of forces which produce, or tend to produce, motion.

E

e-mail. Mail transmitted electronically.

e-procurement. an electronic means of buying via EDI or INTERNET sites.

early supplier involvement (ESI). Consultations with suppliers at the conception, design or pre-production phases of the development of a product.

earmarked stock. *See* STOCK, ALLOCATED.

ECO labelling. (EU) A scheme for Community-wide positive labelling of consumer goods which are 'environmentally friendly'. The scheme is part of general strategy to reduce pollution and waste caused by consumer goods. Basic objectives are to: define the criteria by which to judge a product; encourage manufacturers to develop products which reach those standards; provide consumers with a guide to such products; encourage 'consumer awareness' of environmental control, ecological disciplines, etc.

ecology. A philosophy which attempts to transform manufacturing companies' existing processes to comply with and surpass the values of environmentally conscious consumers. It does this through a set of practical guide lines. (Dr Matthew 'An ecological way forward', The MFg Engineer vol. 72 No.3).

economic order quantity. *See* QUANTITY, ECONOMIC ORDER.

economics. The study of natural resources, how they are obtained, manipulated and distributed along with the wealth that goes them. 'Macroeconomics' is concerned with the total economy of a country,

economy, centrally planned economy. The economic systems of such economies (as the former Eastern Bloc) based on a system which requires close control of the system in the absence of normal MARKET FORCES.

economy price. *See* PRICE ECONOMIC.

economy, mixed economy. One in which the means of production the provision of services, particularly within the INFRASTRUCTURE, are partly in private hands or in public ownership.

economy, national economy. The means of, and systems for, producing distribution of the needs (material and services) of a society within the area of State bounds. Involves the infrastructure financial structure of the area the 'macro-economy'.

ECU, the. *See* EUROPEAN CURRENCY UNIT.

EDIFACT. The European standard for EDI.

elastic demand. Demand is said to be 'elastic' when a small change in price results in a large change in demand. *See also* ELASTIC SUPPLY.

elastic supply. Supply is said to be elastic when a small change in price results in a large change in supply. *See also* ELASTIC DEMAND. Note: this and similar rules of 'supply and demand' do not always apply to industrial purchasing and supply because demands are usually pre-determined by other factors, e.g. sales and production needs, and, not solely by market forces.

electricity pool. (energy). Industry representative forum responsible for deciding pricing issues in the electricity market in England and Wales.

electronic data interchange (EDI). Means by which information is passed between organizations, or organizational departments, by computer.

electronic funds transfer (EFT). A system of payment whereby businesses may readily settle accounts by means of electronic data transmission.

electronic point of sale (EPOS). A system whereby goods are scanned, usually by a bar code reader, at the sales desk. Inventory records are updated, and a receipt including a description of the goods is produced.

electronic signature. A scanned signature transferred onto an electronic document confirming the authenticity of the document.

embodiment materials. Materials which will be incorporated into some product to be manufactured and which the buying organisation will then sell on.

encryption. A way of ensuring the confidentiality of data transmitted over the internet.

end-product. The final result of a process of manufacture. This may or may not be a finished product but it may become the raw material for further production or process.

endorse. To sign the back of a bill of exchange, promissory note, cheque, warrant, delivery order, etc. The person signing it is termed the 'endorsee'.

energy. The capacity for doing work by a body of matter (e.g. a moving object) or a system (e.g. a stretched spring). The energy capacity is expressed in 'joules'. *See* ENERGY - KINETIC ENERGY *and also* ENERGY, POTENTIAL ENERGY.

energy management. The management of the storage, conversion, distribution and utilization of energy directed to the economic provision of required services and the elimination of avoidable losses.

energy, kinetic. (HS) Energy derived from the motion of an object or quantity of substance.

energy, potential. Energy from the position of an object (or a substance such as a liquid) due to its elevated position. (e.g. dangers from objects stacked insecurely at high level, tanks of liquid feeding inadequate pipework at lower levels, etc.)

enquiry. An invitation to a supplier to submit prices for goods or services by estimate, quotation or tender. *See also* INQUIRY.

enterprise. Any commercial or industrial business venture including those in the private, public and worker cooperative sectors of an economy. (This term is preferred by some to the term 'undertaking' as describing a 'venture, especially one calling for determination and initiative' (Larousse).

enterprise resource planning (ERP). A system for the coordination of planning and execution of business on a wide basis, between links in the supply chain, involving more than coordination.

entrepot trade. Trade through a trading centre or port which is imported and re-exported without incurring duty.

environment. 'Surroundings. Particularly the influences which, may affect growth, development, existence of living things.' (Dictionary definition). In the context of purchasing and supply the term 'environment' has a number of important implications. 1. Compliance with Statutory laws, Directives, Codes of Practice, etc. relating to health and safety of those who may come into contact with supplies and services which have been procured. 2. The ambient conditions in the environment in which goods are stored. 3. The possibilities of pollution arising from processes, handling or storage of supplies.

environment directives. (EU) There are over 350 directives, regulations, and decisions in force at the time of preparing these notes. They include inter alia assessments, storage of HAZARDOUS SUBSTANCES and public access to information.

Environment Protection Act 1990. (HS) Section 33 of this Act (inter alia) makes it illegal to 'treat, keep or dispose of, CONTROLLED WASTES in a manner likely to cause pollution to the environment or harm to human life.' *See* WASTE.

environmental control standards. (BS) This standard specifies the elements of an environmental management system.

environmental declaration. (EU) A declaration by members of the Community to: a. preserve, protect, improve the quality of the environment; b. protect human health; c. ensure prudent and rational use of natural resources; d. take preventative action to repair damage at source; e. ensure the polluter shall pay.

environmental engineering. *See* NOISE (ENVIRONMENTAL), NOISE CONTROL (ACOUSTIC), OPERATING STATIONS, SANITARY ENGINEERING; WATER SUPPLY.

Environmental Protection Agency. An agency operating in the United States to encourage the safeguarding of the environment. The Agency issues certificates of merit to firms which achieve good effective results in environmental control.

ergonomics. The study of the physical relationships between operatives and machines.

escalation clause. A clause in a contract which permits a seller to adjust his price in the event of market changes. Note: in normal times care should be taken to ensure that the clause also covers any fall in costs. *See also* CONTRACT PRICE ADJUSTMENT.

escrow. (law) A contract or deed which does not come into effect until some other condition has been fulfilled.

escrow, software. An arrangement whereby the source code to a piece of software is held by a neutral third party.

estimate. 1. An (approximate) calculation of the charges or cost. 2. Judgement made by calculation, especially from incomplete data, rough or incomplete calculation. *See also* QUOTATION.

estoppel. (law) Implies that, owing to an action by one party, another party is prevented or stopped from completing a task, contract, etc.

ethics. The theory relating to morality of behaviour. Ethical Standards cover conforming with an accepted standard of good behaviour, e.g. in a profession such as purchasing and supply. The Chartered Institute of Purchasing and Supply publishes an ethical code which is widely adopted as the basis for behaviour in this profession.

ethics, in supplies activities. The code of behaviour considered to be appropriate to the functions of obtaining and administration of supplies. See the ethical code of the Chartered Institute of Purchasing and Supply.

Euro. (EU) The Euro is based on a basket of currencies but can be regarded as money in most respects, since it is a means of payment, a medium of exchange and a store of value. The value of the Euro is calculated as the sum of the set amounts of the Community currencies within it. These amounts are set broadly to reflect each country's relative economic size in terms of gross national product and the importance of its trade within the Community. Euro is the official name for the single currency (previously known as the ECU) introduced in the EUROZONE in 1999.

Eurocheque scheme. (EU) A bank scheme whereby cheque cards and bankers cards may be used by their holders to make withdrawals within certain specified limits from those continental banks which cooperate in scheme, within the EU.

Eurodiploma. A diploma in purchasing and supply management initiated by the European Regional Group of the International Federation of Purchasing and Materials Management.

Euroland. (EU) *See* EUROZONE.

Europatents. Patents valid throughout the EU granted by the European Patents Office.

European Committee for Electrotechnical Standardisation, 'CENELEC'. European regional standards organization comprising the International Electrotechnical commission (IEC) and national committees of the EC countries. The UK member, the British Electrotechnical Committee European Council of the BSI. *See also* CEN.

European Committee for Standardisation. European regional standards organization comprising the national standards bodies (members of the International Organisation for Standardisation ISO) of the EU.

European Community. (EU) The 'community' of European States set up under the Treaty of Rome (1957). Prior to 1985 the Community was styled the 'European Economic Community' and the 'Common Market', and

subsequently the 'European Community' (The EC). Finally w.e.f. November 1 1993, under the Treaty of Maastricht the adopted title became The European Union (The EU).

European Community Competition rules. Rules set down by the Treaty of Rome aimed at ensuring equality of treatment of organizations throughout the Community.

European Currency Unit. *See* EURO.

European Journal: 'The Official Journal of the European Communities.' The 'Journal' available in the UK from the HMSO contains DECISIONS, DIRECTIVES, OPINIONS, RECOMMENDATIONS, and REGULATIONS. These all become 'Official' when published in the 'Journal'.

European Monetary Fund (EMF). A fund to be set up as a reserve asset and means of settlement of account via the European Currency Unit.

European Standards. (EU) CEN or CENELEC standards implemented by CEN/ CENELEC members who adopt them as identical national standard and withdrawing any conflicting national standard. *See also* HARMONIZATION DOCUMENT and CEN/CENELEC.

European Union, The (EU). The formation of the European Union arose from the Treaty of Maastricht and took effect on 1 November 1993. The Union is a multi-pillar structure which confers European citizenship on all Citizens of the Union, and which incorporates the European Community with its supranational institutions. THE COMMISSION, THE EUROPEAN PARLIAMENT and the EUROPEAN COURT, together with arrangements for intergovernmental cooperation in foreign affairs and matters of justice.

European Union. *See* EUROPEAN COMMUNITY.

Eurozone. (EU) The member countries of the EU that have adopted the EURO as legal tender.

evidence accounts. A formalized system in trading with the Eastern bloc whereby a record is maintained by the 'FTO' (or an appointed bank) through which all the, transactions will pass or to whom details will be notified and verified.

ex warehouse. *See* EX WORKS.

examining. Looking very carefully and closely (*but see. also* INSPECTION) to discover evident facts, mistakes or, for example, evident damage Of goods received at intake, following an initial check of the condition of the package in which the goods were received.

exception principle. The analysis of what is wrong, difficult, important or exceptional. *See* MANAGEMENT BY EXCEPTION. The exception principle is important in INFORMATION TECHNOLOGY and INFORMATION PROCESSING. In applications, particularly where associated with FEEDBACK, the volume of recorded data may be reduced by 'exceptions'. For example: 'demand changes', 'quality failure', etc. can be 'reported'. This can eliminate vast volumes of data which are 'unexceptional' and upon which no management or administrative decisions are needed.

exception reporting. An important asset resulting from EDP is the ability of a computer (when given a suitable program) to report exceptional events, trends, demands, (such as demands for supply, production outputs, etc.) also quality data. Such reporting can then act through FEEDBACK to correct any digression/diversion from the plan or program which is in operation.

excess stock. (BS) *See* STOCK, EXCESS *and* STOCK LEVEL, MAXIMUM.

exchange rate mechanism (ERM). (EU) A preliminary to membership of EMU in which a candidate currency is fixed against the EURO within a tight band. The currency needs to demonstrate its ability to preserve its value within this band before it can be accepted into EMU.

exchange. A place where merchants and dealers meet to transact business.

exchange rate. The value of one currency in terms of another

exchange, bill of. *See* BILL OF EXCHANGE.

exchange, commodity exchange *See* MARKETS.

exchange, market. *See* MARKET, FUTURES MARKET.

exchanges futures exchange. *See* MARKET, . FUTURES MARKET.

exclusion clause. *See* CONTRACT, EXCLUSION CLAUSE IN CONTRACT.

exclusive buying. An arrangement to purchase or stock only products of one supplier, possibly in return for an exclusive supply arrangement.

exemptions, 'negative clearance'. (EU) Negative clearance is an individual exemption granted by the Commission in respect of an article of Community enactments. *See also* COMFORT LETTER.

exhaust bin level. *See* STOCK LEVEL, EXHAUST LEVEL.

expediting. A term adopted from the USA as a synonym for PROGRESSING or progress chasing. Expediting may be active. 'Chasing' is implicitly reactive.

expeditor. One who expedites.

expendable supplies. *See* SUPPLIES,CONSUM-ABLE SUPPLIES.

expert system. (IT) A computer program that imitates a human expert.

explosion. The listing of the various component parts of an assembly, including the quantities of each component.

explosives. Substances - solids, liquids, gases, powders or particulates, or other forms of substance - which undergo rapid chemical (or nuclear) change. The former produce gas in high volume compared with the volume of the original substances when heated, struck or energised in some other way. Great pressure is generated if the explosion occurs in a confined space. (Hence, the need to avoid storage of explosives such as LPG within a closed space, or installation of dust containing silos, etc. without explosion vents.) *See* SUBSTANCES.

exponential smoothing. (stat) A forecasting method based on exponen-tially weighted moving averages . This system places more emphasis on recent data, the relative weight placed on each observation decreases with increasing age, the 'weights' form an exponential series.

exposed person. (HS) Any person wholly or partially in a DANGER ZONE.

exposure limit, maximum, personal. (HS) The maximum concentration of an airborne substance, averaged over a stated period, beyond which may be hazardous by INHALATION. Levels of concentration.

external good order. A term used in the freight business to convey the assumption that goods tendered for carriage are complete and in good order. *See also* GOODS INTAKE.

external resource management. The management of providers of goods or services, and of relationships with them.

extranet. A part of the INTERNET closed off to public access, and reserved for use only by those authorised.

F

face value. *See* VALUE, FACE VALUE.

facilities management. The contracting out of all activities connected with the organization and control of a facility such as building maintenance, security or catering.

factor of safety. The factor set, or allowed for, in the design of a structure, or plant - such as a silo, storage equipment, handling equipment, etc. - so as to ensure that the operational working stress is safely below the safe permissible limit.

factor, business factor. *See* AGENT, FACTORING AGENT.

factoring of credit. *See* CREDIT, FACTORING OF CREDIT.

Factors Act 1889. Act which is concerned with transfer of title to goods where they have been sold or otherwise disposed of by a factor (or mercantile agent) acting on behalf of the seller. Subject to a number of conditions, any such sale is as valid as if expressly authorized by the seller.

factory order. *See* ORDER PRODUCTION.

fail safe. (BS) A designed property of an item that prevents failures of it being critical failures.

failure mode and effects analysis. An analytical technique to identify hazards and explore the effects of failure or malfunction of individual components within a system.

fair price. *See* PRICE, FAIR.

Fair Trading Act 1973. Act which created the Director General of Fair Trading and Monopolies & Mergers Commission. Director General required to review commercial practices in UK and report to DTI on adverse practices against the public interest. Director-General also required to monitor monopolies and mergers in order to suppress anti-competitive (or potentially anti-competitive) practices. Act has been substantially amended by the Competition Act 1998, with increased powers being given to Director General and the newly created Competition Commission (replacing the Monopolies and Mergers Commission).

fair wear and tear. The deterioration on plant, equipment, vehicles, etc. which has resulted from the normal intended use and with the required maintenance having been carried out.

faith. *See* GOOD FAITH *and* BAD FAITH.

fast moving stock. *See* STOCK, FAST MOVING.

feasibility study. A method for assessing the viability of a scheme, such as extension of a production or process plant.

fee simple. Legal statement for absolute ownership of land.

feedback. 1. The term is commonly used in regulatory systems for comparing 'output' with some standard to be set and usually maintained at a fixed level. e.g. Stock replenishment may be initiated by feedback via computer (or manual) records when the actual physical stock in hand is compared with the 're-order level' set for a particular item of' stock. 2. A system whereby information at an 'output' is compared with forecast and the difference (known as the 'error') is feedback to the input (i.e. 'feedback') and adjusted. *See also* HOMEOSTASIS.

feedback (communication). The return flow of information in a COMMUNICATION NETWORK. May be of an electronic, verbal, numerate or physical nature.

feedback, negative. (IT) In supply control systems, future action is often based upon deviations from the forecast which had been made for the present (or latest) event. *See* STOCK CONTROL BY EXPONENTIAL SMOOTHING.

feedback, positive. (IT) This involves amplification of a signal as distinct from differentiation employed in the application of negative feedback. Positive feedback is acted upon when, for example, increased power is needed for a conveyor or other powered (or power assisted) machinery.

feedstock. Material introduced into a plant in order to be processed.

fiduciary. Referring to trust or trusteeship,

fifth freedom (air transport). The right, allowing an airline to set down and pick up passengers, cargo or mail in an intermediate country before flying on to the country of destination.

final assembly. An assembly to which no further parts need be added. *See also* ASSEMBLY, SUB-ASSEMBLY.

financial sanction. *See* SANCTION, FINANCIAL.

finished goods. (CIMA) Manufactured goods, ready for resale or despatch to a purchaser, agent, etc. *See* CURRENT ASSETS *and* END PRODUCTS.

finished goods stock. *See* STOCK, FINISHED GOODS STOCK.

firewall. A means of controlling access to one computer network from another. Used as a defence against unauthorized interference with data.

firm offer. *See* OFFER, FIRM.

first-in, first-out (FIFO). The materials management discipline to ensure that oldest stock is used first so as to avoid STOCK LIFE exceeding SHELF LIFE. *See also* STOCK VALUATION, FIRST-IN, FIRST-OUT; PRICE, FIRST IN, FIRST-OUT PRICE.

fitness for purpose. In the sale of goods legislation, the term which means that goods sold/purchased must not only be of satisfactory quality, but must also be suitable for the purpose for which they are intended.

fixed assets. *See* ASSETS: FIXED.

fixed costs. *See* COST, COST FIXED.

fixed order interval. An inventory control approach where orders are placed at regular fixed intervals, the order quantity being varied. *See also* CONTRACTS: ADMINISTRATION *and* ORDERS & CONTRACTS: VARIETIES OF.

fixed order quantity. An inventory management approach where the same quantity of materials is ordered at varying intervals. *See also* CONTRACTS: ADMINISTRATION *and* ORDERS *and* CONTRACTS: VARIETIES OF.

flag of convenience. Registration of a ship in a country other than that of its owner, usually to take advantage of a more favourable tax regime.

flash point. The temperature at which a substance gives off a gas which at this temperature will then ignite.

flats. A term for flatbed or platform vehicles or containers, and sometimes for timber, cases and similar goods.

flexible manufacturing system. *See* PRODUCTION.

float. A sum of money provided or set aside for some specific purpose.

flow chart. (stats) (adm) A process chart using appropriate symbols, setting out the sequence of flow of a product (or of supplies in the context of purchasing and supply), or of procedures, in an administrative context, by charting all events under review.

force (f). 1. A dynamic influence that changes (or tends to change) an object from a state of rest to a state of motion, or to change the rate of motion of the object. (e.g. the force applied to a truck or other mobile stores handling equipment) in order to produce motion]. 2. A static influence that produces strain upon an object or system. (e.g. the force producing strain in an overloaded beam or shelf).

force majeure. Circumstances beyond the reasonable control of either party to a contract, e.g. government intervention, a strike or lock-out. *See also* ACT OF GOD.

force, tractive force. *See* TRACTIVE FORCE.

forecast. (CIMA) A prediction of future events in the light of circumstances expected to prevail. *See* EXPONIENTIALLY SMOOTHED FORECAST.

forecast, rolling forecast. (CIMA) A statistical method of forecasting whereby at the close of each period actual results are recorded, noted and adjusted forecasts are made for the next period (or periods) ahead.

forecasting horizon. The longest future time interval covered by a forecast; this may be divided in to forecast periods.

foreclose. To seize a security in the event of an unpaid mortgage or debt.

foreign bill. Any bill of exchange, drawn and payable outside the British Isles, or drawn within the British Isles on a resident outside.

forfaiting (forfaitieren). A form of credit whereby the forfaiting bank purchases an exporter's 'receivables', discounting them, usually at a fixed rate.

forge. To offer with the intention to deceive, e.g. offer something as genuine which is fake.

fortran. Abbreviation for 'formula translation'. A computer language appropriate for mathematical and scientific problems.

forward allocation. Arrangement for ALLOCATION STOCK or advance orders for future delivery to ensure availability of supplies when required. *See also* FUTURES.

forward allocation of supply/stock. Arrangements to allocate deliveries of supplies/or quantities of stock to meet specific needs. *See also* STORE, ALLOCATION STORE

forward delivery. Goods to be delivered at a later date but in an agreed period.

forward supply arrangement. *See* ORDERS AND CONTRACTS A-Z.

forwardation. (com) *See* CONTANGO.

forwarding agent. *See* AGENT, FORWARDING.

Fossil Fuel Levy. (energy) A surcharge on electricity bills, linked to the need to reduce atmospheric pollution, duty or charge imposed.

foul bill. *See* BILL OF LADING.

framework agreement. An agreement, not necessarily a contract, whereby a supplier or service provider undertakes to supply goods or services up to a certain value, over an agreed period of time, at an agreed price. These are also known as CALL-OFF ARRANGE-MENTS.

franchise. The licence (i.e. the right) given by a manufacturer to a distributor to market his products. May include certain territorial or other rights and obligations such as after-sales service, standards, etc.

fraud. Criminal deception, dishonest artifice or trick. To succeed in an action on contract it must be shown that it was: 1. a false statement regarding fact; 2. made knowingly or recklessly; 3. intended that the plaintiff should act upon it.

free market (economy). One where price is determined by the free play of MARKET FORCES such as SUPPLY AND DEMAND without intervention or control by governments. *See* CENTRALLY PLANNED ECONOMY.

free of all average. On a marine insurance policy which is so endorsed, only a claim for total loss can be considered and dealt with; partial loss will lie solely with the owner of the goods lost alone. *See* AVERAGE.

free of general average. On a marine insurance policy which is so endorsed underwriters need not make any contributions towards the general average in the event of loss.

free of particular average. The underwriters are not liable for partial loss unless it is the result of accident or some unavoidable cause. *See* AVERAGE.

free port. 1. A port where goods intended for re-export can enter duty free. 2. A port open equally to all commercial vessels.

free-issue materials. *See* FREE-ISSUE SUPPLIES.

free-issue supplies. *See* SUPPLIES, FREE-ISSUE.

free-issue system. A system by which stock is held available in store and is issued for use on demand without a stores requisition, or other documentation *See also* STOCK, FREE-ISSUE STOCK.

freight/freightage. 1. Commercial transport that is slower and cheaper than 'express'. 2. The price charged for freight transport. 3. The goods transported. 4. A cargo or part of it. *See also* HAULAGE.

freight absorption. The arrangement by a supplier to include freight charges in his price.

freight forward or freight collect. Freight payable by consignee on arrival of the goods.

freight forwarder. *See* AGENT, FORWARDING.

freight note. Bill for freight charges.

freight outward. Freight included in the price and paid by the seller.

freight release. An endorsement on a bill of lading to indicate that freight has been paid.

freight tonne (FT). Base tonnage upon which freight charges are calculated. The symbols 'W' and 'M' are often added to signify whether the freight has been calculated on the basis of weight or physical measurement, e.g. in cubic metres.

freight, backfreight. Freight payable by a supplier for goods to be returned to him for any valid reason such as rejection for non-compliance with contract, etc.

freight, inward paid. Charges for delivery to the purchaser paid for by the seller,

65

or refunded to the purchaser on delivery.

freight, shortfall freight. Increased charge by a carrier to cover extra costs where freight charged on a pro-rata basis fails to achieve the minimum as per his tariff.

freighter. A ship or aircraft designed for carrying cargo.

frequency curve. (stat) A frequency curve can be produced where there are many items and small intervals ('classes') developed from a HISTOGRAM. When the top centre of each pipe is joined the lines may form a continuous curve.

frequency distribution (BS) The relationship between the values of a characteristic and their absolute or relative frequencies. The distribution is often presented as a table with special groupings (classes) if the values are measured on a continuous scale.

frequency polygon. A simple HISTOGRAM in which the number of items (classes) are too few to produce a true FREQUENCY CURVE. Whilst a frequency polygon is seldom adequate for close mathematical and statistical manipulation it can have practical applications to study, for example: supplier's delivery performance; frequency of damage in transit; analysis of loads transported and their frequency, etc.

friable. Liable to crumble or disintegrate.

frustration of contract. *See* CONTRACT, FRUSTRATION OF CONTRACT.

full line forcing. Efforts by a seller to force his customer to accept a full range of goods which he has on offer.

functional profile. The profile of administrative functions operating in an enterprise which is organized on a functional administrative basis. For example, the profile may include specialist areas such as production, marketing, accounting, purchasing, and personnel.

fund, sinking. A fund into which sums are paid (usually) at annual intervals to provide for meeting a future commitment such as the repayment of a loan or the replacement of machinery or of some other asset and to cover

future goods. *See* GOODS, FUTURE GOODS.

futures. 1. Commodities which are the subject of a FUTURES CONTRACT. 2. Contracts of a standard nature under the auspices of a FUTURES MARKET to buy or sell commodities for delivery at a future date, e.g. a contract for next season's crop, or copper due to be mined in say six months' time. *See also* ORDERS & CONTRACTS A-Z.

futures contract. *See* CONTRACT, FUTURES CONTRACT.

futures exchange. *See* MARKET, FUTURES MARKET.

G

Gantt chart. A diagrammatic time-scaled chart. As used for production, scheduling of supplies, etc. It comprises a diagram in which each horizontal line relates to (e.g.) a supply of goods. Vertical lines divide the chart into periods of time. Horizontal bars inserted at each appropriate line indicate 'targets' set and the achievements (or failure) by suitable signals.

gap analysis. (CIMA). A method used to analyze the gap between the final objectives which have been set for the achievement of a task, project or other aim, and the short-fall (or over-achievement!). This assumes existing performance is maintained until the time set for its fulfilment is reached. The analysis then proceeds to identify the extent of the changes needed and the ways by which the gap can be closed.

general administration cost. *See* COST, ADMINISTRATION, GENERAL.

General Agreement on Tariffs and Trade (GATT). An agreement established in 1948 as a multinational trade treaty embodying reciprocal commercial rights and obligations as a means of expanding and liberalizing world trade. Also embodies a code of practice for fair training in international commerce. Now World Trade Organisation.

general average. *See* AVERAGE: GENERAL AVERAGE

general store. *See* STORE, GENERAL STORE.

gifts and favours. A phrase usually associated with BRIBES and bribery. No valid CONTRACT can arise from gifts and favours but their acceptance becomes a bribe when their intention or effect is seen to affect a contractual situation.

glut. There is said to be a glut in a market when owing to a superabundance of supply or a diminution of demand the quantity in the market greatly exceeds what is required for the ordinary trading demands.

goods. Commodities that are tangible and usually capable of being moved or transported. In supplies terminology the term is usually used in the plural form whereas economists and others frequently refer to 'a good'.

good faith. 'A thing is deemed to be done in good faith when it is in fact done honestly, whether it is done negligently or not'. Sale of Goods Act 1979. *See also* BAD FAITH.

goods intake (also goods inwards, goods receiving). The place where goods are received into an enterprise. Provisions required for vehicular access, security, facilities for off-loading, sorting, checking, etc. *See also* CHECKING, INSPECTION *and* GOODS INTAKE, SIGNING FOR.

goods intake, signing for. An important function when receiving supplies. In addition to signing goods received notes the goods intake staff may be required to sign the haulier's CONSIGNMENT NOTE endorsed either 'unchecked', 'unexamined', 'subject to examination', 'suspected damaged' or other phrase. *See also* EXAMINATION *and* CHECKING.

goods inwards sheet. A document on which details of incoming deliveries are recorded before the packages are examined.

goods received note. (Known colloquially as a 'GRN'.) A form recording all details relating to a receipt of materials (supplies) from an outside source. Note: a variety of names is given to this by different organizations.

goods, ascertained. Goods identified and agreed upon after the making of a contract. Note: where there is a contract for sale of ascertained goods no property in the goods is transferred to the buyer until the goods have been ascertained. Sale of Goods Act 1979. *See also* GOODS, UNASCERTAINED GOODS.

goods, attractive. Those goods which although they may not be valuable or costly are attractive to pilferage or theft from the workplace or store.

goods, bonded. Imported goods on which duty has not yet been paid. *See also* WAREHOUSE *and* STORES, BONDED.

goods, capital. Goods which involve the expenditure of capital and generally those which are for the purpose of manufacturing and processing to convert materials into saleable products.

goods, dry. Collective noun for domestic goods such as clothing, hardware, etc. but excluding groceries.

goods, durable. Collective noun for domestic goods which are used but not consumed, e.g. motorcars, TVs, washing machines, etc.

goods, examination of. *See* EXAMINATION.

goods, factored. (CIMA) Goods bought for resale.

goods, finished. Goods ready for use or consumption.

goods, future. Goods to be manufactured or acquired by the seller after making the contract for sale. *See also* GOODS, FUTURE GOODS.

goods, hazardous. *See* HAZARDOUS GOODS.

goods, intermediate. A term sometimes used to describe partly finished goods and materials.

goods, receiving. *See* GOODS INTAKE.

goods, specific. (law) 'Goods identified and agreed upon at the time a contract of sale is made'. Sale of Goods Act 1979.

goods, unascertained. Goods to be grown, manufactured and/or supplied in the future. Also goods which are (according to a legal judgement) 'an unidentified part of a specific whole'. *See also* GOODS, ASCERTAINED GOODS.

goods, valuable. Goods of high intrinsic and/or high financial value which need special security in storage and preservation. *See also* GOODS, ATTRACTIVE GOODS *and* STORE, SECURE STORE.

goodwill. The intangible assets of the reputation of business. These are difficult to evaluate but include many aspects of vendor analysis in relation to relationships with, and services to, purchasers.

grace, days of. The days (usually three) allowed above the actual term of a bill except where this is not drawn 'on sight' or 'on demand', or if the days of grace are specifically excluded. *See* BILL OF EXCHANGE.

grade, contract. (com) The physical properties or standards established by a commodity exchange that must be maintained by those offering commodities for sale.

graft. Abuse of one's position (e.g. in business) for personal gain. *See* CORRUPTION.

gravity racking. Racking where the contents move to the picking face lay gravity. Usually based on roller conveyors.

green purchasing. Briefly, purchasing with environmental considerations in mind.

grey imports. goods which are purchased for delivery to one country, but then re-exported to another.

grid technique. A quantitative method which facilitates the discovery of the least cost centre for locating a factory or warehouse.

gross. Total measure of any quantity such as weight (gross tonnage) value (gross value), etc. with no deductions such as packaging in the first example or discounts in the second example.

gross domestic product (GDP). The total value of all goods and services produced in a country during a year. The figure excludes indirect taxes such as VAT, etc.

gross registered tonnage. *See* DEAD WEIGHT TONNAGE.

gross weight. The total weight of goods and package or a vehicle and contents before making any allowance.

group contracts. *See* ORDERS & CONTRACTS A-Z.

groupage. A system by which an agent (usually a **FREIGHT FORWARDER**) groups together small consignments to make up a full load. Savings are: cheaper full load rates and simpler documentation, such as a single BILL OF LADING.

guarantee. (n) A commitment by a supplier that the goods or services he provides will meet the specifications of performance and/or description agreed in the contract. *See also* WARRANTY. (V) TO GUARANTEE, TO MAKE A GUARANTEE COMMITMENT.

guarantee period. *See* WARRANTY PERIOD.

guarantor. One who gives a guarantee.

H

hacking. Gaining, or attempting to gain unauthorized access to a computer system.

haggle. To cavil, wrangle when negotiating a bargain.

Hague Rules. (law) Legislation by international convention covering the transportation of goods by sea. It is embodied in UK law under the Carriage of Goods by Sea Act 1924 re-enacted 1971.

Hamburg Rules (1992). An international shipping code devised to attempt the reconciliation of interests of carriers and owners of the cargoes they carry. The Hamburg Rules replace the Brussels Protocol of 1968 which revised the Hague Rules.

handling cost rule. *See* COST, HANDLING COST RULE.

handling, manual handling. The handling of materials, goods, etc. without the aid of power or mechanical equipment. *See* HANDLING, POWERED HANDLING.

handling, materials handling (IM). A branch of industrial engineering and MATERIALS MANAGEMENT defined as 'the techniques employed to move, transport, store or distribute materials with or without the aid of mechanical and/or powered equipment'.

handling, mechanical handling. The use of mechanical aids to handling, such as hand trucks, pallet trucks, rollers, the lever, etc. without necessarily the use of power.

handling, powered handling. (log) The application of power to handling operations.

handling, straddle handling. Systems of handling in which the load to be handled (transported, raised, lowered) is carried between the points of support thus providing stability in operation. Examples are: straddle trucks, straddle carriers and cranes of the gantry and Goliath types.

hard sell. Pressure applied to a purchaser by sellers who may be facing poor market conditions or heavy competition. (See also under NEGOTIATION other eventualities in this area.)

hard standing. A place, such as a concrete apron to an unloading or loading bay, lay-by, or access to a site, of sufficient load bearing strength to support vehicles and their loads (e.g. plant, cranage, etc).

hardening of market. *See* MARKET, HARDENING OF MARKET.

hardware. General term for 1. metal tools, domestic goods, etc. 2. the components of a computer (but not the program or associated stationery which is referred to as 'software'), 3. military equipment (guns, tanks, etc.) and (sometimes) for heavy mechanical equipment in a large project, e.g. excavators in a quarry. *See also* MATERIAL.

harmonization documents. (EU) A harmonization document constitutes a CEN/CENELEC Standard. It (an HD) carries the obligation to withdraw any conflicting national standards. BUT, the public announcement of its number and title is otherwise sufficient. Harmonization documents are established if transposition into national standards is unnecessary - because, [for example] a CEN or CENELEC standard is already adopted.

haulage. The charge made for carrying goods. Does not usually include loading and unloading. *See also* FREIGHT.

hazard. (HS) (n) The hazard (danger, risk, etc.) presented by a substance is its potential to cause harm. (To persons or to other matter.)

hazard rate. (HS) A measure of the instantaneous failures and hazard per unit time.

hazard signs. (HS) *See* SIGNS, HAZARDS. Health and Safety at Work Act Safety at Work Act 1974.

hazardous goods. (HS) Those which in transit, storage, handling, etc. present a danger to other goods, property or persons.

hazardous substances (goods, etc.). *See* SUBSTANCES.

hazards, measurement in reliability tests. (HS) The ratio of failures during a measured period divided by the size of the sample at the start of the period.

Health & Safety at Work Regulations. General notes. At first sight the HSWA and REGULATIONS (EU) may appear not to affect purchasing and supply, but, the following should be noted: 1. their effect is to establish a level playing field throughout the Community and thus costs for and prices in ESTIMATES and QUOTATIONS; 2. the purchaser must: 2.1. buy/provide suitable PERSONAL PROTECTIVE EQUIPMENT' for workers, 2.2. arrange suitable safety labelling for hazardous supplies - incoming and outgoing; and, for safe handling - including MANUAL HANDLING, 2.3. provide PACKAGING subject to the same rules, 2.4. have regard to any STORAGE hazards and precautions for same; 3. comply with Statutes including those arising from DIRECTIVES of the Community.

Health and Safety at Work Act. (HS) 1974 (HSWA). The Health and Safety at Work Act together with subsequent regulations, codes of practice, etc. lays down stringent conditions for the maintenance of plant and equipment in a safe operational condition. (For handling and stores the chief implications are the regular testing, certification and marking of lifting and handling appliances.)

Health and Safety Audit. (EU)(HS) A review of the effectiveness of Health and Safety (HS) policy, paying particular attention to: 1. degree of compliance with H & S performance standards including legislation, 2. areas where standards are absent or inadequate, 3. achievement of stated objectives within a stated time scale, 4. data on injury, illness and incidents, 5. analysis of immediate and underlying causes, trends and communal features.

Health and Safety Codes of Practice. (HS) These codes provide practical guidance on the requirements of Sections 2 to 7 of the HSWA, or in health and safety regulations, or in any of the existing statutory provisions. Special status of approved codes of practice is provided by Section 17 of the Act, Sections 23(2) and 21, 22 apply to Codes of Practice in respect of prohibition notices, etc. H8C7.

Health and Safety Commission. (HS). A Commission consisting of representatives of both sides of industry and local authorities. It takes over from government departments the responsibilities for developing Policies in the health and safety field. (Sections 10 and I I of HEALTH AND SAFETY AT WORK ACT. bibl. HSC4.)

Health and Safety Executive. (HS) The statutory body set up by the HEALTH AND SAFETY COMMISSION which works in accordance with the direction, and guidance given to it by the Commission. The Executive enforces legal requirements, provides an advisory service to both sides of industry, and embraces all major inspectorates in the health and safety field. (Sections 10 and I I of the Health and Safety at Work Act apply). bibl. HSC4.

health and safety, hazard studies. (HS) Such studies involve safety, health and environmental consideration at each stage. (Purchasing and supply and Standards are likely to be involved at each stage also.)

health and safety, related system. (HS) A system wherein the functioning, or malfunctioning, of the system may affect safety.

health and safety, Safety-Critical (Control) System. A control system the function of which is to assure safety of the system it controls.

health and safety: planning and setting standards for health and safety. 1. Identify HAZARDS, assess RISKS, plan their elimination or control. 2. Comply with all HS laws, codes of practice, and DIRECTIVES and the corresponding UK Regulations. 3. Agree targets with all staff. 4. Take HS into account in purchasing and supply policy. 5, Design tasks, processes, equipment, products, services taking account of HS. 6. Set standards against which performance, can be measured. 7. Apply standards to: 7.1. premises, place of work and ENVIRONMENTAL CONTROL, 7.2. plant and substances, purchase, supply, transport, storage and use, 7.3. procedures, design of jobs, way work is done, 7.4. people, training and supervision, 7.5. products, services, design, delivery, transport and storage.

hedge, buying hedge. The buyer covers his risk that uncovered sales will result in a loss if prices rise. In this case he buys FUTURES to mature at the time he requires the supply.

hedging. A manoeuvre to reduce risk by making opposing (i.e. counterbalancing) speculations, e.g. a buyer using a commodity exchange can safeguard the price he must pay at the time he needs the commodity by purchasing equivalent FUTURES (i.e. the 'hedge') which the buyer will sell on the 'exchange' when the due date arrives. He can then set off any gain or loss against the rise or fall in price at the due date. The buyer thus pays the amount he originally expected plus any charges for the use of the market.

heuristic methods. (BS) Procedures based on experience to rank activities and/or schedule activities to produce a feasible solution. Note: usually time-based information derived from the time analysis of the network(s) is used. The term can also involve search for a goal (or solution) by steps, or by trial and error, or by a suitable computer program using, e.g. a BINARY CODE.

hire. 1. Wages paid for any service. 2. Price paid for temporary use of any item. *See also* ORDERS & CONTRACTS, HIRE PURCHASE.

hiring. A way of achieving the use of an asset whilst another party (the hirer) retains ownership. Items are usually hired from an organisation specialising in the class of goods hired. *See* LEASING.

historical costs. *See* COSTS, HISTORICAL.

holding costs. *See* COSTS, STOCK HOLDING COSTS.

holding out. (law) The action of a person presenting themselves, falsely, as authorized to act officially on behalf of an enterprise. (Can be a serious business risk in purchasing and supply). Unauthorized persons may deliberately or inadvertently commit the company to an unauthorized and inadvertent CONTRACT.

home use entry. An order for the removal from a bonded warehouse of goods required for consumption in the home country.

homeostasis. The process of balancing or holding steady the parameters essential to the effectiveness of a system despite disturbances or 'buffeting' to which the system is subjected, e.g. maintenance of availability of supply/stock despite changes in rate of consumption, demand, deliver lead times, etc.

honour, to honour (contracts). (v) to respect and carry out in full TERMS and CONDITIONS agreement freely entered into (e.g. of a purchase contract).

hopper. A storage container which allows bulk loading of loose materials (e.g. grain) from the top, with a controlled discharge from the bottom.

horizon, planning horizon. (BS) The longest time ahead for which plans are normally made. Note: period varies with subject being planned and the planning organisation, e.g. it may be 10 years for facilities and one year for materials.

horizons. The periods over which (particularly, long term) supplies, production and/or sales can be forecast and planned.

housekeeping, industrial housekeeping. An important aspect of storage, handling and distribution. It implies the maintenance of clean, well-lit stores and areas such as loading bays; clearly marked aisles and hazards with correct and well-positioned signs; aisles and walkways clear of obstructions of any kind, etc. Savings from good industrial housekeeping almost invariably far exceed costs of accidents, spillage, and wastage which may otherwise occur.

hub. The centre of a network of computers or peripheral devices.

hub airport. An airport that serves as a destination for long haul flights; dispersing passengers or freight locally by smaller aircraft or carriers.

hygroscopic. The tendency to absorb water.

identification (of supplies). The process of systematically defining and describing items, e.g. stock, of all kinds, supporting goods and all commodities used in a firm.

ideogram. *See under* CODES.

idle stock. *See* STOCK, IDLE STOCK.

idle time. (BS) The period of time for which a workstation is available, for production but is not utilized due to shortage of tools, materials, or operators.

ignition. The action of causing a substance to ignite (or explode) when and if the temperature of the substance(s) is raised to the ignition point (i.e. the FLASH POINT).

illegal. Contrary to law. The legal code draws a distinction between contracts which break a criminal law, and those which are contrary to public policy. The former are wholly void, the latter only in respect of those portions contrary to public policy.

immiscible. *See* SUBSTANCE.

impartiality. A lack of prejudice towards any particular side in a study or debate. An important quality in all who are engaged in interdepartmental services, such as those provided by the staff of purchasing and supply. *See also* OBJECTIVITY, VALUE ENGINEERING, VALUE ANALYSIS, etc.

implied terms (contract law). *See* CONTRACT, CONDITIONS, LEGAL CONDITIONS.

import licences. *See* LICENCE, IMPORT LICENCE.

importer. For customs' purposes this includes the owner or any other person possessed of or beneficially interested in, the goods at any time between their importation and their clearance from customs' charge.

imports. Goods and services which one country buys from another.

imposts. Taxes, particularly those on imports.

imprest. A method for controlling cash needed for small payments (or stock) of very low value by provision of a fixed sum (or stock) at the beginning of a period and its replenishment at the end of that period equal to the amount spent (or issued). *See* STOCK-CONTROL, IMPREST.

improvement curve. *See* LEARNING CURVE.

in ballast. A ship is said to be in ballast when she carries no cargo but only water or heavy material to maintain stability.

in bond. Goods subject to duty stored in a BONDED WAREHOUSE under the control of the customs' authorities until the owner pays the duty. When goods in bond are sold the buyer must pay the customs' duties in addition to the value of the goods.

in house. A term used for work done within a plant instead of buying from outside source or PROCUREMENT from another plant of the same GROUP. *See also* MAKE OR BUY.

in transitu. On the way from one place to another; in transit.

incentive clause. A contract clause which rewards the contractor for better performance.

incentives. (BS) A motivating influence or stimulus. In the business context a legitimate offer of a bonus or discount to encourage the establishment of a contract. Illegitimately it may be a bribe for acceptance of which criminal proceedings may follow. A procedure designed to encourage a desired response from people.

inclined plane. The description of a surface which is at an angle to the horizontal. The angle may be used to calculate the force required to move (say) handling equipment (e.g. a gravity conveyor), or to examine the safety (or otherwise) of storage or handling on a sloping surface.

Incoterms. International rules (published by the International Chamber of Commerce) for the interpretation of terms used in foreign trade contracts and recognised by buyers and sellers worldwide. Detailed guidance on the interpretation of these terms is contained in their publication 'Incoterms 2000'. There are 13 terms, briefly explained below. Readers are advised not to rely on these outline explanations, but to use ICC publications or advice if they are involved in the practical use of the terms.

CFR. cost and freight . . . named port of destination. Seller's obligations end when goods reach their destination.

Buyer bears all risks from the moment the goods pass over the ship's rail at the port of destination.

CIF. cost, insurance and freight . . . named port of destination. As COST AND FREIGHT but seller insures goods to their destination.

CIP. carriage and insurance paid . . . named place of destination. As CARRIAGE PAID TO but seller responsible for insurance.

CPT. carriage paid to named place of destination. Seller delivers goods to the carrier nominated by him, but the seller must bear the cost of bringing the goods to the named destination.

DAF. delivered at frontier...named place. Seller's obligations end when he has, at his own risk and cost, delivered the goods at the intake side of the frontier post.

DDP. delivered, duty paid...named place of destination. Seller bears all risks and costs including duties through to destination in country of importation.

DDU. delivered duty unpaid... named place of destination. Seller delivers goods to the buyer, not cleared for import and not unloaded at the named destination.

DEQ. delivered ex quay . . . named port of destination. Seller's obligations end when he has, at his own cost and risk, made the goods available to the buyer at the quay at the destination.

DES. delivered ex ship . . . named port of destination). Seller's obligations end when he makes the goods available to the buyer on the ship at the destination. Seller bears full costs and risks up to that point.

EXW. ex works . . . named place. The seller delivers when he places the goods at the disposal of the buyer at the seller's premises.

FAS. free alongside ship . . . named port of shipment. Seller's obligations end when he has placed the goods alongside the ship on the quay or in a LIGHTER.

FCA. free carrier . . . named place. Seller's obligations end when he at his own risk and cost delivers the goods to the carrier at the named port.

FOB. free on board . . . named port of shipment. Seller's obligations end when he has placed the goods on board. Buyer's obligations start when goods have passed over the ship's rail.

increment. An amount added to a previous amount, e.g. a sum added to the value of a contract to cover a contingency such as inflation, the escalating cost of transport, etc.

incremental cost. *See* COST, INCREMENTAL.

indemnity. Security against loss or damage; legal exemption from penalties incurred.

indent. A word sometimes used as a synonym for a REQUISITION or a PURCHASE ORDER. Strictly speaking it refers to the indenting of legal documents and agreements.

index numbers. A statistical device to facilitate comparison between DATA at different times obviating the need for repetition of the full data for each period. Thus, for example, in purchasing and supply one may take a typical price at a selected (or seasonal) date or one which has been calculated (say) over twelve months. Using this price (or other data) as basic, then subsequent annual (or other) prices

can be expressed as a percentage of this basic figure (price), e.g. a basic price at a basic year is (say) £100. If next year the price is £105. The increase is 5% and this is the index number.

indifference curves. These are devices for making choices between alternatives, such as the proportion or mix of two similar sources of supply in which it is desired to select the optimum mix based on price or other considerations.

indirect. A term which, when applied to goods or materials means that they are not to be embodied in a finished product. *See* MRO.

indirect expense. *See* COSTS, INDIRECT.

indirect labour. Those wages which cannot be directly traced to a particular job or contract. One of the items included in works ONCOST.

indirect materials. (CIMA) Materials costs other than DIRECT MATERIALS COSTS.

indirect oncost. A term used in connection with departmental oncost, and which represents items of any works oncost which cannot be directly traced to any single department.

indirect stock. *See* STOCK, INDIRECT STOCK.

inductive technique. (adm) The process of drawing general conclusion from a number of known facts by objective and rational reasoning and discussion. *See also* INQUIRY AND INVESTIGATION TECHNIQUES.

industrial classifications. Standard government classification of the 21 main groups (and numerous subgroups) of industry, designed to promote uniformity and comparability in the official statistics of industry in the

UK. The, classifications follow the general principle of the International Standard Industrial Classification by activity and not by commodity. They can be of considerable assistance in purchasing research. *See also* CENSUS OF PRODUCTION.

inert. *See at* SUBSTANCES.

inertia selling. *See* MARKETING. inflation (price inflation). An economic condition where prices are rising generally.

inflation accounting. *See* CURRENT COST ACCOUNTING.

information agreement. Agreements whereby information is circulated between firm, party to an agreement in respect of: 'prices charged, terms of supply, costs, quantities or descriptions of goods, processes of manufacture or places and persons supplied.' Such agreements are (in nearly all cases) contrary to the Restrictive Trade Practices Act and conditions for trading within the European Union.

information processing. A specialist activity performed by the administrative organization of an enterprise. It is concerned with the systematic recording, arranging, collating, processing, filing, retrieval and dissemination of facts relating to the, physical/financial events occurring in a business. *See also* DATA PROCESSING *and* MANAGEMENT INFORMATION SYSTEMS.

information technology (IT). The application of technological means for processing and transmitting information. Such means include the use of computers, telecommunication, microelectronics, the web.

information theory. The study of information flow. Initially applied to communication systems. More recently applied universally to business systems. It concerns the flow of information, capacity of channels, and many other factors relevant to use If information technology in business. Information theory is therefore important to purchasing and supply organizations where these rely on the use of information technology.

infrastructure. Originally a term coined by French railways, later adopted as a military term for basic military equipment associated with logistics. Latterly its use has become associated with basic needs of a developed economy. These needs include: transport networks, communications, provision of water, power, education, health needs.

ingestion. The taking of substances into the digestive tract through the mouth. *See also* INHALATION.

inhalation. The drawing of substances (gases, dusts, etc.) into the lungs.

inherent vice. *See* VICE, INHERENT.

injunction. (law) A court order to a person, company, etc. engaged in litigation, the order may: 1. prohibit something being done, e.g. forbidding details of a contract being passed on to a third party, or 2. be a 'mandatory' instruction, something to be done, e.g. to complete a contract against a purchase order.

inquire (v) **inquiry** (n). To make a search or an investigation in depth. Some examples of techniques which may be appropriate to inquiry are: DELPHI TECHNIQUE, questioning technique, inductive technique, VALUE ANALYSIS and VALUE ENGINEERING, BRAIN STORMING, etc. *See also* ENQUIRE *and*

ENQUIRY. (Appropriate terms for an invitation to a supplier for a QUOTATION or ESTIMATE, etc.)

inquiry technique, inductive technology. A method of collecting many facts (or data) which appear relevant to a problem or investigation and classifying and analysing them, e.g. in VALUE ENGINEERING, COST BENEFIT ANALYSIS. *See also* BRAIN STORMING.

inquiry technique, questioning technique. (adm) (BS) First stage, primary questions, e.g. the need for each activity (or other matter under investigation), its means, sequence, place and person, etc., justification sought for each reply. Secondary questions: the second stage examines remaining essential activities (or other matters). These are further questioned to determine alternatives and to select those that are practicable and preferable. The techniques are applicable (suitably modified) for purchasing negotiations, materials management problems, work study in stores and handling, etc.

Insolvency Act 1986. Act which consolidated previous legislation relating to company insolvency and winding up, insolvency and bankruptcy of individuals, the functions and qualifications of insolvency practitioners, the public administration of insolvency and the penalization and redress of malpractice and wrong-doing.

insolvent and insolvency. A person is deemed to be insolvent within the meaning of the Sale of Goods Act 1979 if he either ceases to pay his debts in the ordinary course of business or he cannot pay his debts as they become due, whether he has committed an act of BANKRUPTCY or not.

inspecting orders. Documents authorizing the official in charge of a bonded warehouse or other storehouse to grant permission to the holder to view the goods.

inspection. (BS) The process of measuring, examining, testing, gauging, or otherwise comparing the item with the applicable requirements. *See also* CHECKING *and* EXAMINING.

inspection and test. A technical process which uses a specified procedure to measure one or more characteristics of a product [or service]. A major activity undertaken during design, product development, manufacture and product (service, service or use).

inspection certificate. *See* QUALITY CONTROL, CERTIFICATE OF CONFORMITY.

inspection clause, in a contract. A clause inserted into a contract for construction or for plant. It gives the purchaser the right to inspect the working of the contract and its progress at all reasonable times and to reject any part which does not comply with the contract. A similar clause may be applied to contracts for products, where appropriate.

inspection, 'hold point'. The stage during a contract beyond which the supplier must not proceed without the operation being overseen by the designated inspector.

inspection, by attributes inspection (BS) Inspection whereby certain characteristics of an item are assessed without measurement and classified as conforming, or not conforming, to specified requirements. An 'attribute' is a characteristic which is appraised in terms of whether it meets or does not meet a given requirement (e.g. 'go' or 'not go'

inspection, stores inspection. The formal inspection of stores by a qualified person (such as the stores superinten-dent) to examine the condition of all stock, its effective housing, stacking, security, safety, fire, vermin, contamina-tion, etc. (Sometimes misleadingly referred to as a 'stores audit'.) *See* STORES INSPECTION.

insurance stock. *See* STOCK, SAFETY STOCK.

insurance, in contracts. The provision of financial protection in the event of certain foreseen contingencies which may arise in the performance of a contract, such as: loss or damage in transit; failure in completion of contract; loss, damage or injury to personnel or members of the public.

intake. *See* GOODS INTAKE.

intent, letter of. *See* ORDERS AND CONTRACTS, LETTER OF INTENT.

intention (legal). An essential component for a valid contract. The parties must have intended to create legal relations. Intentions in any contract must be clear and unequivocal. In the absence of such conditions the court will seek to discover the intentions of the parties to the contract at the time it was made. The test is 'what would a reasonable man understand to be the intention of the parties, having regard to all the circumstances?'

Inter-firm Comparisons. A 'pyramid' or 'tree' of ratios starting at its head with ratio of 'profit: capital employed' and analysing progressively each ratio of 'costs to sales' at each cost and profit centre of the firm. A chief authority (set up by the Institute of Management and the British Productivity Council as the Centre for Interfirm Comparison.

inter-state trading. Trade between members of the European Union and States outside the Union. *See also* INTRA-UNION.

interest. (fin) 1. Payment by a borrower for the use of a sum of money loaned to him. 2. As payment for risk in making a loan. 3. As recompense for overdue settlement of an invoice, etc.

interest, annual percentage rate, APR. (fin) Annual percentage rate of charge is a measurement of the TOTAL cost for credit expressed as an annual rate. Unlike most other rates in the past, APR includes the interest on the loan itself and any other charges which may be due as a condition of obtaining the loan (for example: documentation fees, maintenance charges for items on hire purchase). (Office of Fair Trading).

interest, financial. (fin) The charge for the use of credit, overdue payment for purchases. Usually expressed as a percentage of the sum outstanding per unit of time it is outstanding.

interest, legal. (fin) A legal or financial stake, right or title to a thing or moneys, capital, etc.

interest, vested. The interest of (usually) an individual, with a strong personal concern in some matter, or thing, which it may be expected will influence their judgement or the course of events in which they are involved and over which they have influence. Such an interest may involve a 'declaration of interest' where it is supposed that the 'vested interest' may adversely affect a decision.

interim certificates. Certificates signed by a person authorized in the contract confirming the progress of a project (plant or building) so that STAGE (or PROGRESS) PAYMENTS may be made by the purchaser.

intermediary. Third party who provides services in connection with the movement of goods and payment between buyer and seller. Example of intermediaries include banks, shipping companies, freight forwarders.

intermediate bulk containers. *See* CONTAINERS.

intermediate goods. A term sometimes used to describe partly finished goods and materials.

intermediate stock. *See* STOCK, INTERMEDIATE STOCK.

intermodal units. Units and unit loads, e.g. containers, capable of transfer between systems, e.g. sea-borne containers delivered finally on a road vehicle. *See* CONTAINERS.

internal lead-time. *See* LEAD-TIME.

internal rate of return. (fin) A percentage discount rate obtained from discounted CASH FLOW used in the appraisal of capital investment appraisal which should bring the cost of a project, or plant, and its future cash inflows into equality.

International Maritime Dangerous Goods Code. A code published in four loose-leaf volumes by the International Maritime Organisation - United Nations body headquarters in London.

International Standards Organisation (ISO). Organization established in 1947 at United Nations conference to promoting the development of standardization throughout the world with a view to facilitating exchange of goods and services and to increase international collaboration. Now concerned with making of consensus based standards for world-wide application.

Internet. The Internet is a global collection of interlinked computer networks. Most of the Internet is accessible to anybody with the necessary equipment.

interruptible supply. (energy) An arrangement between customers and suppliers whereby the former receive gas at a lower price if they are prepared to allow their supply to be cut from time to time.

Intra-Union. (EU) Trade within the Union between member states. *See also* INTER-STATE and THIRD COUNTRY.

Intranet. A private computer network. Usually a part of the Internet, protected by FIREWALLS.

intrinsic value. *See* VALUE, INSTRINSIC VALUE

inventory control. Alternative term for STOCK CONTROL, common in the USA and some public authorities for the quantities of stock and/or its value held by the authority.

invitation to tender. *See* TENDER, INVITATION TO TENDER.

invitation to treat. *See* TREAT, INVITATION TO TREAT.

invoice. A priced list of goods or services supplied, showing the sums due from a purchaser.

invoice, certified invoice. One issued by a firm and certified as a true copy of the original.

invoice, consular invoice. One certified by the consul of the importing country who is situated in the exporting country to enable correct import duties to be charged.

invoice, pro forma invoice. One prepared by a seller to show the sum due from the purchaser in a transaction, usually before shipment is made or the service is rendered.

inward goods. *See* GOODS RECEIVING, GOODS INTAKE.

irrevocable credit. *See* CREDIT, DOCUMEN-TARY LETTER OF CREDIT.

Ishikawa diagram. Also known as a cause and effect diagram or fishbone diagram. A graphical tool which can be used to discover the root causes of problems. This is done by posing a series of what? where? when? and why? questions and presenting possible answers

issue (usage take-off). (BS) The actual results of stores activities expressed in terms of quantities issued in a given period. 2. The number of issues made per day, per week, or per production period, etc. *See also* SUPPLIES THROUGHOUT, SUPPLIES TURNOVER OF SUPPLIES *and* STORES SERVICE FACTOR OF STORES, etc.

issue note. (BS) A document recording the issue of products or raw materials from stores and which authorizes the revision of (stock) records in terms of quantity and value.

issue, units of. *See* UNITS OF ISSUE.

issuing bank. (SITPRO) A bank which issues a LETTER OF CREDIT on the instructions of the importer (purchaser). Usually the importer's own bank.

item (of production). An identifiable item, sub-assembly or equipment supported by a manufacturer's part or drawing number.

item, (in supplies). Any finished or partly finished product or raw material which can be identified as an individual item.

J

jerque. Examination of a ship's cargo by a custom's officer known as a jerquer, to ensure that it and the captain's list agrees with that of customs. When he is satisfied the 'jerquer' issues a certificate known as a 'jerque note'.

job. That work which is undertaken to meet a customer or production order and which, for production control (and purchasing) purposes, has a unique identification.

job analysis. Detailed analysis of a job to agree the best method and qualities needed by the operatives/staff.

job breakdown. An up-to-date, step-by-step account of the operation(s) being, or to be, performed. Often associated with WORK STUDY and associated with a study of effective and/or standard methods.

job costing. That form of specific order costing which applies where work is undertaken to purchasers' special requirements.

job description. A statement of the purpose, scope, organizational relationships, responsibilities, authority and tasks that constitute the job, for which the personnel must satisfy the job specification.

job evaluation. The determination of the relative. standing of jobs within an organization. Four basic systems are: 'classification/grading' - placing tasks within the appropriate grades where these are established in the organisation; 'factor comparison, - analysis based on requirement of job, skill, mental ability, physical requirements, responsibility, working conditions; 'ranking placing jobs in order of importance or value; 'rating, points rating'- analysis of full description of work to be done and full range of factors involved.

job lot. 1. Production. A relatively small number of specific types products produced at one time. The part or product may be a standard item that has been, and will again be produced, or a special item destined for an individual customer who has not ordered it before and may not do so again. 2. Purchasing. a. Goods arranged in separate portions or parcels for sale by auction. b. A collection of odds and ends for sale. c. A lot offered for sale by a merchant being a special 'once off' line not usually repeatable.

job satisfaction. The extent to which the desires and hopes of a worker are fulfilled as a result of his or her work.

job specification. A specification of the qualities, abilities, character and skills needed by the person being considered for a job so that they may meet the requirements of the JOB DESCRIPTION.

jobbing, engineering production. The manufacture of customers' orders by the job, usually in small lots or batches, and of different Products within the range and capacity of the enterprise.

joule. The SI Unit of work/energy applied when the point of application of a force of one newton is displaced through a distance of one metre.

just in time (JIT). A production philosophy whereby what is needed is made when it is needed, and not before.

K

kaikaku. Japanese term meaning significant, if infrequent gains in productivity. A key feature is the removal of MUDA.

kaizen. Japanese word translating into English as 'continuous improvement'.

kanban. Japanese term which translates literally as 'card', meaning something like 'sign' or 'flag'. It is the signal which triggers deliveries of specific quantities of supplies in a JUST IN TIME system. The term is often used erroneously for 'just in time'.

keiretsu. Japanese term denoting a grouping of companies around a major bank and held together by cross-shareholdings.

kitemark. A symbol by the British Standards Institution authorized to be used by manufacturers on products which comply with British Standard Specifications.

kitting. *See* PRE-ASSEMBLY.

knocked down. 1. A machine or article supplied unassembled usually to facilitate transport, etc. 2. Term used when an auctioneer or salesman accepts a bid and assigns the lot to the person bidding; the lot is said to be knocked down.

kyoryoku kai. Japanese term for SUPPLIER ASSOCIATION.

L

labour, direct labour. Productive wages which can be definitely traced to a particular job, contract or process.

lading, bill of (through bill of lading). Form of bill used where the carrier takes on the entire transit from door to door.

lagan. Goods or wreckage found on the bed of the sea. Provision may be made for its recovery.

landed terms. The price including LIGHTERAGE and DOCK DUES until goods are landed at the port of destination.

landfill. (env) Placing of waste materials into (usually) worked out excavations such as old quarries or mines.

landing order. A document given by a customs authority to the captain of a ship authorizing him (after the dues have been paid) to hand over the goods for landing.

landing (or landed) weight. The actual weight of cargo removed from a ship.

last in, first out. *See* STOCK VALUATION.

Late Payment of Commercial Debts (Interest) Act 1998. Act entitling small businesses (fewer than 50 employees) to charge 8% above prevailing bank rate as interest on late payment.

Law Reform (Frustrated Contracts). Act 1943 Act setting out the rights and liabilities between the parties where a contract has become void through the application of the doctrine of frustration.

law, case law. The principles of law laid down in cases heard in the higher courts.

law, common. That part of law based on established customs and usages recognised by the courts including CASE LAW. (*See also* STATUTE LAW.)

law, equity. Addenda to Common Law, largely concerned with the equitable interpretation of contracts, agreements, documents, etc.

law, maritime. That portion of commercial law that deals with ports, harbours, docks, ships, seamen, navigation, pilots, lighthouses, etc.

law, mercantile or commercial. The term generally used to denote those portions of the law that relate to the rights and obligations arising out of the transactions of mercantile persons.

law, statute. Laws derived from statutes enacted by Parliament. It is 'written law'. In buying and selling and in industry such laws increasingly derive from international agreements, DIRECTIVES from the European Union and other sources.

lay days. The number of days allowed for the unloading of a ship.

lay hours. (log) The period allowed for the time a ship may be lying off-shore before being able to dock. Usually 'lay hours' will be negotiated into the relevant contract. *See also* DEMURRAGE.

lead time. This term is used in a great variety of ways, and should always be considered in context. Typical interpretations are: 1. the administrative purchasing office time taken from the receipt of the indication of a need by the purchasing department to the, placing of the purchase order to meet that need; 2. the time taken by a supplier from receipt of an order to meet that order.

leads and lags. An expression to describe the activities of those who hasten or delay payment to take advantage of anticipated changes in the rates of exchange. (Such speculative trading is uncommon in normal purchasing practice where stability of price and cost are preferred.) *See also* PRICE.

leakage or breakage. A mercantile term sometimes included in a CHARTER PARTY or BILL OF LADING to protect the captain of a ship from claims on these counts where the cargo is particularly subject to these risks. It excludes protection for, a captain's own negligence.

lean production. *See* PRODUCTION, LEAN.

lean supply. *See* SUPPLY, LEAN.

learning curve. The rate at which the CYCLE TIME decreases or is expected to decrease with increasing, experience.

lease. (n) An arrangement whereby a lessor puts property, plant, etc. at the disposal of a lessee for an agreed period after which the subject of the lease returns fully to the owner (the lessor). The lease is also the document of contract. *See* ORDERS & CONTRACTS A-Z also LEASING OF PLANT.

lease, full pay out. One where the total cost is repaid during the primary period of the lease. At the end of the lease the lessee may be able to continue by renting the item for a period to be agreed or indefinitely, for an agreed sum (or a nominal amount to be agreed), there may also be a credit for a portion of the final disposal of the item.

lease, residual. One in which the full cost of the leased item is not repaid during the primary period of the lease. (Leasing payment may be lower than with a FULL PAY OUT LEASE, but the lessee may find additional costs after the end of the primary period.)

leaseback. (fin) A financial arrangement under which the owner of property or plant sells it to a purchaser (usually a finance house) and retains the use of it under a leasing arrangement.

leasing of plant and equipment. Contracts giving possession of plant and equipment for a specified period for which the lessee makes payments during that period to the lessor. At the end of the lease the lessee usually has the option to purchase at a nominal or other agreed charge. *See also* ORDERS & CONTRACTS A-Z.

least-time track. Flight navigation technique to find the best flight path to avoid head -winds and take advantage of tail winds.

ledger, purchase, or bought. (CIMA) The record of creditors, individual accounts and transactions.

less than containers load Containerization term used when there is less than a full container load for a single complete shipment. *See* GROUPAGE.

letter of credit. *See* CREDIT, DOCUMENTARY LETTER OF CREDIT.

letter of indemnity. 1. One containing an undertaking on the part of the writer to be responsible for any loss or damage or other specified claims in the circumstances detailed. 2. One sent by an exporter agreeing to make good any loss due to faulty packing, etc., thus ensuring a 'clean' BILL OF LADING.

letter of intent. *See* ORDERS & CONTRACTS - LETTER OF INTENT.

letters patent. Right granted by the Patent Office to protect an invention or process from being copied.

levels, stock levels. *See* STOCK LEVELS, MAXIMUM, RE-ORDER, PROVISIONING, DANGER/ WARNING, SAFETY, STOCK-OUT, DEFICIENCY, ETC.

leverage. 1. The ratio between the debts of a business and its capital assets. 2. A term to describe the negotiation potential which a purchaser possesses over a supplier to ensure a satisfactory and competitive outcome to negotiations. 3. A state of obligation, such as liability for breach of contract if a supplier fails to deliver or a purchaser refuses to accept delivery to him. *See also* FINANCE.

liability, product. *See* PRODUCT LIABILITY.

licence, software A licence which is sold with a software package to give a user exclusive rights.

licences (import). Licences granted for the import of goods. Such are: 1. open general licence for specified classes of goods which may be freely imported by any trader from any country or from designated countries of origin; 2. open individual licence authorizing a trader to import unlimited quantities of specified goods from any country or from a designated country of origin; 3. specific licence authorizing the designated trader only to import the stated quantity of specified goods within the time stated on the licence.

lien (general). The right to retain the possession of property or goods until all debts due have been paid.

lien (particular). The right of the possessor of goods, who has not been paid for his services in connection with them to retain those goods (but these only) until he has been paid for the debts relating to them.

lien, carrier's lien. The right of a carrier, road, rail, etc., to detain release of goods to the consignee until e.g. freight has been paid.

life cycle assessment. (env). The systematic, comprehensive objective assessment of the impact on the environment by a product or process throughout its life cycle

life cycle. The expected useful life of plant and equipment. In many instances life cycle of plant has inherent features at different phases of the cycle: initial teething troubles and breakdown, rising output associated with a LEARNING CURVE, later increasing repair costs and down-time costs leading in final phases to rapid increases in such costs, fall in output and loss of competitiveness in relation to new technical developments when available.

life cycle costs. *See* COST, LIFE-CYCLE COSTS.

life, useful life. (BS) The period from a stated time, during which, under stated conditions, an item has an acceptable failure rate, or until an unrepairable failure occurs. Note: the useful life of an item may also be determined for reasons other than failure. *See also* COST, LIFE-CYCLE COSTS.

lift table. Device, usually hydraulic, for lifting heavy loads so they can be placed on trucks, etc.

lift trucks. (BS) The term is used here to signify a wide range of handling machines (known as 'fork trucks' or 'forklift trucks'. In modern practice such machines are equipped with many handling attachments besides forks for handling pallets and palletised loads. The ancillary equipment includes attachments such as: crane jibs, clamps for timber and bales, roll clamps, reach forks, and many more to provide the almost infinite variety of handling needs in industry, commerce and services.

lifting accessories (mobile machinery and lifting equipment. Directive). (EU) (HS) 1. 'Lifting accessories', means components or equipment not attached to the machine and placed between it and the load in order to attach it. 2. 'Separate lifting accessories' are those which help to make up or use a slinging device e.g. eyebolts, shackles, rings, eyehooks. 3. 'Guided load' is one where total movement is made along rigid or flexible guides whose position is determined by fixed points.

lighter. A vessel, usually a barge, used for conveyance of goods to or from a ship lying off shore.

limitation clause. A clause which suppliers, particularly of a service, may seek to insert into a contract, which, while not excluding liability for BREACH OF CONTRACT or negligence, seeks to restrict liability to a specific sum. *See also* EXCLUSION CLAUSE.

limitations, statute of limitations. Legal enactment which establishes the period in which legal action must be brought in order to enforce a right.

limits. *See* QUALITY CONTROL LIMITS.

line organization. (adm) One in which AUTHORITY is DELEGATED from top management to departmental heads of staff who are given full (or stated) authority within their department.

linear programming. An operational research technique which can be used to determine an optimum solution within the bounds imposed by constraints upon the decision.

liner. A means of transport proceeding at regular times between specified destinations, particularly a ship.

link, hot. A part of a Web page that enables a direct link with another Web silt, such as that of a related organization.

liquid assets. (CIMA) Cash and other assets readily convertible into cash. Very little of normal industrial stock fails into this category.

liquidated damages. *See* DAMAGES, LIQUIDATED DAMAGES.

liquidation. The WINDING UP of the affairs of a business when it ceases from trading and appoints a liquidator to set its affairs in order, realise its assets, and with the proceeds pay its debts and distribute any surplus to its shareholders. (com) The sale of a contract to offset a previously made purchase.

liquidity ratio. *See* CURRENT RATIO, ACID TEST RATIO,

load board. (BS) The collective term for any portable platform with or without a superstructure, for the assembly of goods to form a UNIT LOAD, or for handling and storage by mechanical appliances (powered or manual). *See* BS 3810 FOR TERMINOLOGY OF COMPLETE RANGE OF HANDLING EQUIPMENT.

load factor. (energy) In the energy supply industries, the relationship between consumption and maximum demand.

load line (the Plimsoll Line). The level below which a vessel may not be permitted to sink when fully laden in any waters into which it may sail.

log book (transport, etc.). A book in which are recorded the arrivals and departures of vehicles at an enterprise, giving details such as: vehicle registration number, name of haulier, date and time of arrival and departure, etc., along with other relevant particulars.

logistics. The process of managing both the movement and storage of goods and materials from their source to the point of ultimate consumption, and the associated information flows.

long. The position of a trader who owns physical commodities which he has not hedged, or one who has bought 'future'.

Lorenz curve. A graphic method of measuring divergence from an average. Originally devised for measuring the distribution of wealth it also applies to supplies analyses and can be used as an alternative, or supplementary to PARETO'S PRINCIPLE, and ABC ANALYSIS but showing how blocks of stock (or supplies) may vary from the mean.

loss (constructive total loss). This is said to occur where the subject matter of goods insured is justifiably abandoned because its total loss appears inevitable, or where it is so damaged that it is uneconomic to repair it.

loss leader. Item offered at cost or below cost in order to attract business. *See* PRICE, LOSS LEADER PRICE.

loss, consequential. A loss due to breach of contract (through accident or similar event) which is in addition to the direct loss such as destruction of stock or property, It may result in loss of profit, losses due to interruption of business. Consequential loss is not normally covered in a contract unless special terms make it so.

loss, partial loss/total loss. Liability in marine insurance covered by the peril against which insurance has been arranged. 1. Partial loss is a loss other than total loss. 2. Total loss, 'total actual loss', is where the subject of the claim and the insurance cover is destroyed or so damaged as to be no longer the kind of thing insured. 3. Total loss 'CONSTRUCTIVE TOTAL LOSS' is a situation where the thing insured has been abandoned because 'total actual loss' appears certain.

lot. A definite quantity of some commodity manufactured or produced under conditions which are presumed uniform, and for production purposes passing as a unit through the same series of operations. In some industries 'lot' and 'batch' are not regarded as synonymous. Where they have distinctly different meanings, these should be defined. Where it is unnecessary to retain the distinction, the word is preferred. In purchasing and supply the term 'lot' may be related to quantity for storage, handling, packaging, inspection, test, transportation, sampling, etc. It also has the commercial connotation of an article, or set of articles, offered for sale at an auction. *See also* BATCH.

loyalty discount. *See* REBATES, LOYALTY REBATE.

loyalty rebate. *See* REBATES, LOYALTY REBATE.

lump sum. *See* PAYMENT, LUMP SUM PAYMENT.

M

machine down time. *See* DOWN TIME, IDLE TIME *and* WAITING TIME.

machine utilization index. *See* UTILISATION FACTOR.

machinery: code of safety practice. (EU)(BS) In order to comply with the relevant Directive all machinery purchased, imported, exported or used must satisfy the essential health and safety requirements set out in annex B of the Directive. Not only must purchasers of machinery comply with the Directive but may also need to consider relevant national standards.

macro-economics. *See* ECONOMICS.

maintainability. (BS) A function of the rapidity and ease with which maintenance operations can be performed to help prevent malfunctions or to correct them if they occur.

maintenance. (BS) The combination of all technical and corresponding administrative actions intended to retain an item in, or restore it to, a state in which it can perform its required function.

maintenance history. (BS) A history record used for the purpose of maintenance planning. May be combined with the PLANT REGISTER and also helpful in PROVISIONING.

maintenance materials (supplies). Those supplies specially PROVISIONED for, or carried in stock for, maintenance. They usually require priority action to ensure continuity of production. They are sometimes referred to as MRO (maintenance, repair and operational) materials.

maintenance period. A period (usually 12 months) during which plant supplied and installed under a CONTRACT WITH ERECTION will be maintained by the contractor. *See also* WARRANTY PERIOD, RETENTION MONEY, *and* ORDERS & CONTRACTS A-Z, 'TURN KEY' CONTRACT.

maintenance, corrective. 'The maintenance carried out after a failure has occurred and intended to restore an ITEM to a state where it can perform its required function.

maintenance, emergency. (BS) Maintenance which it is necessary to put in hand immediately to avoid serious consequences.'

maintenance, planned. (BS) Maintenance organized and carried out with forethought, control and the use of records to a predetermined plan.

maintenance, preventive. (BS) Maintenance carried out at predetermined intervals or corresponding to prescribed criteria and intended to reduce the probability of failure or the performance degradation of an item.

maintenance, remedial, corrective. (BS) Maintenance carried out after a failure has occurred and intended to restore an ITEM to a state where it can perform its required function.

maintenance, repair and operating materials (MRO). Materials for support operations, not to be embodied in the finished product. *See* INDIRECT MATERIALS.

maintenance, routine. *See* MAINTENANCE, SCHEDULED MAINTENANCE.

maintenance, running. Maintenance which can be carried out while the item is in service.

maintenance, scheduled. (BS) The PREVENTIVE MAINTENANCE carried out to a predetermined interval of time, number of operations, mileage, etc.

maintenance, repair and operating materials (MRO). used up in the running of the organisation. Similar to 'consumables', or 'indirect materials'.

management (cf. administration). The formulation of strategy, policy, and direction of an enterprise in all its vital functions, with effective communication and rapport with those appointed by management to ADMINISTER the execution of such strategies, policies and directives.

management accounting. (CIMA) The preparation and presentation of accounting information in such a way as to assist management in the formulation of policies and in the planning and control of the activities of the enterprise.

management by exception. (adm) The, application of the 'exception principle' under which managers and staff concentrate time and effort on the 'vital fewer' matters and less upon the 'trivial many'. (For examples see ABC ANALYSIS and the PARETO PRINCIPLE. But, note that in purchasing and supply some apparently 'trivial' items, e.g. spares, may be vital to the continued functioning of production or a process).

management by objectives. (adm) The technique under which targets are fixed as a basis for achieving greater effectiveness throughout part or whole of an enterprise. May involve motivation of personnel by involving them in setting targets of performance, etc.

management/executive development.

(adm) The systematic process of developing effective managers and executives at all levels required in an enterprise. It involves the analysis of present and future management/executive requirements, assessing existing and potential skill of managers/ executives and devising the best means for their development to meet these requirements.

manifest. (mar) A document completed by the captain of a ship before it leaves port, and containing the record of the cargo the ship carries and its destination. It is handed in to the authorities at the port of departure.

Manual Handling of Loads Directive. Implemented by UK wef 1.1.1993. (Manual Handling Operations Regulations 1992). This UK Regulation has wide implications and particularly for storage, handling and distribution embraces a wide range of manual handling practices and risks. Key provisions include three main steps for employers to take to protect the health and safety of their employees: 1. avoid hazardous manual handling where possible; 2. assess those operations which are unavoidable; 3. reduce the risk of injury as far as possible.

manual, departmental, (supplies, stores, etc). A handbook detailing procedures, administration, duties, policies and all other information needed by staff for efficient and harmonious working.

manual, technical. (BS) 'A document providing information explaining use, maintenance and repair of any material or product. Technical Manuals are provided for those involved with management maintenance, operation, and provisioning'. *Also may include* INSTRUCTIONS; INSTALLATION, COMMISSIONING, OPERATING.

manufacturer's agent. *See* AGENT, MANUFAC-
TURER'S.

manufacturing resource planning. Usually
known as MRP2. This is a development
from 'materials requirements planning'
and encompasses the planning and
scheduling activities associated with
production resources to match output
needed and supplies available.

marginal costing. (CIMA) A principle
whereby MARGINAL COSTS of units
are ascertained. Only variable costs are
charged to cost units, the fixed costs
attributable to a relevant period being
written off in full against the CONTRI-
BUTION for that period. Note: it is
recommended that the term be applied
only where the routine system incorporates the marginal principle.

Marine Insurance Act 1906. Act which
codified the law relating to marine
insurance.

maritime law. *See* LAW, MARITIME LAW.

mark up, mark down. (CIMA) A term used
in commercial business (retailing,
wholesaling, factoring etc.) adding
('up') or reducing ('down') a selling
price to effect a sale. Often expressed as
a percentage.

market economy *See* FREE MARKET
ECONOMY.

market forces. Forces acting in an
economy which affect prices through
pressures on demand for the supply of,
goods and services. Market forces may
include, for example: 1. forces: exerted
by marketing activities; 2. demands for
changes: in domestic habits, fashion,
etc.; 3. technological change, development, or obsolescence; 4. state intervention, pressures, Statutes, quotas,
controls, etc; 5. international pressures,
controls, regulations, Directives, etc. *See
also* note at COMPETITION.

market grades and grading. Grading of
materials sold on COMMODITY
MARKETS. These take place according
to recognised and accepted standards
using samples in the case of crops and
ASSAY in the case of some minerals.

market leader. The enterprise with the
largest share in the market of a particular product.

market overt (open market). A market
open to the public (originally between
sunrise and sunset) where goods are
displayed in bulk. Gives the purchaser
certain rights of the TITLE regardless of
the title of the seller.

market research. A systematic investigation into the actual or potential market
for a particular product, commodity or
service.

market testing. Using cost analysis to
determine whether an internally
provided service might be more
economically provided by an external
organization.

market value. The prevailing price as
determined by MARKET FORCES
applied to goods and services bought
and sold under free market conditions.

market, buyer's. Market conditions where
supply exceeds demand and prices tend
to fall to the advantage of buyers.
Typical of conditions changing from
boom to recession in a free market
economy. (Seller's market is the
converse of a buyer's market.)

market, commercial. Place where sellers
offer goods and purchasers come to
buy. *See also* MARKETS: COMMODITY,
MARKET FUTURES.

market, commodity. One where (usually) natural products e.g. minerals and crops are bought and sold on the world or regional market basis. Often situated at centres of importation, e.g. London, Chicago, etc. Such 'organized markets' tend to develop when the COMMODITY is fairly durable, traded in large consignments, and subject to price fluctuations.

market, commodity market auctions. Procedures for sales of non-standardized graded natural commodities. Catalogues are circulated and samples made available for inspection. Trade associations set terms and conditions of trading and brokerage charges. The seller's contract takes the form of a 'sold note' against which the broker issues a 'bought note' and delivery is made against a 'warehouse warrant'.

market, economic market. The trade in commodities and goods for which buyers and sellers are in free competition.

market, futures. Commodity markets where 'futures' contracts are arranged between producers, purchasers and speculators.

market, hardening of market. A market situation where prices tend to rise and become inflexible to negotiation for reduction, e.g. price will harden if a supplier discovers he is in a monopoly position vis-a-vis the market, or his customer or that the purchasing officer is committed to buy from him.

market, perfect. A theoretical condition where many sellers and buyers are in continuous close contact so that their combined activities tend to produce a uniform price after allowing for distribution costs.

market, share of. (CIMA) A firm's share of a market as a percentage of the total market available.

market, terminal market. FUTURES MARKETS are sometimes called terminal markets because the dealings in them are for specified 'terms,' i.e. in periods of time.

marketing. The creative management function that promotes trade by assessing consumer needs and initiating research and development to meet them, it co-ordinates the resources of production and distribution of goods and services; determines and directs the nature and scale of effort required to sell profitably the maximum production of goods.

marketing costs. *See* COSTS, MARKETING COST,

marketing, distance selling. Marketing to (mostly) domestic areas which may then enter into contracts for goods and services at a distance as a result of remotely operated marketing. Domestic postal consumers may expect protection through new DIRECTIVES but these may not apply to business contracts.

marketing, inertia selling. The supply of unsolicited goods or services. Applies chiefly to domesti.c consumers for whom protection is proposed by a 'Distance Selling Directive' from the Commission.

marking (of packages). The process of applying to a container such particulars as: 1. destination; consignee and special transportation markings;, 2. consignor, 3. quantity, 4. nomenclature, 5. package number, 6. invoice or other document details as may be necessary.

mass production. *See* PRODUCTION, MASS PRODUCTION.

master production schedule. The plan for production of completely finished products or assemblies.

material. (BS) Equipment, stores, supplies and spares that form the subject of a contract, chiefly those used by armed services, e.g. NATO. This generic term is often used for large scale PROCURE-MENT and avoids the necessity of repeating items covered in this definition. *See also* MATERIAL *and* SUPPLIES.

material (supplies). *See also* MATERIAL. In a supplies context materials are substances in solid, liquid, powder, gaseous or other form and which have a recognizable identity for use in production, process or other function.

material control. (BS) Procedures and means by which the correct quantity and quality of materials and components (SUPPLIES) are made available to meet production needs.

material costs. *See* COSTS, MATERIAL COSTS.

material utilization control. (BS) Procedures and means set up to ensure that materials provided for the production plans are used most effectively.

materials cost analysis sheet. (CIMA) A record showing the total materials cost charges for a period and detailing the separate amounts relating to different COST UNITS or COST CENTRES.

materials credit note. A document used internally giving details of surplus materials returned to store from a production department.

materials direct. Those materials consumed or converted which may be traced to a particular job or contract.

materials handling. *See* HANDLING, MATERIALS HANDLING.

materials management. The concept requiring an organizational structure which unifies into one functional responsibility the systematic planning and control of all materials from identification of the need through to delivery to the customer. Materials management embraces planning, purchasing, production and inventory control, storage, materials handling and physical distribution.

materials requirements planning (MRP). A method of provisioning which depends upon a master manufacturing schedule as distinct from statistical predictions. The 'schedule' defines when finished batches and items are needed for production. It is then broken down into components and subassemblies, etc. and each of these broken back to provision (purchase or supply) raw materials or parts. *See also* MANUFACTURING RESOURCE PLANNING.

materials requisition. *See* REQUISITION.

materials returned note. A document which records the return of unused material to stores.

materials transfer note. (CIMA) A document which records (and may authorize) the transfer of material from one store to another, or from one COST CENTRE to another.

max-min system. *See* STOCK-CONTROL, MAX-MIN.

maximum stock. *See* STOCK LEVEL, MAXIMUM.

mean, arithmetic mean. (BS) The sum of recorded values divided by the number of values recorded.

mean, moving, exponentially weighted. *See* EXPONENTIAL SMOOTHING.

measurement, Units of Measurement Directive. (EU) This Directive (adopted 11/89 by HMG UK) extends the use of metric units throughout the Community.

mercantile agent. *See* AGENT, MERCANTILE AGENT.

mercantile bills. Bills of exchange drawn by one merchant on another.

mercantile law. *See* LAW, MERCANTILE LAW.

mercantile person. One engaged in an area of buying and selling as distinct from manufacturing.

merchandise. (n) A generic term usually applied to commercial goods and stocks of all kinds.

merchandizing. The practice particularly in the retail area, of seeking to increase sales by publicity and attractive displays of goods in shops, market places, etc.

merchant. Strictly a person who imports goods on his own account, applied also to persons in the home trade who buy and sell on their own account, or sell another's goods on commission.

Merchant Shipping (Dangerous Goods) Rules 1965. Lays down the classification of dangerous goods under IMO classifications.

merchantable quality (law). *See* QUALITY, MERCHANTABLE QUALITY.

merger. The union of two or more enterprises by which either 1. one is absorbed by the other and terminates its separate legal existence, or 2. the identities of the existing enterprises are extinguished and a new combined enterprise is formed.

method engineering. (BS) 'The systematic recording and critical examination of the factor, and resources involved in existing and proposed ways of doing work, as means of developing and applying easier and more effective methods and of reducing costs

metrology. (BS) The field of knowledge concerned with measurement. Legal metrology treats units of measurement, methods of measurement, measuring instruments, in relation to mandatory technical and legal requirements.

micro-economics. *See* ECONOMICS.

microfiche. Flat filing system for small-scale photographic transparencies.

microfilm. Film often used for storing small-scale photographic images, often of document, or drawings.

middleman. Any WHOLESALER, MERCHANT, BROKER, AGENT, DISTRIBUTER, STOCKIST, who has to do with the distribution of supplies. *See also* AGENTS.

milking. The practice of a supplier, who may have a MONOPOLY of MISREPRE-SENTATION supply, who excessively inflates profit by extortionate pricing of his product.

minimum stock level. *See* STOCK LEVEL, MINIMUM STOCK LEVEL.

mio. abb. Currency dealer's abbreviation for million.

Misrepresentation Act 1967. Act which extended available remedies (in particular, the award of damages) where an innocent misrepresentation has been committed. Attempts to exclude liability for misrepresentation subject to the test of reasonableness.

misrepresentation. An untrue statement of fact made by one party to another, e.g. during the course of negotiations, as to some existing fact or past event, and which acts as a material inducement to the other party to enter into the contract.

misrepresentation, fraudulent. A false statement which the representor himself did not honestly believe to be true.

misrepresentation, innocent. A statement made by one party to another in which the party making the statement genuinely believes it to be true.

mission approach. Management across functional barriers in an enterprise in order to meet and achieve particular organizational goals. e.g. the introduction of specialists in purchasing and supply administration and management in a growing firm so as to co-ordinate the total SUPPLY aspects and needs of the enterprise.

mistake. Legal doctrine recognises three classes of mistake only: 1. Common mistake - includes circumstances where for example, unknown to either party, the subject of the contract no longer exists. 2. Mutual mistake - here both parties mistake the nature or subject matter of the contract, which may then become void. 3. Unilateral mistake - here the mistake may be in the person with whom the party believes himself to be dealing. Lawyers assume that when people enter into a contract they know what they are doing and mean what they say in the contract.

mnemonic. *See* CODES, MNEMONIC CODE.

mobile machinery and lifting equipment, directives. (EU) (HS) Most mobile machinery and lifting equipment made, sold, imported into UK has to: 1. satisfy wide ranging HS requirements on

WORK STATIONS, controls, protection against mechanical hazards; and 2. in some cases be subject to TYPE-EXAMINATION by an APPROVED BODY; 3. carry the 'CE'MARK and its relevant information; 4. the manufacturer (or his authorised representative in the Union) must draw up and keep available, a technical file of the MACHINERY. Failure to comply will be a criminal offence.

mobile racking. *See* RACKING, MOBILE RACKING.

mock up. A model (not necessarily 'working') made up to display (usually) physical size and proportions and other characteristics of the final product, e.g. an aircraft fuselage.

mode. The value of an item which occurs most frequently in a range of observations, or 'the most frequently occurring value in a distribution'. The 'mode' is not suitable for mathematical calculation buy may be used as a means of assessing quickly, action required on PROVISIONING, dealing with production rejects in QUALITY CONTROL, etc.

modification. An alteration made to a physically existing product usually resulting in an improvement in performance and generally carried out as the result of a design change (e.g, replacing a plain bearing by a sealed roller bearing).

modification order. *See* ORDER AND CONTRACTS VARIATION ORDER.

momentum ('P'). The impetus of a body (such as e.g. a fully laden truck) resulting from its motion.

monitoring, health and safety, reactive monitoring. The monitoring of health and safety after things have gone wrong.

(Investigation of cases of illness, property damage, 'near misses!!' - identifying in each case why performance was sub-standard).

Monopolies and Mergers Act 1965. (law) This Act extended the functions of the Commission under monopoly investigations to the consideration of supply of services as well as goods. At the same time mergers of business were brought within its scope and the Commission was renamed the Monopolies and Mergers Commission.

monopoly. (econ) A market situation in which an enterprise or a number of enterprises acting in concert control a large proportion of a market in such a manner that they can fix prices and terms of trade to a large extent without regard to competitors. *See also* DUOPOLY *and* OLIGOPOLY.

monopoly, absolute monopoly. (econ) The control of total output/supply of a commodity or service for which there is no substitute, by a single enterprise, state or CARTEL, etc.

monopsony. The reverse of monopoly, many suppliers but only one purchaser.

Monte Carlo method. (BS) A method of obtaining an approximate solution to a numeric problem by the use of random numbers and simulation.

muda. Japanese term translating as 'waste', or 'that which does not add value'.

multinational. An organization which has branches or operations in more than one country

multiple sourcing. *See* SUPPLIES, SOURCING OF SUPPLIES.

multiplier, the multiplier. The degree to which extra spending power injected into an economy is spent a number of times over, and the proportion saved each time the money passes from one individual to another.

mutagenic. (HS) A substance which may result in risks of hereditable genetic defects if INHALED or INGESTED.

mutagenic substances. *See* SUBSTANCE.

mutual relationship. A relationship between buyer and seller whereby it is felt that mutual support, advice, technology sharing, etc. can create benefits for both cf PARTNERSHIP SOURCING.

narcotic. (HS) A substance (a drug) which tends to induce sleep if taken into the bodily system. *See* SUBSTANCE.

National Accreditation Council for Certification Bodies (NACCB). A Council formed to report to the Secretary of State for Trade and Industry concerning the competence and impartiality of CERTIFICATION BODIES, leading to their accreditation and ability to display the National Accreditation Mark alongside their own certification mark, 071 233 71 1 1.

National Measurement Accreditation Service (NAMAS). A service provided by the National Physical Laboratory to give formal accreditation to calibration and testing laboratories. A list of accredited laboratories world-wide is available from NAMAS and from Department of Trade and Industry.

National Quality Information Centre. The Centre is operated by the INSTITUTE OF QUALITY ASSURANCE in order to assist industry and commerce to obtain information and improve quality in their corporate activities and in the products and services they provide.

negative clearance. (EU) An individual exemption granted by the Commission of the EU in respect of an article of Community enactments.

negligence. (law) 1. Want of care. 2. 'Culpable negligence', a degree of negligence deserving censure and blame. 3. 'Gross negligence', the want of even the slightest care.

negotiable instrument. A document entitling the holder to a sum specified upon it. It can normally be transferred to another party, usually by endorse-ment. Examples are cheques, bills of exchange, etc.

negotiate (v) To communicate, discuss and bargain with the objective of reaching an agreement.

negotiating bank. (SITPRO) The bank specifically nominated in the letter of credit to purchase the bill of exchange (draft) drawn by the beneficiary, or a drawee other than the negotiating bank. If a letter of credit is freely negotiating any bank willing to do so can be the negotiating bank. *See also* ADVISING BANK.

nemawashi. Japanese term which may be loosely translated as 'consensus decision taking'. Essentially it may be regarded as a way of ensuring that middle managers keep their superiors informed, the theory being that senior management is then able to make better decisions.

nemo dat quod non habet. Legal expression, 'no one can give what he does not have', i.e. if you do not have title then you can not pass title to another.

net. The amount of any charge, weight or other measures which remain after all allowances have been made. Also spelt 'neat' and less accurately 'nett'.

net cash. *See* PRICE, NET PRICE.

net present value. *See* VALUE, NET PRESENT VALUE.

net price. *See* PRICE, NET PRICE.

net profit. *See* PROFIT, NET PROFIT.

net registered tonnage (NRT). The gross registered tonnage (in cubic tons) of a ship less allowance for space not available for cargo (e.g. engine room, crew's quarters, etc.). Usually about 55-65 percent, and used for assessing harbour dues, etc.

net weight. Gross weight of goods less TARE, i.e. after deducting the weight of box and package, etc.

network (project network). (BS) A representation of activities and/or events with their interrelationships and dependencies.

network analysis. (BS) A group of techniques for presenting information to assist the planning and controlling of projects. The information, usually represented by a network, includes the sequence and logical inter-relationships of all project activities. The group includes techniques for dealing with time, distances, resources and costs. Note: the term 'critical path analysis' refers to a particular technique of product network analysis, and should not be used as synonymous.

network code. (energy) A set of terms and conditions implemented in 1996 giving access to and use of the national gas pipeline system

new electricity trading arrangement. Introduced in the UK in 2000 to allow traders more opportunities for contracting, easier adjustment of contract prices and better balancing of the supply system.

Newton (F). The SI unit of force which imparts to a mass of one kilogram an acceleration of one metre per second per second. Of importance when calculating the effects of collisions or similar events with moving plant, e.g. fork lift trucks, vehicles, etc.

noise. An 'inhibition' which may induce unwanted signals which intrude into a telecommunications system. 2. Random variations to be discounted in forecasting.

nominal price. *See* PRICE, NOMINAL PRICE.

nominal price. *See* PRICE, ECONOMIC PRICE.

non-tariff barrier. A barrier to free trade that does not involve the imposition of customs duties. Export or import licencing schemes are examples.

noxious substance. *See* SUBSTANCES.

O

Orders and Contracts

O&C all-in contract. A contract which covers all aspects of a job including design, provision of prototypes through to commissioning. Also known as 'Turnkey Contract'. *See also* DESIGN AND DEVELOPMENT CONTRACT.

O&C amendment order. *See* VARIATION ORDER.

O&C automated purchasing. *See* AUTOMATED PURCHASING *at* A.

O&C barter. Direct exchange of goods without transfer of cash. Goods bartered may be part of a major transaction. Often favoured by states with controlled economies. *See* COUNTER TRADE.

O&C batch and batch schedule ordering. A production, linked ordering system in which purchase orders (and/or their deliveries) are so scheduled that INTAKES are in accordance with the production or process schedule for which they are required. *See also* 'JUST IN TIME' TECHNIQUE.

O&C blanket orders. Orders covering or 'blanketing' a range of goods from a supplier, e.g. an order covering a range of tools from a tool supplier. As with other similar arrangements enables user to obtain goods and services at known price, specification and delivery,

O&C bulk/contract order. 1. A contract for bulk materials. 2. A contract in which a number of requirements are bulked together to achieve price/delivery advantage.

O&C buy, sell and lease back. A form of capital financing whereby the purchaser of a large unit plant (such as a ship) sells the unit at the time of purchase to a finance company from whom he then leases it back for his own use. *See also* LEASE BACK.

O&C call off. *See* DRAW OFF ORDERS.

O&C cancellation order. Notification to a supplier that the purchaser intends to break the contract by cancelling his order. As with **VARIATION ORDERS** these should be in writing and agreement of the other party is needed.

O&C cash and carry. Buyer pays cash and collects, loads and carries away the goods he has purchased. More usually applicable to the domestic market.

O&C cash on delivery. Buyer pays cash when he receives the goods. Mostly confined to domestic trading.

O&C cash with order. Goods are only despatched if the buyer sends cash with his order. Generally restricted to retail firms between wholesalers and new retail accounts. *See also* PAYMENT PROFORMA. PAYMENT AGAINST.

O&C cheque-order. System of ordering where the order form has a cheque attached which the supplier detaches and passes to his bank. For security the cheque should have the amount filled in. Restricted to suppliers with whom the purchasing company has regular transactions.

O&C computer ordering. *See* COMPUTERISED ORDERING SYSTEMS AND AUTOMATED PURCHASING.

O&C consignment stock order. The supplier places goods in the purchaser's stores to be drawn off and paid for as used. For use with forward supply arrangements, etc. on high-use items. Assures supply and saves investment by the purchaser. Supplier may seek to recover his investment costs.

O&C consortium buying orders. Orders by a consortium which shares a secretariat to collate requirements of the members. Enquiries are placed on behalf of the consortium members. Often used to purchase important items common to a number of enterprises.

O&C cost plus orders/contracts. A purchase contract in which final sums invoiced are based on prices paid by the supplier for materials with an estimated or actual addition for cost of labour. Used in construction industries and where the precise estimates of price are impossible.

O&C cost reimbursable. Payments are made against claims for actual costs of work done and incurred in carrying out the work. Costs may be based upon pre-agreed rates or targets, as in the case of contracts on a time and materials basis. Applications are mostly as for lump sum contracts.

O&C delivery note acceptance ordering. The supplier uses specially printed delivery notes for requirements of customer whose authorized named persons collect goods. Delivery notes are priced, and used as invoice and order. Used for routine purchases from wholesaler, etc. for (e.g.) spares for maintenance, small tools, resale items, etc. Not for large value items as a rule.

O&C design and development contract. An order or contract placed purely for design and/or development of a complete product, prototype, etc. Used where design, etc. is beyond the capability of the purchaser, and he wishes to retain freedom of negotiation

and choice of supplier. Regularizes the use of supplier's expertise by the purchaser.

O&C draw-off order, call-off order. Order used to 'draw off' requirements from FORWARD SUPPLY CONTRACTS and/or FORWARD SUPPLY ARRANGEMENTS. Branches, stores, etc. authorized to issue these according to need at regular intervals or according to stock levels. Can be used for all classes of supplies from raw materials to miscellaneous but standard factory needs.

O&C enquiry-proceed ordering. An enquiry carrying instructions to put preliminary or complete work in hand. An order number is reserved and mentioned on the enquiry but only released on agreement of quotation. Used in similar circumstances to those for LETTER OF INTENT, but of smaller requirements, such as urgent spares.

O&C fixed order quantity cycle. Method of ordering on a fixed order quantity (e.g. See EOQ) when FEEDBACK from STOCK CONTROL or production/process indicates need for further supply.

O&C fixed price order/contract. One which has been subject to a firm quotation and no price variations are allowed for. For long-term contracts some clause for re-negotiation in the event of market changes may be essential.)

O&C forward buying contract/order. One placed in advance of actual need. Delivery may be 'as available' or planned for future. Object may be to secure supply from the source, for seasonal requirements, to profit from seasonal price changes, etc. (This form of contract needs a firm price, otherwise a CONTRACT PRICE

ADJUSTMENT formula will be needed.) *See also* FUTURES CONTRACT.

O&C forward supply arrangement (FSA). An arrangement for the future supply of specified goods and services to be drawn off as required. Such arrangements may be open-ended in regard to quantity and/or time. Some commitment on supplier and buyer. Can be used for class 'C' and sometimes class 'B' requirements where quantity and/or time are indeterminate. May have value in pegging price and specifications. *See also* MAIN (*and* FORWARD SUPPLY) CONTRACTS below.

O&C free-issue order. An order raised by a supplier's purchasing department on his firm's customer (in agreement with him) for the procurement from him of embodiment materials to be used in the supplier's production. Often includes details regarding inspection, etc. Regularizes the transaction and provides valuable record. Harmonises the supplies procedures with those of all normal transactions.

O&C futures contract. A contract made with a FUTURES EXCHANGE or TERMINAL MARKET for supplies to be available on maturity of the contract. Used for basic raw materials, metals and natural products. Hedging techniques can establish final price.

O&C group purchasing. The channelling of requirements for a group of companies into bulk contracts, etc, Means of gaining improved prices, deliveries, specifications, etc. (May break competition rules of the European Union).

O&C hire contracts (plant). Either a normal style order with special terms and conditions appropriate to hire or more usually a special contract form presented by the plant hire company.

Contract conditions should be studied with great care. The hire firm should service and maintain the plant hired.

O&C hire purchase contract (also known as lease purchase contract). The bailment of goods (usually) plant and equipment, under which the hirer becomes the BAILEE and to whom ultimately upon the completion of the contract the property in the goods will pass.

O&C in-plant stores arrangement. A kind of forward supply arrangement in which a supplier (sometimes a stockist) keeps a section of the customer's stores replenished at regular intervals, or 'on call', or as stock levels dictate. Employed for small miscellaneous requirements, usually class 'C'. *See also* STOCK, CONSIGNMENT STOCK.

O&C incentive contracts. Contracts which include a clause authorizing the payment to the supplier of additional money on the contract price for early delivery, improved performance, etc. For major contracts where completion date, delivery or performance is vital.

O&C job lot. A term sometimes used for a BATCH ORDER covering requirements for a PRODUCTION BATCH. More correctly, the term should be used to describe a miscellaneous assortment of goods sold as a lot and often of a low price and trivial nature.

O&C lease, hire. The hire of plant, buildings or equipment for rent.

O&C leasing (financial) contract. An arrangement whereby a finance house advances cash to the lessee so that the latter can obtain plant, etc. which he retains in possession and full use, but the property in which rests with the lessor during the period of lease.

O&C letter of intent. A written communication to a supplier leading to a contract and instructing him to take some action such as: 1. reserving production capacity or 2. putting preliminary work in hand, or 3. proceeding with work, etc. The letter of intent must usually be subject to a firm order being placed by a pre-agreed date or to cancellation at that date if work is not to proceed further.

O&C loan order. Used for borrowing tools, jigs or other equipment from a neighbouring factory or a main contractor to whom the user is a subcontractor. Standard small-value or local-purchase order forms can be used.

O&C local purchase order (LPO). As SMALL VALUE ORDERS but restricted to use with local suppliers.

O&C long-term contracts. Those contracts for supplies or services which may extend over a number of years as distinct from the normal twelve month period. There may be a number of objectives such as continuity of supplies or services of consistent quality and delivery at agreed prices.

O&C lump sum contract. A method of contracting usually restricted to civil and construction works. A single price and payment is quoted and paid for the whole job.

O&C measurement contract. Based on a BILL OF QUANTITIES with a schedule of rates, payments being made against certificates at various stages or upon completion of the contract. Used mostly as for LUMP SUM CONTRACT.

O&C memorandum buying. A system of purchasing mainly confined to retailing activities. The system permits the retailer to sell the goods before he pays the supplier. (May be coupled with a 'sale or return' clause agreed in advance with the supplier.)

O&C modification order. *See* BELOW, VARIATION ORDER.

O&C open order. An order wherein one or more features of a full contractual commitment are missing, usually in respect of time of completion, or quantity or both as in many FORWARD SUPPLY ARRANGEMENTS. *See* ABOVE.

O&C open-ended order/contract. A form of running order/contract arrangement having no fixed date for termination. (It is usually essential to include a clause, such as a BREAK CLAUSE, enabling the purchaser to terminate or modify the arrangement).

O&C package deal. *See* ALL IN CONTRACT.

O&C parallel working contracts. A representative part of a project is fully designed with full bills of quantities. Remainder is planned in outline with approximate bills. Details are then worked out and firm tenders obtained. Large projects where it is neither practicable nor desirable to design the whole job from the start e.g. local authority housing schemes.

O&C periodic ordering or hatching. To reduce the number of orders per week, or other period, requirements are held and collated into an order placed or reviewed for placing at a fixed rate, or when a viable quantity is reached, c-9. routine items or miscellaneous items on a wholesaler.

O&C petty cash purchases. Purchasing method by which purchases are made for cash and the sum recovered from firm's petty cash fund. Very small low value items in the fixed price range.

O&C pound cost averaging. Where regular imports are made at a fixed/stable commodity price the EXCHANGE RATE may vary. Under this arrangement, a fixed sum is allocated for each period. If the exchange rate varies adversely, the intake is reduced so as to keep expenditure within the fixed amount of finance allotted for the period. If the exchange rate varies in favour of the purchaser he may take advantage of this to build stocks to the value of the finance which is allotted. (Such SPECULATION needs close control by the financial management of the enterprise. Also it may not fit production or process demands).

O&C prime cost contract. One in which the contractor is reimbursed for his proven costs plus an addition to cover his overheads and profit, either a percentage on that cost or a fixed fee.

O&C priority order. An order which is identified as taking precedence over other orders to ensure its completion in the minimum time or to meet a fixed DEADLINE.

O&C procurement systems contract. An arrangement made between buyer and seller whereby arrangements are made in advance of the actual need arising, enabling the buyer quickly to acquire material as and when required against the arrangement. These arrangements often take the form of the provision of CONSIGNMENT STOCK, held at the customer's premises, and are sometimes referred to simply as ' systems contracts'.

O&C production reservation arrangements. Purchasing arrangements whereby the purchaser earmarks his supplier's production capacity, usually by monetary value or by machine hours, etc. Advance reservation is firmed up before each production period. Used for major requirements often with varying specifications but usually within the same product group.

O&C quasi contract. *See* CONTRACT, QUASI CONTRACT.

O&C reciprocal trading contracts. Purchase contracts which are related to the sales of other goods to the supplier. Each side buys from, and sells to, the other.

O&C requisition/order. A requisition / order form is so designed that after preparation by the user it may be sent to the purchasing department for editing, signature and forwarding to a supplier. 'Authorized persons' and other limits should be applied. Employed in companies, etc. where requisitioning on a central purchasing department is required. This obviates typing orders.

O&C run-on contracts or serial contracts. Project planned in reasonably continuous phases.

O&C sale and lease-back. A method of acquiring the use of a major asset without owning it. The buyer sells off the asset for cash, thus eliminating any call on his own cash flow or other resources. He then leases back the asset for his own use and takes over the risks in use of it. The technique is used for acquisition of capital items such as factory premises, plant, ship, etc.

O&C sale or return. A purchase on sale or return is an arrangement whereby the purchaser and seller agree that in the event of the goods not being sold they may be returned and the price credited.

O&C sample, order for sample. Order for samples free or on charge. It regularizes the transaction and provides valuable record.

103

O&C self-regulating/forward planning. A system whereby orders are placed periodically according to need and monitored against forecast and checked cumulatively. For major class 'A' needs, particularly for process-plant work. May be monitored by means of '2' CHARTS.

O&C serial contracting. A system whereby a contractor (subject to satisfactory service) tenders for a series of projects on agreed terms. The rates of prices on the first job may be used as the basis for the remainder of the programme.

O&C service contracts. As hire contracts as regards type of order. The same warnings apply. Also essential to study tariffs, etc. with great care. Used for specified tasks, e.g. to carry out a specific overhaul programme, undertake a specific duty, i.e. security service.

O&C severable contract. One involving deliveries by instalments where failure to deliver any one instalment may render the whole contract broken. Otherwise, in a normal contract a court will treat separate instalments as separate contracts, but in the case of a breach the court will look for the INTENTIONS of the parties.

O&C small value order (SVO). Simplified ordering system. Smaller (usually) order forms in tear-off manuscript pads may be used. Have a limited cash validity. Only issued for use by 'authorized persons', foremen, etc. May be restricted to, say, £25-£30 or other limit. Technique used in non-recurring small value orders, or those drawn from forward supply arrangements and needed for day-to-day or occasional use.

O&C sole supplier contracts. Contract with named supplier to the exclusion of others. A form of restrictive trading. May incur the attention of legal author-

ities if in breach of state or EU regulations.

O&C standing order or contract. An order for regular delivery of goods or services for an indefinite period. A single original instruction normally suffices.

O&C stock production order. (BS) A production order to manufacture a product to replenish stock in a store.

O&C stock purchase order. An order on a supplier for stock replenishment.

O&C stock schedule order. A schedule, often of standard parts, used as an order. Schedules sent to suppliers either at regular intervals or on demand for specified materials.

O&C subcontracts. Arrangement whereby a main contractor (or supplier) authorizes a second (or more) to undertake part of the order he has secured, Or, subcontract for supplies outside the purchaser's own production or because his production is overloaded.

O&C supplier's order form. Order form provided by supplier. The form is completed and signed by the purchasing officer of the purchasing firm. (Not recommended unless full safeguards are applied. Only used in routine and regular orders, if at all.)

O&C supplier's pre-printed order schedule. As above, a pre-printed (or duplicated) schedule of items supplied by a supplier. Employed for miscellaneous small regular items. May be used in conjunction with stock items, consignment stock, in plant stores, etc.

O&C turnkey. *See* ALL-IN.

O&C variation order. A purchasing instruction to a supplier to vary the substance (e.g. the instructions) on a purchase contract, e.g. quantity, specification, delivery, etc. Note: a variation order should always be in writing and a price should be agreed at the time of the variation order. The term VARIATION ORDER is preferred to the term MODIFICATION ORDER as this may have a double meaning. It is synonymous with 'amendment order'.

O&C verbal orders. Orders given verbally by telephone or face to face. Legally binding once accepted by the supplier and acted upon, Should always be confirmed by written order unless of totally insignificant value.

O&C volume versus exchange rate contract. For this type of contract a datum rate of exchange is agreed as basic to the contract for importation of supplies. When the exchange rate rises above this level intake may be increased and stocks built up to take advantage of the favourable rate of exchange. When the exchange rate falls below the datum the purchaser reverts to HAND TO MOUTH buying of the minimum possible and using stocks where available.

O&C volume versus market price contracts. A system of buying in which timing of each contract is adjusted according to the market price forecast.

O&C work and materials orders. Those orders which fall outside the scope of a contract for sale or hire purchase, e.g. a contract for maintenance or installation of plant but not its purchase.

objectivity. The study, consideration or discussion of subjects or problems based upon facts, untrammelled by SUBJECTIVE emotional or prejudicial influences. An important character-istic/quality of those engaged in administration and management to ensure that subjective considerations do not override commercial or technical aspects of a problem or a purchase.

obsolescence, functional obsolescence. The measure of loss of value of a FIXED ASSET due to various causes: 1. Asset superseded by one which is superior to it, technically or in performance. 2. Cessation of need in consequence of change in the market or a change in production method. 3. In the purchasing supply context it may imply that supplies, equipment and spares have ceased to be readily available even although the plant requiring them is still in use. 4. On the way to becoming OBSOLETE.

obsolescent. Not yet obsolete but becoming so.

obsolete. 1. Supplies, plant or equipment which have passed OBSOLESCENCE and are completely out of date, out of use. 2. Supplies which are no longer available and cannot be replaced.

ODETTE. A standardised format for transport labels, employing bar coding as well as plain language information. Used internationally in Europe.

offcuts. Residual materials left after machining, turning, cutting, shearing, etc. Represent a loss centre in supplies and call for effective materials manage-ment and control.

offer (in a contract). An offer is a communication of definite intention to enter into a contract; it may be written or verbal for an), value under English law. It is a vital component of a contract

and must be met by an unqualified acceptance.

offer, by tender. *See* TENDERS AND TENDERING.

offer, counter-offer. An offer made in response to the offer from another party in a negotiation. The communica-tion by an offeree (e.g. a purchaser) to an offer or a (supplier) seeking to modify the terms of an acknowledge-ment by the latter, is in law, a 'counter offer' and deprives the contract of an 'unqualified acceptance'.

offer, firm. One which has been made by a supplier for supplies of a specified quality, quantity, price or delivery date and which allows of no variation from that stated. It binds both supplier and buyer and as common with most offers is usually open for acceptance for a limited and stated period, usually 30 days.

offeree. A person to whom an offer is made.

offeror. A person who makes an offer.

Office of Fair Trading (OFT). The statutory body responsible for overseeing of British industrial and commercial life and its 'fair trading'. Examples of its remit include prices charged for supplies and raw materials and the impact of take-overs. It can launch investigations, revoke licences, refer matters to the MONOPOLIES AND MERGERS COMMISSION (MMC), highlight malpractices and make recommendation to the govern-ment. While it must be noted that this and other similar Acts exist primarily to protect the public, they can also have implications for purchasing and supply activities if these impinge upon the domestic supply area.

Office of Government Commerce (OGC). A body concerned with the development and dissemination of good commercial practice in the UK Civil Service. Formerly the Central Purchasing Unit.

Official Journal of the European Community (OJEC). Electronic publication in which most European public sector purchases where the anticipated value exceeds the relevant threshold must be advertised.

offset. (com) The elimination of a current long or short position by the opposite transaction.

ogive (cumulative frequency curve). (stat) A curve of characteristic shape, similar to the letter 'Z'. It is used in purchasing and supply when (for example) plotting comulative values of a range of demands/usages on the vertical axis against time on the horizontal axis in periods of (say) weeks, months, production periods, etc. In purchasing and marketing e.g, the upper curve can represent the twelve month moving mean of consumption or sales; the lower curve the monthly take-off or sales; the curve sloping upwards from left to right, the cumulative sum of take off or sales.

oligopoly. (econ) The occupation of a market, or a large part of a market, by a small number of enterprises, each of which has significant economic power which it exercises independently, at the same time taking account of the conduct in the market by other enterprises. *See also* DUOPOLY *and* MONOPOLY.

oligopsony. (econ) A buyer's market situation, where for a certain good (or range of goods) there are so few buyers that they are able to influence the price paid in their favour.

on line. The term used in information technology for the immediate access to information through electronic process facilities. (Of particular importance for instantly updating stock control records, movement of transport, etc. immediately as it takes place.)

oncost. *See* COSTS, OVERHEAD COSTS.

one-for-one. *See* STOCK CONTROL, ONE-FOR-ONE'.

open access bins. Bins (or other containers) usually at work centres from which operatives can take supplies without formal paperwork control. The level is usually maintained by visual stock control by imprest and/or by regular (daily) replenishment. *See also* OPEN ACCESS STORES.

open credit. Name given to a letter of credit when it contains an unconditional request to pay money to another person. *See also* DOCUMENTARY CREDIT.

open market. *See* MARKET OVERT.

operating profit. *See* PROFIT, OPERATING. PROFIT.

operating ratio. Operating costs of a (transport) service expressed as a percentage of receipts. The higher the percentage the lower the profitability.

operation costing. (CIMA) Basic costing methods applicable where standardized goods or services result from a sequence of repetitive and more or less continuous operations or processes to which costs are charged before being averaged over the units produced during the period. *See also* CONTRACT *and* JOB COSTING.

operational research. The application of methods of science to complex problems arising in the direction and management of large systems of people, machines, materials and money in

107

industry, business, government and defence.

operator. (adm) The person or persons given the task of installing, operating, adjusting, cleaning, repairing or transporting MACHINERY.

opinions. (EU) Such (e.g. from the Union) have no binding force but merely state the view of the institution that issues them.

opportunity cost. See COST, OPPORTUNITY COST.

optical character recognition. Electronic method whereby an instrument recognises outlines of characters and can transmit them into a computer.

option. The right of choice, particularly in contracts, where an offer (or some part of an offer) may be taken or not taken at the choice or option of the offeree.

order cover. The sum of stock physically on hand and on order, less any reserved stock.

order processing time. See LEAD TIME, INTERNAL LEAD TIME, etc.

order, production order. BS A written internal instruction to proceed with the manufacture of a product or the provision of a service, normally specifying quantity, delivery date, etc. Also referred to as: 'works order', 'manufacturing order', 'factory order', 'shop order'.

order, purchase order (written). (BS) A written instruction to a supplier to provide a product or service normally specifying: quality, quantity, delivery-date required and price. Note: a purchase order does not need to be in writing in order to create a valid contract.

ordering costs. See COSTS, ORDER PREPARATION COSTS, etc.

organization and method (O&M) (BS) The application of WORK STUDY to the detailed administration, clerical and office work with the objectives of improved methods and procedures. Methods include examining: 1. needs for and of procedures/operations; 2. effectiveness of procedures/operations.

Organization of Petroleum Exporting Countries (OPEC). A prominent example of an international commodity PRODUCERS' ASSOCIATION.

out-of-phase, in supplies. The condition where INTAKES are out of step with DEMAND. This can result in glut when replenishments arrive and yet fail to prevent stock-out later in the production cycle. The difference between stock level and USAGE represents financial loss (usually unseen) to the enterprise.

outage. The state of an item e.g. plant being unable to perform its required function.

outgoings. A term sometimes used for EXPENSES.

outsourcing. Placing non-core activities with external contractors. The theory is that concentrating on core functions and leaving more peripheral but nevertheless essential activities to external specialists leads to greater efficiency

over-specification. A specification in which TOLERANCES, LIMITS, performance or other features are specified more closely or rigidly than the end-use demands.

overcharge. An amount in excess of the sum agreed in a contract. It must be noted that those costing for sales owe the same obligation to their enterprise to avoid an undercharge as does the purchasing officer to prevent an overcharge.

overhaul. (BS) A comprehensive EXAMINATION and RESTORATION of an ITEM, or a major part thereof, to an acceptable condition. *See also* REPAIR.

overhead costs. *See* 'COSTS, OVER-HEAD COSTS.'

overload. A load, electrical or mechanical, which exceeds the normal (stated/indicated) capacity of the plant or equipment. 'Overload capacity' may be negotiated by the purchaser. In this case the supplier should state the extra capacity above the normal rating which will be available and for an agreed (specified) time under specified operating conditions.

Overseas Trade Magazine. A free periodical from the DTI. Gives export news and opportunities in European markets.

overtrading. (CIMA) A term applied to a business which enters into commitments in excess of its available resources, e.g. a supplier may accept purchase orders for which he has inadequate means of paying for the supplies needed to execute the work.

own account operator. One who provides his own service, particularly transport, on his own account instead of using other available sources for the service he provides.

owner's risk. *See* RISK, OWNER'S.

ownership. *See* TITLE.

P

package. Anything in which goods are contained for transit or storage, etc.

package deal. *See* ORDERS AND CONTRACTS, 'ALL-IN' CONTRACT.

package register. A record of movements inwards and outwards of packages (e.g. drums, cylinders, pallets, containers, handling tackle) which are sent by the supplier and will be charged for and invoiced and must be returned for credit and items which are free but returnable. Copies of package notes will be required by the invoice checking section.

packaging. The design of, and the materials involved in, the packing of articles or commodities for carriage, storage and delivery.

packing note (packing list). A document packed inside individual packages of a consignment listing the actual goods in that package..

packing. (v) The operations of packaging whereby articles or commodities are enveloped in wrapping and/or enclosed in containers or otherwise secured.

page, home. The first page that appears when visiting a Web site.

paladin bins. Circular waste bins on wheels for local authority and industrial waste

pallet. (BS) Portable platform with or without superstructure for the assembly of a quantity of goods to form a unit load for stacking and handling by mechanical appliances particularly by pallet truck and fork lift truck. *See also* LOAD BOARD, *also* STILLAGE.

pallet invertor. Device for transferring the load from one pallet to another by making a sandwich then turning it over.

pallet loader, lorry bed type. Roller tracks in vehicle beds to facilitate the movement of pallets along the vehicle thus obviating the necessity for lift trucks to operate on the vehicle deck.

pallet racking. *See* RACKING, PALLET RACKING.

pallet truck. Wheeled device for moving pallets horizontally (but not vertically). May be manual or powered.

pallet, box type. Pallet with solid sides for small goods or those requiring protection

pallet, cage. Pallet with mesh sides, one of which may drop or be hinged for access

pallet, flat. One which comprises a single flat platform or load board.

pallet, post. One with fixed or demountable posts at each corner and suitable for self-stacking

pallet, roll. Usually two or four cage-sided on four castor type wheels. May be fitted with couplings for towing.

palletization. The arrangement for housing goods and material on pallets for handling, transportation, storage and use.

palletize. Mechanical equipment for loading and/or wrapping pallets.

paperless trading. (IT) The practice of communicating trade information by electronic data interchange (**EDI**) instead of using paper documentation.

parameter. (stat) A mathematical term, frequently used as a synonym for BOUNDARIES or LIMITS etc.

Pareto's Principle. In a study of distribution of national wealth, Pareto noticed that a large proportion of national wealth was under the control of a relatively small number of people. He based on this the rule that: 'In any series of elements to be controlled, a selected small factor in terms of the number of elements almost always accounts for a large factor in terms of effort'. *See* ABC ANALYSIS.

part (or component). (BS) A uniquely identifiable product that is considered indivisible for a particular planning or control purpose or purchasing.

particular average. *See* AVERAGE, PARTICULAR AVERAGE.

particulates. Separate small particles of materials.

partnering. An approach to sourcing through which mutually profitable long-term relationships between suppliers and their customers are sought, based on openness and trust. It is important to note that this approach is not intended to allow the 'partners' to become relaxed and perhaps therefore less competitive, but instead to become more competitive through cooperation in the avoidance of waste. This approach is sponsored and supported by Partnership Sourcing, a body jointly sponsored by the DTI and CBI.

Partnership Act 1890. Act which codified the law of partnership. It defined partnership, created tests for establishing its existence, and defined rules by which the external and internal relations of the partnership were governed. Often allows partnerships to agree otherwise. Contains rules governing the dissolution of partnership.

parts list (bill of materials, parts schedule). (BS) A list of all parts, sub-assemblies and raw materials that constitute a particular assembly, showing the quantity of each required.

parts per million. (PPM) Self-explanatory, now commonly used (parts per million defective) as an indicator of quality where substandard parts are rarely encountered.

patent. *See* LETTERS PATENT.

Patents Act 1977. Act reforming patent law including rules governing requirements for successful patent applications and procedures for application and registration, employee inventions, licences and infringements. Part Two gives effect to certain international conventions on patents.

payback. (CIMA) A method of PROJECT ASSESSMENT by comparison of investment projects by calculating for each project the periods in which the profits earned will equal the original capital outlay.

payee. (SITPRO) The party nominated by the drawer of a bill of exchange (draft) to receive payment.

payer. The person who pays the money due, by initiating a document such as a bill of exchange, etc.

paying bank. (SITPRO) A bank nominated in a DOCUMENTARY LETTER OF CREDIT to which documents (and sight bill of exchange, if called for) must be presented for payment.

payload. That portion of a load which contributes to revenue for the transport enterprise.

payment. The final stage in a contract whereby the purchaser completes his side of the contract. There may however be residual aspects committing the supplier: MAINTENANCE PERIOD, RETENTION MONEYS, ADJUST-MENT MONEY, etc.

payment against documents (cash against documents). (SITPRO) The shipper (exporter) does not release the goods or the bill of lading on arrival until full payment has been made. When a contract includes this clause, the captain of the ship will not, on arrival in port, hand over the bill of lading and documents of title, or the goods until the covering draft from the consignor has been paid.

payment, cash with order. *See* ORDERS & CONTRACTS, CASH WITH ORDER A-Z.

payment, down payment. One made by a purchaser as an initial instalment for a purchase, or as a DEPOSIT. *See also* PAYMENT, STAGE PAYMENT.

payment, lump-sum. A single payment in cash, usually for a large sum. Also remuneration paid to a ship owner for charter of a ship or portion of it irrespective of the quantity of cargo loaded.

payment, prepayment. (CIMA) A clause by a seller that payment is to be made before delivery.

payment, pro-forma. Payment made against a PROFORMA INVOICE before goods are released or delivered.

payment, progress payments. Payments which may be made for work done during the progress of a contract. The amounts due are in proportion to the work so far completed, and the proportions are agreed between the buyer and seller at the time the contract is let, or are as laid down in standard national agreements for various trades. Payments are made against certificates for work so far completed at the various agreed stages of manufacture or construction. *See also* PLANNING AND PROGRESSING.

payment, prompt. *See* PRICE, PAYMENT AND TIME RELATED.

payment, spot cash. Payment to be made on ACCEPTANCE OF CONTRACT for goods wherever they may be lying and not necessarily waiting for delivery to be effected.

payment, stage payments. Payments made at planned stages of a civil engineering, or construction or plant contract against certificates signed by an authorized person to vouch that the work has been done. *See also* PAYMENTS, PROGRESS PAYMENTS.

penalty (penalty clause). (law) A term sometimes used for a clause in a contract which stipulates a sum to be paid by a supplier in the event of his default in a contract. A penalty clause ('in terrorem') cannot be enforced in a court of law. *See* DAMAGES LIQUIDATED *and* DAMAGES UNLIQUIDATED. Note: on applying a penalty clause a plaintiff can, as a rule, only recover the direct damage resulting from a BREACH of the contract.

perfect competition. *See* COMPETITION, PERFECT COMPETITION.

performance bonds. *See* BONDS, PERFOR-MANCE.

performance, specific performance. (law) The carrying out of all TERMS and CONDITIONS of a contract. An order by a court may call for specific performance by a supplier, i.e. to complete his contract with the purchaser, instead of awarding DAMAGES to be paid to the latter who has suffered loss.

perils of the sea. (ins) A marine insurance clause relating to dangers which may occur to a vessel and its cargo during a voyage, the risks of which, on being accepted in a bill of lading, is undertaken to cover by the insurers.

period, production period. See PRODUCTION PERIOD.

periodic stock check. See STOCK CHECK, PERIODIC STOCK CHECK.

peripheral. A device attached to a computer to carry out a specialised function such as scanning or printing.

perishable goods. Those which deteriorate if not used within their SHELF-LIFE or stored under (special) suitable conditions to preserve them.

permits, bilateral transit. (EU) Bilateral permits, usually for one 'there and back' trip only, enable transits across EU and non-EU states. Further permits are, needed to cross intervening states. Conditions of granting the permits varies from state to state.

perpetual inventory. Americanizm for STOCK-CONTROL, CONTINUOUS. See also INVENTORY, and STOCK-TAKING.

perpetual stock record. See STOCK RECORD CONTINUOUS STOCK RECORD.

perquisites. Fees or emolument allowed by law for some specific purpose, usually of a casual nature and beyond normal salary or wages for services rendered.

personal protective equipment. See PROTECTIVE PERSONAL EQUIPMENT.

petty cash. (fin) A small sum set aside for minor expenses and purchases. From the standpoint of administration of purchasing and supply the control of purchasing through the use of petty cash is difficult. It can lead to abuse, fraud and error, one solution is the use of LOCAL PURCHASE ORDERS. See under ORDERS & CONTRACTS, VARIETIES OF.

photodegradation. (env. ecol). Degradation of certain substances by absorption of light particularly ultra-violet rays. Applies chiefly to fibrous textiles, etc. Usually the degradation is accompanied by a loss of strength in the material owing to breakdown of the polymers. Suitable protection from ultra-violet light is therefore needed when storing such materials.

picking, order picking. Colloquializm for the act of removing goods from their storage location for issue.

picking list. Colloquializm for a parts list or schedule set out in such a manner as to facilitate order picking from stores.

pictogram. Diagram which displays statistical information by pictorial representation of the items under consideration, e.g. in purchasing and supply. For example, a diagrammatic map showing origins of sources of supply from different areas with colours or shading to indicate (e.g.) pricing or transport, etc.

piece goods. Name applied to goods sold by the piece, such as sheetings, canvas, etc.

piece parts. Components manufactured from raw materials, to make assemblies or sub-assemblies. The term is often applied to parts made in a manufacturer's own works.

piece rate. A method of remuneration by which the worker receives a definite sum for performing a stipulated quantity of work. Originally, goods or material made 'in the piece', now applied to components used in manufacture and assemblies.

pilot run and/or prototype. May be required before the start of a major contract.

pipeline. 1. Large diameter tube for long distance conveyance. 2. Used metaphorically for ideas similar to SUPPLY CHAIN.

place utility. The value added to a product by moving it to where it can be used.

planning. The setting of targets, whether of production, sales, supplies, profits or other features, or the plant and structures needed for their attainment.

planning cycle. The sequence by which planning, implementation, evaluation and revision of plans take place.

planning horizon. (adm) (BS) 'The longest time ahead for which production plans are normally made'. *See also* PURCHASING PLANNING HORIZON.

planning policy. (adm) Decisions of an important nature usually wider in scope than strategies or tactical planning and of long HORIZON, i.e. a decade or more.

planning, corporate. The study of long-term (long HORIZON) objectives and strategy of an enterprise as a corporate entity.

planning, distribution requirements and resource planning (DRP). A system for forecasting or projecting requirements for finished goods at the point of demand. From these projections, aggregated, time-phased requirements schedules can be derived. DRP is a 'pull' system depending upon assessments of the demands of end-users of the supply concerned.

planning, long-term strategic. The formulation, evaluation and selection of strategies involving a review of the objectives of an enterprise, its environment, strengths, weaknesses, opportunities, threats, etc. so as to prepare a long-term plan.

planning, strategic. Overall planning to meet main overall objectives and taking account of tactical planning which should contribute to the overall strategy.

planning, supplies. PROVISIONING to suit the planning policies of the enterprise on a time scale to suit the HORIZONS of the main planning policies of the enterprise.

planning, tactical. Planning decisions usually in a particular field or activity and which may be of shorter duration than other planing - a year or less.

plant. The assemblage of tools and equipment to manufacture goods, chemicals, power, etc. and usually situated in a fixed location for a particular operation, or mobile as is the case of handling equipment.

plant numbers, plant numbering. The numbering of units of plant and equipment with individual numbers. These facilitate the keeping of maintenance and performance records. Plant numbers can also assist the functions of purchasing and supply in the provisioning and storage of spares and maintenance contracts.

plant register. (CIMA) A record showing the details of each item of plant purchased and used by a business. A valuable record for maintenance purchasing, record and control of spares, etc.

plating, of vehicles. The fixing to vehicles of the various signs showing their size, type, capacity, load, dangerous goods, hazard signs and so on.

Plimsoll Line. *See* LOAD LINE.

policy. The objective, the mode of thought, and the body and principles underlying activities and organization in the light of changing circumstances.

policy stock. *See* STOCK, POLICY STOCK.

population. (BS) The totality of ITEMS under consideration e.g. the total of all the ITEMS in a RANGE. Note: 'range' may be misleading if used as a measure of demand for future stock building, control or purchasing unless due care is taken regarding exceptions at each extreme of a range.

portal. A website acting as either a gateway to the web, or as a focus for users with specific interests

post date. To date a document with a date later than that upon which it was prepared, or signed, etc. In the latter instance and in regard to contracts and similar documents there may be legal implications. But the action may be warranted where a cheque is post dated to ensure it will not be cashed until funds are available or some other contingency such as delivery has been successfully achieved.

post-tender negotiation Negotiation after receipt of formal tenders and before letting final contracts with a view to obtaining more favourable terms. The practice is widely regarded as ethical unless it puts the tenderer at a disadvantage.

Powers of Attorney Act 1971. Act making new provision in relation to powers of attorney and the delegation by trustees of their trusts, powers and discretions.

practicable. Able to be achieved at the current state of knowledge.

pre-packing. (BS) The operation of packing goods ready for sale or issue immediately they are required.

pre-paid. *See* PAYMENT, PRE-PAYMENT.

pre-standards. *See* EUROPEAN PRE-STANDARDS.

precision. *See* QUALITY CONTROL.

preferred numbers. A technique devised by Charles Renard using the principle of geometric progression in sizes of particular items of supply. The choice of sizes depends upon the number, and range of sizes needed. Applied to plant, preferred numbers provide means to greater interchangeability, e.g. of spares. The technique helps to create uniformity and assists VARIETY REDUCTION.

premium. (fin mkt) A margin deducted from a spot exchange rate reflecting the dearer forward value of one currency against another.

preservation. The prescribed protection or other preparation of an item so as to maintain it in good condition during transit and in stores.

preventative maintenance management. A proactive approach to maintenance under which plant and machinery is maintained and overhauled on a scheduled basis. The performance of equipment is usually monitored under this kind of maintenance regime.

prevention cost. *See* COST, PREVENTION COST.

price. Amount of CONSIDERATION to be paid or given for an article, goods, service or something desired, offered or purchased. *See also* COST, for which price is not a synonym.

price analysis. The examination of a seller's price without examination of the separate elements of cost and profit making up the price.

price break. The point at which a supplier's price changes in response to a change in quantity, (e.g. there may be a reduction in price when a certain quantity of supply is ordered.)

price fixing. The process by which prices are set in advance or by agreement between producers, viz. PRICE RING, or by governmental edict, rather than through the operation of a free market. Now illegal in most free market economics.

price index. A figure, usually expressed as a percentage, and showing the relationship between a current price and the price at some prearranged date. *See also* STATISTICS, INDEX NUMBERS.

price list. A vendor's list of articles he has for sale with the prices at which he makes an INVITATION TO TREAT with prospective purchasers.

price, 'conference price'. Adjusted price by means of a rebate given to shippers who agree to restrict shipments to a destination to the sailings of the shipping lines in the conference serving that destination.

price, all round. One which covers various costs which would normally be charged as 'extras'.

price, at despatch. The normal method of pricing where the purchase order fails to specify an agreed price at the time it is placed. *But, see also* PRICE, PRICE AT INVOICE DATE.

price, average. A price which represents the average (mean) of a number of prices. This may be based upon the simple or weighted average. *See also* COST, AVERAGE COST.

price, basing point. A method of pricing where identical freight charges are made to all customers in a particular area irrespective of their distance from a point selected by the supplier and known as the basing point.

price, basis point. A price taken for the basis of comparison or for further calculation.

price, basis price. The difference between the price of a commodity for a specific future month and the SPOT PRICE for the same commodity.

price, bonded or in bond. The price of goods as they lie in a bonded warehouse, the buyer to pay duty on them.

price, cash and carry. Orders priced in this manner require the buyer to pay cash and carry away the goods he as purchased with no credit allowed. *See* ORDERS AND CONTRACTS.

price, cash on delivery. Orders priced in this manner require the buyer to pay cash when the goods are received with no credit allowed. *See* ORDERS AND CONTRACTS.

price, cash. The price at which a vendor is prepared to sell provided the purchaser is prepared to make immediate payment. (In making the DEAL the purchaser may or may not also be required, or wish to take immediate delivery.) *See* PRICE, CASH AND CARRY.

price, catalogue. The price quoted in a catalogue or price list as an 'invitation to treat' by the prospective purchaser. Such lists were originally taken as CURRENT PRICES, but this assumption can no longer be made without a specific statement to that effect being given by the vendor.

price, contract, adjustment price. A final price of a contract whereby the original contract price has been adjusted for changes in wages and materials during the course of the contract and calculated by a formula agreed between the parties to the contract. Also referred to as an ESCALATION CLAUSE.

price, cost insurance and freight. Price applicable to shipping contracts on this basis. *See* COST, INSURANCE AND FREIGHT *and* INCOTERMS.

price, cost. A price based purely upon cost of goods without allowing profit, etc.

price, current. 1. The established price 'for the day' in a market. *But see also* SPOT PRICE. 2. The up-to-date catalogue/price list. (But note, unless stated otherwise such prices are 'invitations to treat' with no commitment as to the validity of the price shown). *See* TREAT, INVITATION TO TREAT.

price, cut. Incentive pricing at a figure usually below true cost and competitor's prices to obtain business or dispose of surplus, etc.

price, discriminatory. The offering of similar or identical goods at different prices to different buyers.

price, dishonoured. One where a supplier who has accepted a FIRM PRICE order

later claims an increase for which no provision for adjustment has been made in the contract.

price, dumped. The sale of goods (usually) in an overseas market at a lower price than in the borne market.

price, duty paid. The price of goods (e.g. in a bonded warehouse) including duties.

price, duty. The price defined by customs as customs landed price or open market value at the point of entry.

price, economic net. A price which results in equilibrium between profit and loss to the supplier.

price, elastic demand price. A situation is regarded as elastic when a small change in price results in significant increase In demand or vice versa.

price, equilibrium. The theoretical price which arises in a 'perfect' market when supply demand are equal.

price, estimated. One which is based upon an ESTIMATE and may therefore not be the final price required for the goods or service offered and ordered.

price, ex warehouse. Warehouse price includes cost of goods and packing, and loading on to the customer's vehicle but not carriage to the customer.

price, fair. That price which allows a producer to pay fair wage rates, buy and use the correct materials, carry out adequate research, and maintain adequate capital investment in plant acid equipment and earn a reasonable return on capital so invested.

price, firm. A price which will not be varied during the term of a contract.

price, first-in, first-out. The price paid for supplies first taken into stock is used for pricing purposes, costing, invoicing, etc. Note: such 'historical pricing' is not reliable for estimating purposes.

price, fixed. A price which cannot be varied by the efforts of the buyer in negotiation as distinct from a price which can be so negotiated in the course of offer and counter-offer between buyer band seller.

price, forward. One offered by a supplier for a supply against an order to be confirmed at a future date. *See also* PRICE, FUTURES PRICE.

price, 'franco'. Free delivery to buyer's warehouse.

price, free alongside, free on board, etc. *See* INCOTERMS.

price, free. A price which is arrived at by the effects of free unfettered MARKET FORCES.

price, futures. (com) Price estimated by brokers for FUTURES based on options to buy and sell a commodity on an exchange.

price, indifference. The price at which a buyer, if he has the option whether or not to purchase goods, will be indifferent whether or not to proceed with purchase or seek a better bargain. *See* BREAK-EVEN POINT, COST BENEFIT ANALYSIS and PRICE, EQUILIBRIUM PRICE.

price, invoice date, price at. The order will be priced as at date of invoice not necessarily at date of despatch. (A delayed invoice may thereby include a price increase after the completion of the contract).

price, leader. A ruse used by a price ring to evade the law. One member's price is followed by others, based on 'reported price' communicated to all members. Illegal in most free market' economics. *See also* PRICE, LOSS LEADER PRICE.

price, limits of. The limits, normally above (e.g. a TARGET PRICE) which should be specified on a purchase order so as to avoid overspending on a project or budget.

price, list price. Price given in a suppliers published PRICE LIST.

price, loco. Price wherever lying, buyer to pack and load.

price, loss leader. A price applied to a sales item (or range of items) which is near or below COST PRICE in order to induce additional sales.

price, loyalty. A concessionary price given to a customer in consideration that he will make all or an agreed proportion of his purchases from the supplier who gives the concession. Usually such concessions are in the form of a rebate.

price, marginal. The price for one more article than the previous quantity quoted for, manufactured or purchased.

price, mark down. The price which has been reduced from normal selling or list price shown by a retailer or a distributor to increase sales.

price, market. 1. Price current in open market; 2. Economic equilibrium price resulting from SUPPLY and demand in open market.

price, mean. The mean price calculated from a series of values. Used in some stock account valuations.

price, monopolistic. Price based on ability of monopolist to control price against the natural forces of supply and demand, or the efforts of a purchasing officer.

price, net. The price at which a bargain may be made with no further discounts or additions. (Old usage was neat price.)

price, nominal. An arbitrary price may be a very low one applied to an item of goods or a service, etc. *See also* PRICE, NOTIONAL PRICE.

price, normal or natural. (fin) That price which arises through the interplay of free market forces. *But, see also* PRICE ECONOMIC PRICE *and* PRICE, FAIR PRICE.

price, notional. A hypothetical price (or cost) taken into account to represent a benefit enjoyed in respect of which the actual known price (or cost) can be ascertained.

price, on site. A price which includes plant or goods being delivered and set down on a prepared site or hard-standing. The contract must state if other requirements apply such as, if to be 'erected', 'tested', 'set to work', etc.

price, open price agreement. The practice of some businesses to exchange information regarding prices and/or price changes in the field. The method adopted has to avoid the need to report the arrangement to the RESTRICTIVE PRACTICES COURT. Illegal in most free market economies.

price, opportunity. The price at which the benefit from the purchase breaks-even with the disbenefit of foregoing the acquisition of the item. *See also* COST, OPPORTUNITY COST.

price, overdue account. A 'penalty' price applied by a supplier upon customers who are late payers - usually claimed by a percentage on the account - but, must be stated when the order is accepted, otherwise it is void.

price, payment and time related. A price which takes account of time or times at which payment is to be made. *See also* STAGE PAYMENTS.

price, premium. A price set above the normal or list price, etc, paid to a supplier so as to gain some advantage.

price, progress payments. Price structures which contain this clause will require PROGRESS (or stage) PAYMENTS during the term of the contract to which they apply. Such progress or stage payments usually require certificates authorised by the purchaser or his duly appointed agent, to certify that the work has been satisfactorily executed to that stage of its completion.

price, progressive rebated price. *See* REBATES.

price, prompt cash. A price reduce below LIST (or normal) price of the supplier to encourage prompt payment of his account. Usually given in the form of a discount. *See also* PAYMENT.

price, quantity. One based upon profitability of quantities bought and/or manufactured. Usually offered as an inducement to order in larger quantity. (May be given by discount, rebate, etc.)

price, quoted. Price submitted in quotation or tender. Usually valid 30 days or other stated period.

price, re-opener clause. A clause which a purchaser may write into a contract so that a new lower price can be negotiated if, for example, the quantity required turns out to be greater than the original estimate or an improved method of manufacture, packaging or handling, etc. is discovered; or higher if the purchaser changes his specification, quantity or other factor(s) which may have price cost implications.

price, reasonable. *See* PRICE, FAIR PRICE. PRICE, RECOMMENDED PRICE.

price, recommended. A price suggested by a supplier (manufacturer or major distributor) for sale of his goods in the domestic market. The former method of establishing fixed prices for goods has been banned in most free market economics in the interest of stimulating competition.

price, replacement. (CIMA) The price at which an asset, identical to that which is being replaced or revalued, could be purchased.

price, reported. Members of a trade association (or price ring) report quoted prices to one another. Illegal in most free market economics.

price, resale. Price recommended by supplier for resale.

price, reserve(d). The lowest price at which an owner will sell. Term usually applied at an auction.

price, ring. Price fixed by price ring. Illegal in most free market economics.

price, ruling. The price generally understood to be that ruling at the date of despatch or other date specified and agreed. *See also* PRICE, INVOICE DATE, PRICE AT.

price, seasonal. A price (or prices) adjusted to meet seasonal conditions, either variations in seasonal demand or conditions of shortage or glut, or stringency such as difficulties of transport, harvesting or numerous other factors.

price, settlement. (com) The average price on the closure of a trading day.

price, small quantity. A PREMIUM PRICE charged (Or claimed) for a smaller than normal quantity ordered or delivered in smaller batches than usual, or more frequently.

price, spot. Price on the day or quotation for immediate delivery. Term used when trading in a commodity market.

price, standard. (BS) A predetermined price fixed on the basis of a specification , if all the factors affecting that price.

price, statutory (legal). A price set by governmental decree as a form of control.

price, survival. A special price offered by a supplier to secure an order or contract with. out which his business will fail unless he secures it.

price, target. A price given to a supplier either in an enquiry or purchase order where the precise value of the contract may not be precisely known when the order is given, e.g. an urgent plant repair. It may also be the price given to a purchasing officer to ensure the competitiveness of a sales project or quotation by his company. *See also* PRICE, LIMITS OF.

price, trade. Price usually given to buyers in same trade or for resale. (Usually given by special discount) .

price, transfer (and transfer pricing). The price used when supplies or services are transferred from one department to another in the same plant or between companies firms within the same group nationally or internationally.

price, upset. The lowest (or reserve) price an owner will accept at an auction.

primage. Percentage on the freight paid to owners of freighters or vessels to cover commission for chartering and other expenses, e.g. lights, pilots, wharves, etc.

prime costs. *See* COSTS, PRIME COSTS.

prior indication notice (PIN). (EU) Contracting authorities are required to make known, by means of an indicative notice in the Official Journal of the European Community to be published as soon as possible after the beginning of their budgeted year, each contract over the relevant THRESHOLD they are considering awarding during the coming 12 months.

private finance initiative Introduced in 1992 with the object of improving the quality and quantity of public sector capital projects and putting more efficient public services in place. These goals are promoted by promoting partnership arrangement and making use of the wide range of assets and services available in the private sector.

privity of contract. A legal doctrine which avers that a contract is a private relationship between the contracting parties and that no other person can acquire rights or incur liabilities in it.

pro rata. At a certain rate of and in proportion to a total. e.g. 50p in the £1.

proforma. *See* INVOICE.

proactive. Tending to initiate change rather than reacting to events.

probabilistic systems. Systems with characteristics which are predictable and controllable but only between defined limits, such as maintaining production or supply within limits, e.g. at maximum and minimum stock control levels. *See also* HOMEOSTASIS. Also known as STOCHASTIC SYSTEMS. They are distinct from deterministic systems which have fixed and clearly predictable limits such as an engine (or other prime-mover) controlled by a governor.

probability. A measure of the likelihood of an event to occur. Statistically its value lies between the limits of 'zero' and 'one'. '0' represents impossibility. 11, represents certainty. Probability is calculated by dividing the number of favourable events by the total number of possible events considered.

procedure, negotiated. (EU) Applicable to tendering situations where certain limited circumstances exist, e.g. where there is only one source of supply, or where no suitable bids have been received under the open procedure.

process mapping. Investigation and modelling, usually by means of a graphical representation, a process or problem with a view to improvement or solution.

process planning. (BS) The activity which determines the operations required, and their sequence to produce a part or assembly (or operate a process).

process plant industry. Second stage in overall SUPPLIES CYCLE, where basic materials (usually) from extractive industries (e.g. oil) are converted (usually) for further manipulation and processing before the final END-PRODUCT is reached. The end products of most process plants provide the raw materials for the next stage in the overall supplies cycle.

121

processing, information processing. (adm) A specialist activity performed by the administrative organization of an enterprise. It is concerned with the systematic recording, arranging, collating, processing, filing, retrieval and dissemination of facts relating to the physical/financial events occurring in a business. *See also* INFORMATION TECHNOLOGY.

procurement. The obtaining by various means (e.g. loan, transfer, hire, purchase, etc,) of supplies and services with or without CONSIDERATION.

procurement card. *See* PURCHASING CARD.

procurement cycle. The overall cycle of obtaining supplies from the origin of the, need through the purchasing or other means, e.g. loan etc, to the intake of correct requirements and final consumption and disposal.

procurement lead time. *See* LEAD TIME, TOTAL.

producer goods. Plant, buildings and equipment, etc. equipped for manufacturing purposes as distinct from CONSUMER GOODS.

producers' associations. Organizations for cooperation among enterprises producing or marketing the same commodity.

product. (BS) An end item or output from a work station, factory or other organizational group. 'Any industrially manufactured product and any agricultural product'. (DTI).

product group. A number of products with one or more common characteristics which make it convenient to combine them for planning and control purposes, for example products using similar resources or products with similar marketing requirements.

Product Liability Directive. (EU) This Directive makes manufacturers and importers liable for injuries caused by defective products. (A UK 'option' provides a balance between the right of compensation to those injured and the need to see that innovation is not hampered).

product liability. (HS) The onus on a producer or distributor for the condition of a product that causes an event by which someone suffers loss or harm.

Product Safety Directive. (EU) This Directive introduces a general obligation on producers, importers and distributors, to supply safe consumer products. (Adopted by HMG.UK wef 29.6.1994).

production. The creation of goods or materials by manufacture, manipulation and/or process, and also the provision of SERVICES.

production cycle time. (BS) The time required to complete an operation on a BATCH. Also 'floor-to-floor' time.

production down time. (BS) The period of time for which a work station is not available for production due to a functional failure.

production item, an item (of production). An identifiable item, sub-assembly or equipment supported by a manufacturer's part or drawing number.

production line. The layout of production plant and equipment in the direct line in which the production process events take place. (May affect the points at which additional supplies are fed into the process from stores).

production overheads. Indirect materials, supporting goods, indirect wages, and expenses incurred in production.

production period. The length of time which forms the basis for production or process plant operation. May be the number of hours, days weeks, etc. the plant will operate continuously, e.g. on one production run or one batch of feedstock in a process plant.

production pilot run. The initial throughput of units or process material to check 1. suitability for manufacture; 2. costs; 3. tooling; 4. robotics; 5. material supplies, etc.

production planning and control. (BS) Procedures and means by which manufacturing programmes and plans are determined, information issued for their execution and data collected and recorded to control manufacture in accordance with the plans.

production pre-production/assembly operations. Operations, which in the context of purchasing and supply administration may be performed prior to and in preparation for production/process, within a stores complex, e.g. cleaning of components, deburring of castings, counting and weighing batches, loose assembly and other operations of a preparatory nature. Pre-production kitting may take place.

production programme. (BS) A list or chart showing products and quantities which are to be produced and given time.

production progress control. The function that is concerned with: 1. recording of actual production progress, **its** comparison with planned production, and the feedback of warnings, and/or instructions to enable the correction of deviations; 2. the EXPEDITING of production orders which have to be fulfilled in less than the normal LEAD TIME. The production definition is equally applicable in

the fields of purchasing and supply and marketing.

production resource planning. *See* MANUFACTURING RESOURCE PLANNING 'MRP2'.

production waiting time. (BS) The period of time for which an operator is available for production but is prevented from working by shortage of materials or tooling, or breakdown, etc.

production work centre. (BS) 'A set of WORK STATIONS grouped for convenience of PLANNING or work-flow'.

production work cycle. (BS) Work study. Work cycle is the sequence of elements which are required to perform a job or yield a unit of production output. The sequence may include 'occasional elements'. Such occasional elements are intermittent and may not occur in every work cycle of a job, but, may occur at regular or irregular intervals (e.g. stores staff may be required to leave stores from time to time to assist incoming traffic to unload, etc.).

production works order. (BS) A written instruction detailing work to be carried out.

production, 'Census of Production'. A summary of information about British industry. It provides valuable statistics on: sales, output per employee, inputs of supplies, usage of energy on all the major industrial product groups.

production, batch production. Production of quantities in BATCHES which do not reach quantities needed for mass or continuous production and which may, or may not, be in standardized form.

production, capital intensive. A method of production which uses relatively more capital investment and capital goods, e.g. machinery, than labour, per unit produced.

production, changeover time. (BS) 'The time taken to change a work station from a state of readiness for one operation to a state of readiness for another and different operation.' Note: changeover time may be less than the sum of breaking down and setting up times. May incur additional costs to a purchaser where an urgent or emergency measure is needed for supply in crisis.

production, flexible manufacturing system (FMS). A system which enables a manufacturer to switch rapidly from the output of one product to another. A common situation in general jobbing engineering. May be helpful to those purchasing urgent and various supplies but the manufacturer (supplier) needs close control of stocks and supplies and logistics.

production, flow production. A production/process system (usually large-scale) in which products (or materials in process) flow from stage to stage until they reach the final state. (In both product and process flow BUFFER STOCK may be needed to ensure continuous operation, JUST IN TIME technique may be applicable.)

production, idle time. (BS) The period of time for which a work-station is available for production but is not utilized due to shortage of tools, materials, or operators. *See also* DOWN TIME *and* WAITING TIME.

production, 'just in time'. *See* JUST IN TIME. *See also* KANBAN.

production, lean. A system pioneered by Toyota in Japan whereby production takes place in small quantities as

determined by immediate demand only. Skilled and dedicated personnel, using appropriate equipment and methods, avoid defective production and other forms of waste. Facilities are arranged to enable smooth flows of work. JUST IN TIME ideas are employed.

production, manufacturing resource planning (MRP). This technique is usually known by the acronym 'MRP2'. It is a development from 'materials resource planning' (MRP), and encompasses the planning and scheduling activities associated with the allocation of production resources themselves. *See also* MATERIAL RESOURCE PLANNING.

production, marginal. Manufacture where the cost of production equals the cost of the goods, i.e. with no profit or other allowance. *See also* COST/COSTING MARGINAL COST.

production, mass. The production of ENDPRODUCTS or COMPONENTS, etc. on an intensive, repetition basis to a standard specification.

production, master production schedule. The plan for production of completely finished products or assemblies.

production, modular. A method of production by which items are produced to modular dimensions enabling them to be used in a number of applications.

production, operational duration times. The period of time required to carry out an operation on a complete BATCH exclusive of SET UP TIME .

production, optimised production technology (OPT). The OPT method seeks the balance of component parts of the manufacturing process through control of flow by technological means.

OPT can avoid bottlenecks common to batch production if numerous different products are in course of manufacture simultaneously.

production, set up time. (BS) 'The time required to prepare a work station from a standard condition to readiness to commence a specified operation'. Also has implications for purchasing and supply. *See also* COSTS, SET UP COSTS.

production, stock production order. (BS) 'A production order to manufacture a product to replenish stock'. The same disciplines regarding STOCK CONTROL will usually apply to both manufacturer as to purchaser.

production, work in progress. (BS) Stock (or other supplies) upon which work has been performed or has been made ready for work to be started, but which is not available for supply to an external consumer.

production, work measurement. *See under* WORK.

production, work station. (BS) The smallest set of resources for the purpose of planning and control that form a productive unit at a particular location.

production, 'zero defects' in production. A motivating discipline which encourages the sense of responsibility and pride of achievement in production staffs when producing output with ZERO DEFECTS.

profit. The financial gain resulting from a transaction or combination of transactions, or a set period of business activity being the excess of sales revenue over related costs.

profit centre. A division of an organization to which both expenditure and revenue are attributed and in respect of which profitability can be assessed.

profit, net. (CIMA) 1. The profit remaining after all expenses and/or losses have been deducted from the OPERATING PROFIT and further revenues added. 2. The profit of a business before distribution but after deducting from net sales all direct and indirect costs incurred in making the sale. Net profit can be stated 'before' or 'after' taxation.

profit, operating. Profit arising from the normal activities of and enterprise, such as the sale of manufactured goods and services, before taking account of extraneous in transactions such as those of a purely financial nature, e.g. interest on bank loans, etc. to

profitability. An assessment of the actions or transactions which tend to lead to profit, or the 'ability' to produce a profit.

program(me) evaluation and review technique (PERT). A form of NETWORK ANALYSIS used to programme, progress and review the stages of a complex project towards its final completion.

progressing, 'progress chasing'. The activity of monitoring the progress of purchase orders with suppliers to ensure that delivery to the purchaser is as-and-when needed and in the quantities required. The activity may involve EXPEDITING or retarding delivery or re-scheduling to suit production or sales programmes. *See also* CONTRACT MANAGEMENT.

progress payments. *See* PAYMENTS, PROGRESS PAYMENTS.

progressive rebate. *See* REBATE, PROGRESSIVE.

prohibited goods. Those which are forbidden to be exported from or imported into a country.

125

prohibition notice. (HS) A notice issued by an inspector of the Health and Safety Executive who discovers a contravention of one of the provisions of the Health and Safety at Work act or related legislation. The notice is issued if there is a risk of serious injury or pollution etc., to stop the activity giving rise to this risk until remedial action specified in the notice has been taken. It can be served on the person undertaking the activity, or on the person in control of it at the time the notice was served. *See also* IMPROVEMENT NOTICE.

project assessment. The assessment of the viability of a project.

project. (BS) An enterprise involving a number of interrelated activities.

promissory note. (CIMA) A signed unconditional document containing a written promise to pay a specified sum on demand, or on a certain date to a specified person.

prompt cash payment. *See* PRICE, PAYMENT AND TIME RELATED PAYMENT.

property, intellectual. Any material, written, drawn or otherwise produced and which is the unique result of intelligent, intellectual effort.

proposals. (EU) Proposals are made by the Commission of the Community to the European Parliament and to the COUNCIL OF MINISTERS for discussion and implementation by the latter, if approved. Proposals have no legal force until and unless passed by the Council of Ministers.

proprietary goods. Goods manufactured and sold and distributed under a trade name, brand, trade mark, etc.

protective and preventive measures. (HS) Those measures which can be identified by the employer or by the self-employed person in consequence of the assessment of the measures he needs to take in order to comply with his duties under the relevant Statutory Provisions for health and safety.

protective personal equipment. (PPE). (HS) Includes all equipment designed to be worn or held to protect against one or more risks to health and safety. It includes hard hats, safety footwear, lifejackets, eye and hearing protection, high visibility clothing and clothing to protect against adverse weather.

prototype. A full-size working and fully operational model made for appraisal and which when improved, modified, tested and approved can be used as a type for future reproduction.

provisioning. The first step in the SUPPLIES CYCLE which relates to the act of providing, particularly the steps taken beforehand to lay in stocks and provisions for production or for a project. *See also* PLANNING.

provisioning level. *See* STOCK CONTROL, RE-ORDER LEVEL CONTROL.

pull. In purchasing the term is applied to systems whereby material is brought into the organization or production area to replace material already allocated or used.

purchase. (n) The article, goods, material, substance or service which has been purchased in exchange for CONSIDERATION. A similar definition applies to PROCUREMENT except for the lack of 'consideration' in that case.

purchase. (v) To acquire supplies and services by paying money or other CONSIDERATION. (Where acquisition is without passage of CONSIDERATION the term PROCUREMENT can be used).

purchase order. *See* ORDERS & CONTRACTS A-Z.

purchase requisition. *See* REQUISITION, PURCHASE.

purchasing. The obtaining of supplies of goods and services by PURCHASE.

'Purchasing and Supply Management'. (fortnightly CIPS). News of the Institute, and articles on a wide range of topics in the purchasing and supply field.

purchasing audit. An in-depth investigation into every aspect of departmental efficiency and operations. It may be carried out by an internal audit committee or by external auditors usually firms of accountants or management consultants. The audit examines purchasing records and procedures in order to protect the organization against fraud or waste, to ensure the company policies are being adhered to and identify ways in which performance can be improved. The audit should consider every aspect of purchasing activity and present its report to senior management.

purchasing card. A card issued to staff that may be used to purchase goods and services up to an agreed limit from certain suppliers. Similar in operation to a credit card, but there is no credit facility, settlement being made via the issuing company at agreed intervals (usually monthly).

Purchasing Manager's Index'. *See* REPORT ON BUSINESS.

purchasing officer. An official in charge of the whole procurement operation from the receipt of the requisition, through all the stages of negotiation and placing the order, to the final clearance of the related invoices after price checking.

purchasing order. *See* CONTRACTS: ADMINISTRATION OF *and* ORDERS VARIETIES OF.

purchasing policy. A set of principles which guide and influence the purchasing direction of an organization. Typically these will relate to supplier relationships, internal relationships between purchasing and other functions, and strategies in identifying new sources of supply.

purchasing power parities. (econ) The actual worth of currencies in terms of the real amount of goods and services they will buy.

purchasing power, economic purchasing power. The quantity of a good which may be purchased at a specified time by a unit of currency compared with the quantity obtainable from the expenditure of the same unit of currency in another period. *See also* NEGOTIATION, LEVERAGE.

purchasing research. Investigations into improved and more cost-effective purchasing throughout all areas of the supplies/supply cycle. *See also* SUPPLIES RESEARCH.

purchasing, automated. *See* AUTOMATED PURCHASING.

purchasing, backward integration. The acquisition of suppliers by an enterprise wishing to expand or to control the source of supply.

purchasing, central purchasing. 'The steering of demands into prescribed channels, all terminating in one AUTHORITY to ADMINISTER the purchasing and supply function'. *See also* PURCHASING: BULK PURCHASING.

purchasing, forward purchasing. *See* CONTRACTS/ORDERS (FORWARD) *also see* FUTURES UNDER TRADE / TRADING / MARKETS.

purchasing, global. Purchasing strategically on a world-wide basis.

purchasing, green.. Purchasing with environmental considerations in mind.

purchasing, paperless. *See* INFORMATION TECHNOLOGY.

purchasing, partnership. The concept of purchasing as a partnership between enterprises, as, for example, between supplier and manufacturing purchaser. The partnership may be extensive and include the fields of 'design and research', ,value engineering', 'value analysis', etc so as to gain maximum advantage for each party. *See* PARTNERSHIP SOURCING.

purchasing, preclusive. The purchasing of supply, service, or production capacity as a deliberate means of depriving another enterprise from acquiring those supplies, services or production capacity.

purchasing, public procurement - works & supply directives. (EU) These directives apply in the EU to central and local governments and certain other bodies which are funded by such authorities. Above certain value limits they regulate the approach to tendering.

purchasing, public procurement: attestation. (EU) The examination of public procurement purchasing procedures by an independent examiner to ensure that the European Standards for such procedures are adhered to by public authorities.

purchasing, public purchasing directives. (EU) The directives applicable to public bodies, except some nationalised industries, are intended to open up procedures throughout the Community. The directives include: Supplies Directive , Works Directive , Service Directive, Compliance Directive, Utilities Directive, Remedies Directive. (A guide to public purchasing is available from the DTI.)

purpose made. Goods made specially for a specific job or distinct from standard items 'off the shelf. (Also referred to as 'bespoke'.)

purpose, fitness for purpose. 'The totality of features and characteristics of a product or service that have a bearing upon its ability to satisfy a given/stated need'. Where goods are sold in the course of business and the buyer makes known to the seller the particular purpose for which the goods are being bought, there is an implied CONDITION that they are fit for that purpose.' Sale of Good Act 1979 Cl. 12/1 1.

push. In purchasing and supply the term is applied to systems whereby materials are 'pushed' forward to production areas in anticipation of need, as opposed to 'pull' systems where the material is called up to replace material already earmarked or used.

pyramid selling A form of trading in which the seller passes on an obligation or franchise for others to fulfill.

pyrolysis The breakdown of a substance in the absence of air (oxygen).

Q

quality. (BS) The totality of features and characteristics of a product or service that bear upon its ability to satisfy a given need. *See also* QUALITY, MERCHANTABLE.

quality acceptance sampling. *See* QUALITY CONTROL, SAMPLING.

quality accuracy. (BS) The closeness of an observed quality to the defined or true value. Note: accuracy is usually expressed in terms of error or uncertainty.

quality approval, type approval. (BS) The status given to a design that has been shown by type tests to meet all the requirements of the product specification and which is suitable for a specific application.

quality assurance. 1. All those planned and systematic actions necessary to provide confidence that a product or service will satisfy given requirements for quality. Unless given requirements fully reflect the needs of the user, quality assurance will not be complete. 2. For effectiveness, quality assurance usually requires continuing evaluation of factors that affect adequacy of design or specification for intended application as well as verification and audits of production, installation and inspection operations. Providing confidence in quality may also involve the production of evidence. 3. Within an organization, quality assurance serves as a management tool. In contractual situations, quality assurance also serves to provide confidence in the supplier.

quality attribute, an attribute. (BS) A characteristic that is appraised in terms of whether it meets or does not meet a given requirement (e.g. 'go' or 'no go').

quality audit/assessment. (EU) Audits/assessments made to verify that applicable element of QUALITY ASSURANCE programmes have been developed, documented and effectively implemented by the supplier so as to ensure that contractual requirements have been met.

quality certificate of conformity. (BS) A document signed by a qualified person affirming that, at the time of assessment (or INSPECTION) the product or service met the stated requirements. Note: 'release certificate', 'release note', 'certificate of compliance' are considered to be synonymous with certificate of conformity.

quality certification. (BS) The authoritative act of documenting compliance with requirements. Note: the requirements can relate to personnel, processes, organizations and services.

quality circles. (adm) A participation technique where groups of (usually) eight persons from similar working backgrounds meet regularly to: identify quality problems, analyse cause, recommend solutions and in some cases effect implementation of the recommendations. *See also* BRAINSTORMING.

quality compliance. (BS) An indication or judgement that the product or service meets the requirements of the relevant specification or regulation; also the state of meeting the requirements.

quality control. Measures adopted to achieve and keep in place the required level of quality of a service or product. Effective monitoring is a key element.

quality defect. Any non-conformance of an item to specified requirements. Notes: 1. defect is restricted to the requirements of manufacturing, assembly, installation, and final test. 2. this term may require a different definition when applied in connection with product liability. *See also* FAILURE.

quality defect, latent. A hidden defect which could not be revealed by reasonable inspection. The purchaser is (usually*) protected by the law if the defect is revealed later. (*i.e. unless an agreed contractual clause has relieved the supplier of this obligation).

quality defect prevention analysis. The analysis of defects found in an item of supply from past data providing statistics for improvement in future specifications.

quality economic. (BS) The economic level of quality at which the costs of securing higher quality would exceed the benefits of the improved quality.

quality failure analysis. The study of potential failures that might occur in any part of a system in order to determine the probable effect of each on all other parts of the system and on probable operational success. BS 4778 (17.8).

quality failure costs. *See* COSTS.

quality failure mode and effect analysis. Study of the potential failures that might occur in any part of a system to determine the probable effect of each upon all other parts of the system and upon probable operational success.

quality inspection. (BS) The process of measuring, examining, testing, gauging, or otherwise comparing the item with the applicable requirements.

quality inspection and test. A technical process which uses a specified procedure to measure one or more characteristics of a product (or service). A major activity undertaken during design, product development, manufacture and product (service) use.

quality inspection and test, 'hold point'. The stage during a contract beyond which the supplier must not proceed without the operation being overseen by the designated inspector.

quality inspection and test, surveillance. Progressive inspection which takes place during the production/process cycle up to the final inspection and release for shipment of the product, or completion and acceptance of the services provided for in the purchase contract.

quality inspection, variables inspection. BS. Inspection whereby certain characteristics of an item are evaluated against a numerical scale and are expressed as points along that scale.

quality limits, control limits (BS) Limits on control charts that are used as criteria for action, or for judging whether a set of data does, or does not, indicate a lack of control.

quality management. (BS) 'That aspect of the overall management function that determines and implements the quality policy'.

quality policy. (BS) The overall quality intentions and direction of an enterprise as regards quality, as formally expressed by top management.

quality precision. The closeness of agreement between the results obtained by applying defined procedures several times under prescribed conditions.

quality reject note. A note completed as a result of a quality control inspection. It should give details not only of the failure but also of action to be taken, e.g. re-machine, scrap, etc. and if supplies are involved a copy to the purchasing department for replacement supplies to be provisioned.

quality sampling (inspection). The inspection of a limited number of items or of a limited quantity of material, taken at random from the lot or batch according to a prescribed sampling plan.

quality statistical. (BS) That part of quality control in which statistical techniques are used.

quality system. (BS) 'The organizational structure, responsibilities, procedures, processes and resources for implementing QUALITY MANAGEMENT.

quality tests. (BS) Critical trials often involving stress or examination of one or more properties or characteristics of a material, product, or set of observations.

quality test, type tests. (BS) A series of tests directed towards approval of design, conducted to determine whether an item is capable of meeting the requirements of the product specification.

quality, acceptable quality level (AQL). (BS) The maximum percent defective (or the maximum number of defects per hundred units) that, for the purposes of (acceptance) SAMPLING, can be considered satisfactory as a process average.

quality, acceptance number/ quantity. The maximum number of rejects to be permitted should be so specified in a SAMPLE LOT if the total quantity is to be accepted.

quality, certificate of quality (supplier's certificate). A written warranty by a supplier that supplies from him conform to the purchaser's specification and requirements, etc.

quality, conformance of quality with specification. The extent to which supplies received match the quality specified.

quality, costs related. See COSTS, QUALITY RELATED.

quality, economic. (BS) The economic level of quality at which the costs of securing higher quality would exceed the benefits of the improved quality. See also BREAK-EVEN.

quality, physical quality control. (BS) The operational techniques and activities that sustain the product or service quality to specified requirements. It is also the use of such techniques and activities.

quality, satisfactory. Under current U.K. consumer protection legislation, to be satisfactory quality goods must be of a standard that a reasonable person would regard as satisfactory (having regard to the price paid, the description and all other relevant circumstances).

quality, scrap note. A document authorizing the discarding of products or supplies after inspection or test as unsuitable for the intended purpose for which they were bought or manufactured and which are economically incapable of being rectified or salvaged, (In the interests of CONSERVATION to be sorted and classified as WASTE or SCRAP.)

quality, total quality management. A philosophy through which everybody in an organization is expected to deliver defect free products or services to their customer, who might be either internal or external to the organization.

131

quality, 'zero defects'. *See* ZERO DEFECTS.

quality, verification of quality. (BS) The provision of evidence or proof that requirements for policy have been met.

quantity. The designation of measure for supplies to be provided under a contract. Unless specified on an order a court would look for a 'reasonable quantity within the contemplation of the parties to the contract'. *See also* ECONOMIC ORDER QUANTITY, BULK QUANTITY, FORWARD SUPPLY ARRANGEMENT.

quantity discount. *See* DISCOUNT, QUANTITY DISCOUNT.

quantity surveyor. A qualified person who measures the work to be done, prepares the BILL OF QUANTITIES for TENDERS. On the contract he checks work done and advises the client on STAGE PAYMENTS.

quantity, batch. 1. The number of parts or other units of material in a batch. 2. The number of parts or other units of material in each of the batches into which the production programme is divided for processing. 3. The number of parts or other units of material in each of the batches into which a purchase order quantity is divided for.

quantity, bulk. A quantity which can be handled, transported and stored in bulk, and for which the shape and sizes of individual pieces may be of no great consequence: e.g. coal, coke, limestone, pig iron, etc.

quantity, custom of the trade. The units of quantity fixed by a particular trade as the standard (maximum or more usually minimum) unit of supply they will normally provide.

quantity, economic order quantity. That quantity, which having regard to the actual USAGE of the enterprise results in the lowest total of ACQUISITION COST plus HOLDING COSTS.

quantity, fixed order. A quantity of supplies which may be fixed as to quantity on an order from which the supplier shall not deviate or one for which the supplier shall deliver fixed quantities at intervals as specified on the purchase order, or the same or programmed quantities on a sequence of orders to, follow one another.

quantity, supplier's. A quantity which may be negotiated by a supplier because it is his economic batch quantity, the CUSTOM OF THE TRADE, his maximum output or some other constraint.

quantity, units of. A primary component of purchase orders, contracts, stock-control, production and sales. An aspect of supplies and materials administration requiring continuous checking, co-ordination and up dating, with supplies, production and sales.

quantum meruit. (law) ('how much it deserves'). A party may sue in quantum meruit for a reasonable sum for work done, goods supplied, or services rendered where 1. a contract is at an end through default of one party or because it is unenforceable; 2. one party asks someone to do them a service and expressly indicates he is to be paid, although no price is stated or agreed.

quarantine store. *See* STORE, QUARANTINE STORE.

quasi. Something which resembles a recognisable object but it is not actually what it appears. *See* CONTRACT, QUASI CONTRACT at ORDERS & CONTRACTS, LETTER OF INTENT, INADVERTENT CONTRACT.

questioning technique. A technique used in inquiries where intensive investigations are needed. The process is in two stages: 1. 'primary stage': question the need for each activity, its means, sequence, place and person(s) and justification sought for each reply; 2. 'secondary stage': the remaining essential activities are further questioned to determine alternatives and select those which are practicable and preferable. IBS 3138, suitably modified, can be applied to purchasing negotiations and to work-study in stores.

queuing theory. This theory, also known as 'theory of congestion' and 'theory of waiting lines', deals with the problems of congestion and waiting. It has important implications in transportation and in issuing goods from stores.

quota system. 1. Fixed total amount of a commodity to be imported. 2. The maximum to be imported from each country. 3. In trading between enterprises quota may refer to a proportion or quantity of a commodity or service fixed or shared between the parties by agreement. Usually it relates to production or sales, but in the cast of GROUP PURCHASING it could refer also to purchases. May well conflict with UK law and EU DIRECTIVES AND REGULATIONS. *See also* COMPETITION LAW.

quotation. Information from a seller to a buyer (usually the result of an enquiry from the buyer - but may be unsolicited) and an INVITATION TO TREAT (i.e. negotiate). *See also* ESTIMATE. A quotation should give an accurate price for the goods or services offered and should be valid for the period stated by the offer, or for a reasonable period. *See also* ESTIMATE.

R

rack, antler rack. A storage rack for bar, tube and similar materials, designed with cantilever arms to support the stock horizontally.

rack, drive in/through. Pallet racks where fork trucks can be driven into or through the areas of the system not at the time occupied by pallets.

rack, mobile racking. Racking designed so that it can be moved horizontally thus requiring less aisle space than conventional fixed racking.

rack, pallet racking. Steel (usually) framed racking designed to house pallets and similarly other unit containers and loads.

random access. A storage system whereby incoming materials are allocated the next available space. Space is more fully utilized. Tracking of materials needs to be carefully considered, controlled and coded for identification.

range. (BS) The difference between the greatest and smallest values of a quantitative CHARACTERISTIC in a range of data.

rate of return, annual. A method of PROJECT ANALYSIS by assessing the annual rate of return on the capital invested, over the LIFE CYCLE of the project.

rate of stock-turn. *See* STOCK RETURN, RATE OF.

rationalization. In the business context rationalization entails the application of rational decision-making to problems of trade and industry, where for example there is 1. overcapacity; 2. plant no longer produces competitively; 3.

market has shrunk. In all such cases, and others, rationalization calls for reorganization, and the application of remedial actions.

ratios, management ratios. Ratios used in management to establish aspects of management and control such as profitability, efficiency and so on. Reference should be made to Centre for Interfirm Comparisons.

raw material stock. *See* STOCK, RAW MATERIAL.

raw materials. (CIMA) Unprocessed stocks awaiting conversion into saleable/ usable products (part of CURRENT ASSETS). (BS) Materials used as input to a production process resulting in finished products. Note: the finished product from one organizational group may be the raw material of another.

re-cycling. 1. To pass (a substance) through a system again for further treatment and use. 2. To reclaim for further use, e.g. to recycle waste water.

re-order level (provisioning level). The stock level at which a purchase (or production) order must be placed if replenishment is to take place before STOCKOUT occurs provided demand remains reasonably steady and lead time for supply is also reliable and/or steady.

real time (computer). (IT) A computer is said to be operating in real time when it is connected ON LINE to a data processing system and records and processes the data as it is generated, e.g. such a computer may update stock-control records immediately each stock movement occurs.

reasonable care and skill. (law) In a service (or other contract) 'the supplier shall carry out the service with reasonable care and skill'. (Supply of Goods and Services Act 1982 Sect 13). 'It is sufficient if he exercises the ordinary skill of an ordinary competent man exercising that particular art'. (High court judgement).

reasonable price. *See* PRICE, REASONABLE.

reasonable, reasonableness of terms in contract. (law) Tests for: 1. what are the relative bargaining strengths of the parties? 2. could the goods have been bought elsewhere without the terms being applied? 3. did the purchaser know of them, or should he have known? 4. was the clause involving liability of the contractor reasonable? 5. were the goods 'manufactured, processed or adapted to the special order of the purchaser?' (Unfair Contract Terms Act 1977 Schedule 2.) *See also* DEALING, A COURSE OF DEALING.

rebate. A financial allowance on a contract usually based on some relationship to turnover of business over a given period or other conditions. *See* below.

rebate, deferred. A rebate, the credit in respect of which is not paid, or allowed, until an agreed time has elapsed, or a target of expenditure or volume of throughput has been achieved. *See also* REBATE, PROGRESSIVE REBATE.

rebate, flat. A rebate paid at the end of a trading period at a pre-agreed rate regardless of the amount of business.

rebate, loyalty. A special rebate given by a supplier to a purchaser in consideration of some agreement to purchase all (or an agreed proportion of total intake from that supplier, or for a long-term contract. (May or may not be tied to target quantities of business).

rebate, progressive (sliding scale rebate). Rebates paid at the end of a trading period and based upon the amount spent.

rebate, retrospective. The usual arrangement whereby a rebate is paid at the end of a trading period or when a financial or quantitative target is reached rather than at the outset of the trading period.

rebate, stepped or sliding scale. A rebate paid directly each step or target of business is reached. The purchaser receives his rebate immediately instead of waiting until the end of the trading records and processes the data as it is generated, e.g. such a computer may update stock-control records immediately each stock movement occurs.

rebuilding, rebuilt, etc. A term which should commit the supplier to the dismantling and entire rebuilding of equipment completely - or at least substantially, so far as working parts, worn and faulty components are concerned - and of providing a unit in near new condition. *See also* RECONDITIONING.

receipt. A written acknowledgment of having received a sum of money or money's worth.

receipt, clean. A term used when goods put on board a ship agree with the wharfinger's delivery sheet.

receipt, depository. A certificate of physical deposit issued by a warehouse which indicates ownership of the material being stored.

receipt, foul. A term used if the goods put on board a ship do not agree with the wharfinger's delivery sheet.

receipt, mate's receipt. Receipt given by the mate of a ship when goods are put on board ship as she lies in mid-stream, or offshore.

receipt, warehouse *See* RECEIPT, DEPOSITORY

receiver, a receiver. A person appointed by a court to administer the financial affairs of a bankrupt company. He takes into his custody all assets including any which belong to the firm's customers, free issue materials, tools, etc. The receiver may combine his role with that of manager of the firm.

receiving. *See* GOODS INTAKE.

reciprocal trading (reciprocity). The practice (sometimes under a company policy directive) of placing purchase orders with suppliers which are customers of the purchaser. *See also* CUSTOMER-TRADE.

recommendations. (EU) *See* OPINIONS (EU).

reconditioning, reconditioned. Unlike REBUILDING this term may imply merely the replacement of worn and broken parts, cleaning and perhaps testing. It may not include diagnostic work to ascertain causes of failure, etc. It is important that purchase orders are clear in this and in REBUILDING contracts.

record(s). (BS) Collection of related data, e.g. that representing an activity.

record, documents of record. Documents which although not necessarily of legal effect may have implications as evidence in a legal dispute, e.g. a purchase order, goods received note, a reject note, a consignment note and so on.

recovery. *See* SALVAGE AND RECYCLING.

rectification note. (BS) A document which authorises additional operations to bring a substandard product up to specification.

rectify, to rectify. (BS) To perform additional operations to bring a substandard product up to specification.

rectilinear. (stats) *See also* CURVILINEAR. A straight line graph in which a direct simple relationship exists between variables. e.g. HOLDING COSTS in the formula of ECONOMIC ORDER QUANTITY.

reefer. Refrigerated vehicle or ship.

registered stockist. Registered firm, symbols. *See* appendix C.

regression. A term used in statistics to describe the CORRELATION between one VARIABLE and another variable, or variables, which are related to the primary variable.

regulation(s), health and safety regulation(s). Regulations on health and safety are made by the Secretary of State upon advice from the HEALTH AND SAFETY COMMISSION. They may relate to any of the purposes of part I of the Health and Safety Act including any matters set out in Schedule 3. They may be 'general in scope', 'limited', 'functional' or 'industry related'. They maybe detailed in form incorporating references to documents, such as CODES OF PRACTICE, or STANDARDS.

rehabilitation. (BS) Extensive work intended to bring machinery, plant or buildings up to current acceptable functional conditional often involving improvements.

reject. To designate an item or batch as not conforming to specification.

reject note (rejection note). A document which records that an item or batch does not conform to specification.

relationship management. The relationship between buyer and seller is now seen as being of key importance. Attention now focuses on achieving and monitoring the right relationship rather than simple performance measures. *See also* PURCHASING, PARTNERSHIP PURCHASING.

release note. A document recording that products conform to specification and authorizing subsequent issue or processing. BS 4778 gives the following as synonymous with release note: 'release certificate', 'certificate of compliance' and 'certificate of conformance'.

reliability. The ability of an item (or service) to perform a required function under stated conditions for a stated period of time.

reorder interval. The standard interval of time between placement of orders, used in a reorder system of the fixed interval type.

reorder systems. (BS) The methods used to regulate the placing of orders for replenishment of stock. 1. Fixed quantity reordering at variable intervals of time. 2. Ordering at fixed intervals of time, with varying order quantities 3. Ordering at varying intervals and in varying order quantities (e.g. MATERIALS REQUIREMENT PLANNING).

repair. (BS) To restore an ITEM to an acceptable condition by the renewal, replacement or mending of worn, damaged or decayed parts. *See also* OVERHAUL, RESTORATION, REHABILITATION, RECONDITION, REBUILDING.

replacement cost, (accounting by). *See* COST, REPLACEMENT COST ACCOUNTING.

replenish. (v) Renew or replace stocks or supplies which have been issued or used.

requisition, purchase requisition. A document making a formal request to purchase, issued by the person or department requiring supplies to the purchasing department.

requisition, stores/stock requisition. (BS) An internal document to request the issue of product or raw material from a store.

requisition, travelling. A requisition (usually) for replenishment of stock which circulates to and from the purchasing department automatically when REORDER LEVEL is reached without other clerical work being necessary, e.g. ONE-FOR-ONE, or RESERVE PACKAGE CONTROL may use such a document.

resale price maintenance. A practice whereby an enterprise endeavours to enforce a minimum price for the resale of its product. The Resale Price Maintenance Act (1964) rendered void any agreement to fix resale prices unless approved by the Restricted Practices Court and registered with the Director of the Court.

research cost. See COST, RESEARCH.

research operational. *See* OPERATIONAL RESEARCH.

research, applied research. Original or critical investigation undertaken in order to gain new scientific or technical knowledge and directed towards any specific aim or objective. *See also* DEVELOPMENT.

reserve package control. *See* STOCK CONTROL, VISUAL CONTROL.

reserve price. *See* PRICE, RESERVE PRICE.

reserved stock. *See* STOCK RESERVED.

response time. The length of time taken by a system to respond or react to an instruction, input, FEEDBACK, or other communication.

responsibility. An obligation upon a subordinate, to whom AUTHORITY or duties has, been delegated, to use such delegated powers purely for the purposes for which they were intended and in accountability to the person who delegated them. But note: the 'superior is always responsible for the activities of his subordinate and cannot escape this responsibility by delegation'.

responsiveness. The rate at which a system of information technology, or an individual in administration, reacts or replies to a stimulus or communication. Responsiveness in the supply chain is receiving scrutiny as a possible source of advantage. The faster a supply chain can respond to the needs of customers the more potential for cost savings.

restoration. (BS) MAINTENANCE intended to bring an item back to its original appearance or state. *See also* REPAIR, REBUILD, RECONDITION, REFURBISH.

restraint of trade. 'Any contract which interferes with the free exercise of trade or business by restricting the work done for others, or, arrangements made with others in a contract, is a restraint of trade. It is invalid unless reasonable as between the parties and not injurious to the public interest'. *Petrofina v Martin* (1966). *See also* COMPETITION, COMMUNITY RULES. HORIZONTAL RESTRAINTS: those which operate across the board of all products generally. VERTICAL RESTRAINTS: those restraints that apply to a particular or type of goods.

restrictive trade practices. 'Any agreement by two or more firms to fix common prices for a particular commodity or to limit the quantities by the manufacturer or the channels through which they will sell'. Restrictive Trade Practices Act 1976, which consolidated the previous enactment's.

retention money. (CIMA) A sum of money representing an agreed proportion of a price for goods supplied or work completed, such proportion being withheld by the purchaser from the contractor for an agreed period of time as security against failure by the supplier or contractor to fulfil his obligations under the terms of the contract.

retention of title. *See* TITLE, RETENTION OF TITLE.

retrospective rebate. *See* REBATE, RETROSPECTIVE REBATE.

return load. An arrangement for goods to be brought to the factory by a BACK HAUL.

return on capital employed (ROCE). The fundamental ratio for determination of success of an enterprise or plant or other project. The return generated by the capital employed is expressed as a percentage.

return, internal rate of return. (CIMA) A percentage discount rate used in capital investment appraisal. It brings the cost of a project and its future cash inflows into equality.

returns book. (CIMA) The record of details and accounts of goods returned to suppliers. Also, a register of goods returned to a firm e.g. for repair, rectification and so on.

returns, clerical returns. Collections of data or statistics such as weekly stock issues, etc.

returns, physical returns. In supplies, goods which are returned by a purchaser to the supplier, or from a customer to the factory of the purchasing officer for treatment or due to rejection by the customer, etc.

reverse engineering. The production or development of new parts, products or tooling from the study and analysis of existing items.

review. A general survey or report, such as review of performance of a supply department, performance of handling plant and future requirements, etc.

rider. An addition to a document, after its completion; an additional clause to a resolution or verdict.

right first time. *See* ZERO DEFECTS.

ring price. *See* PRICE, RING PRICE.

risk. The combined effect of the probability of occurrence of an undesirable event, and the magnitude or impact of the event.

risk (health and safety). (HS) The likelihood of the potential of a HAZARD being realised. The risk from a substance is the likelihood that it will harm a person in the actual circumstances of use.

risk, buyer's risk. If goods are consigned 'carriage paid', then buyer's risk commences on delivery. If consigned 'ex works' or 'ex wharf or 'ex depot' the risk commences where lying.

risk, carrier's. A term in a contract for carriage under which the carrier undertakes the risk of loss or damage in transit. *See also* RISK,OWNER'S.

risk, in property of goods. 'Unless otherwise agreed, goods remain at the seller's risk until the property in them is transferred to the buyer . . . whether delivery has been made or not'.

risk, owner's. A term in contracts applied to the carriage of goods. In such cases (e.g. as applied to a COMMON CARRIER) where the consignor agrees to relieve the carrier of all liability, save the wilful misconduct or negligence on the part of the carrier's employees, the owner is responsible for the loss and a lower rate of carriage charge is then applied.

risk, process risk. (HS) Risks of outbreak of fire, (explosion or other similar dangerous occurrence) associate with particular substances (or processes).

roadstead. A place where ships can ride at anchor some distance from the shore at whatever state of the tide.

robot. A machine controlled by computer and INFORMATION TECHNOLOGY so that it can sense, grasp, locate and move objects (e.g. tools, work pieces, etc.) in the course of manufacture and process. A similar, but not precise, analogy is the automatic storage and retrieval plant in an AUTOMATED WAREHOUSE/STORES.

robotics. The study, design and use of robots - particularly for industrial purposes, including storage and handling.

roll-on, roll-off (RO-RO) (ship, berth, terminal). Designed so other vehicles can 'roll' on and off. *See* BERTH, RO-RO BERTH. Vehicles on ro/ro ships .

roll-over credit. *See* CREDIT, ROLL OVER.

Romalpa case. *See* TITLE, RETENTION OF TITLE.

routier. Long distance driver.

139

royalties. A percentage of (annual) revenue from sales paid to the person to whom they are due in respect of his invention, patent, proprietorship, authorship, etc.

rummaging. 1. Search by a customs' officer for dutiable goods. 2. Search for packages bearing certain marks and numbers from a pile of landed goods. *See also* JERQUER.

running days. Consecutive days (cf. WORKING DAYS in shipping) without regard to Sundays or holidays.

S

safe working load (SWL). The load or capacity which plant or equipment can safely carry, as determined by design and test. Used in the case of lifting tackle regularly tested and clearly, marked on the plant or equipment concerned. *See also* OVERLOAD.

safe, intrinsically safe. (HS) The design or construction (etc.), chiefly of plant and equipment, so that in the event of MALFUNCTION, however caused (e.g. overload, operator error, breakdown, etc.) it will FAIL SAFE or otherwise avoid any hazard.

safety. (BS) The freedom from unacceptable risks of personal harm.

safety mark. (BS) A triangular symbol authorised by the British Standards Institution to appear only upon products which conform to British Standards specifically concerned with safety or to safety requirements of standards which cover other product characteristics. *See* APPENDIX C.

Safety Signs Directive. (EU) Under this Directive, safety signs for industry include not only written, printed, diagrammatic or other signs of that nature, but also include other means of communication, such as: hand signals, verbal signals, acoustic signals (e.g. fire alarms) and illuminated signs. The Directive requires employers to use safety signs whenever there is a hazard that cannot be avoided or adequately reduced by alternative means.

safety stock. *See* STOCK, SAFETY STOCK.

sale and lease back. *See* ORDERS & CONTRACTS A-Z.

Sale and Supply of Goods Act 1994. Act amending the Sale of Goods Act 1979, mostly relating to rights and remedies for defective performance. Subsequent copies of the 1979 Act contain the amendments.

Sale of Goods Act 1979. Act which consolidated the law relating to sale of goods. Despite later amendments, it is still the basis of statutory provision on sale of goods. Defines sale of goods, sets out rules governing formation of a sale of goods contract, establishes rules relating to transfer of ownership and risk. Further rules govern performance of the contract, rights of the unpaid seller and actions for breach of contract. Frequently allows contractual parties to agree otherwise.

sale or return. *See* ORDERS AND CONTRACTS A-Z.

sale, contract of. 'A contract of sale of goods is a contract by which the seller transfers or agrees to transfer the property in goods to the buyer for a money CONSIDERATION, called the "price".' Sale of Goods Act, 1979.

salvage. (v) Rescue goods or property from loss at sea or from other hazard. (n) Goods, property, scrap materials from production, plant or equipment which can be recovered and disposed of, or recycled or otherwise used. *See* WASTE. *See also* ARISINGS, SCRAP, WASTE, RECYCLING, BY-PRODUCT, etc.

salvage money. A reward paid in recognition of the services rendered in saving a ship or its cargo at sea.

salvage note. A document which authorises the use of a product for a purpose for which it was not originally intended.

sample. 1. A small quantity drawn at random from bulk and taken as representative of the whole. 2. An item held out as an example.

sample size. (stat) The quantity drawn from a LOT that will be inspected in order to determine the quality of the entire lot.

sampling. *See* QUALITY CONTROL, SAMPLING INSPECTION.

sanction, financial sanction. The formal arrangement whereby those in charge of the financial affairs of an enterprise control expenditure on major capital projects, such as plant extensions, etc. The manager of supplies should be involved in costs, delivery, etc. of the plant, also of the supplies needed to feed the new capacity involved.

scale, economy of scale. The gain expected from large scale production, process or purchases. *See also* LEARNING CURVE.

scattergraph (scatter diagram). A graphical representation of data which results in a number of points scattered over a wide area instead of a linear curve. A LINE OF BEST FIT may be found by observation (or calculation). Also, there may be valuable information to deduce from the range between lines marking the boundaries of the maximum and minimum data on the scattergraph.

scheduling. (BS) 'The process of setting operation starting dates and/or finishing dates for jobs'. Applicable also to purchasing and supply and marketing. May also involve component BATCH SCHEDULING, to ensure quantities of components for other

supplies arrive precisely when required, particularly where JIT procedures are in operation. *See also* PLANNING AND PROGRESSING.

scissor lifts. *See* LIFT TABLES.

scrap. Discarded material, having some recovery value, which is usually either disposed of without further treatment (other than reclaiming and handling) or re-introduced into the production process in place of fresh raw material. *See also* BY-PRODUCT *and* WASTE.

seal, container seal. A uniquely numbered seal attached to a TIR vehicle or CONTAINER for through transit across frontiers and which must be seen to be unbroken upon arrival at its destination.

seasonal adjustment factor. A factor introduced into statistical supply calculations so as to take account of and make allowances for regular seasonal fluctuations, such as rate of usage, demand, price, etc.

seasonal index. (BS) A set of numbers, giving relative values e.g. of demand during the periods of a year, which is used to modify forecasts obtained from any forecasting technique which ignores seasonal effects.

secrecy clause, in contract. A clause (where appropriate) inserted into a contract to prevent suppliers (and/or sub-contractors) from divulging any information regarding the subject of the contract to a third party. *See* TERMS AND CONDITIONS OF CONTRACT.

seizure note. (law) A note issued by, customs officer and attached to goods placed in a customs warehouse, when the officer has good reason for believing that such goods were not properly acquired.

sell-by date. A date affixed to a product indicating the date by which it should be sold.

seller. The person who sells, or agrees to sell, goods. Sale of Goods Act. Later Acts refer to 'transferor'.

seller's market. One in which MARKET FORCES tend to be to the advantage of the seller who can dictate price, delivery, quality and so on.

seller's option. The right of a seller to require a buyer to purchase merchandise or other property at an agreed price and within an agreed period.

sellers, over. (com. fin. mkt.) A situation in a commodity market where there are only sellers or more sellers than buyers.

selling cost. *See* COSTS, MARKETING.

semi-manufacturers. Products, such as rubber and steel, which have been processed from raw materials and are intended for use in manufactured articles, such as tyres and car bodies.

semi-variable costs. *See* COSTS, SEMI-VARIABLE.

sensitive commodities. *See* COMMODITIES, SENSITIVE COMMODITIES.

service. (n) A supply of air, gas, electricity, water, etc. (also used in connection with factory cleaning, waste disposal, etc). (v) To replenish the consumables needed to keep an item in operating condition and to make routine adjustments.

service departments. (In industry). Those which provide for the running of an enterprise (particularly one engaged in manufacture, e.g. accounts, stores, maintenance); drawing and design, purchasing (supplies) personnel, transport, safety, materials handling.

service factor. *See* SERVICE RATIO.

service industries. Those which provide supporting services to industry, and those which as part of the national INFRASTRUCTURE control or enhance the quality of life.

service level. The measure of actual success in an operation such as number of successful issues from stores, or supplier's number of occasions when delivery was on time. *See also* STOCK, SERVICE LEVEL: AGREEMENT, SERVICE LEVEL

service ratio (also service factor). The ratio of DEMANDS met to total demands made. e.g. Requisitions submitted for 10,000 of an item but only 9,000 available for issue = service ratio of 90 percent, or if 10 requisitions presented only 8 fully met = 80 percent service ratio.

settlement (energy). In the electricity industry the process used to decide which supplier is responsible for the power consumed by each end user.

ship's manifest. Details of the cargo for customs offices.

ship's papers. Documents establishing ownership, nationality, the nature of the cargo, the CHARTER PARTY, and bills of lading, contract with the seamen, manifest, official log, bill of health, certificate of registry, together with all other papers necessary to comply with the regulations of the governments concerned. Most of the above terms are entered separately.

shipment, short shipment. The goods which cannot be loaded on board either because of lack of space or, through an accident or, for internal transport, the delivery of less than quantity specified.

shipping bill. Manifest of goods on board.

shipping conference. Meeting of the owners of liners with a view to fixing uniform freight rates.

shipping marks. Marks which an importer instructs the exporter to show on his packages (case, crate, plant bale, etc). Usually the importer's initials, the port of entry, the package number and number of packages in the shipment. SITPRO endorses and recommends the simplified four line mark introduced by The United Nations.

shipping note. Delivery or receipt note for goods to be placed on board a ship.

shipping terms. Terms used in the regulation and conduct of transactions for shipment by sea. (*See under relevant sections, such as* FREE ON BOARD, EX WORKS, etc.) The term has also come to include other forms of transit by land surface (rail and road etc.) and by air. *See* INCOTERMS.

shipping weight. The actual weight of a ship's cargo.

shitauke. Japanese term meaning, essentially, partnership in the sense that there are inputs from both sides of a relationship of such things as information, resources, knowledge and trust

shop order. *See* ORDER, PRODUCTION ORDER.

short-termism. (econ) Actions based on decisions taken for immediate gain. It usually implies that little, or no, consideration has been given to long-term effects or results. It is included here because it can have important implications in purchasing policy. These could include finance and economic considerations, effects upon long-term health and safety of workers and/or the public, environmental long-term effects,

scientific effects, metal fatigue, wear, corrosion, chemical action etc.

short. (com) The market position of a futures contract seller whose sale obligates him to make a further purchase.

shortage cost. *See* COST, SHORTAGE COSTS.

shortage, supply. (BS) A shortage of supplies due or overdue demands(s), or part of such demands (s), which cannot be fulfilled immediately.

shortage-time. (BS) The period of time during which an ITEM (e.g. plant) is unable to perform due to shortages of labour, spares, facilities, movement, (supplies), etc.

shrink wrap. Plastics sheet which can be shrunk by heat to wrap and protect and stabilize goods stacked on some form of loadboard. *See also* STRETCH WRAP.

SI Units. Metric units with scales in decimals or sub-decimals employed internationally, e.g. joules, Newtons, etc.

sight draft. (SITPRO) A BILL OF EXCHANGE which is payable on demand, instead of on a time or term.

signs, hazard and warning. Signs often in the form of 'pictograms' or 'ideograms' and used for transit of goods and hazards at the workplace to workers and/or the public. Many are increasingly required under statutory provisions, EU regulations and subject to BSI and ISO standardization.

Simpler Trades Procedures Board. (SITPRO) Sponsored by the Department of Trade and Industry. It works nationally and internationally to remove barriers to trade by the simplification of documents and procedures involved in international trade. Include: advice on simplified commercial, official and transport procedures; export, practice, documentation, finance and payments; advice on standards and techniques for the exchange of information by on-line computers. SITPRO promotes the use of information technology in trading, distribution and payment process.

simplification. The process of eliminating complexities of design by streamlining features or components by their omission or their combination with other features without impairing the functional use of the article. *See also* VARIETY REDUCTION *and* DIVERSIFICATION.

simulation. (BS) The representation of a feature of the behaviour of a physical phenomena by means of a physical or abstract system by the behaviour of another system. A decision-making approach whereby a mathematical or other model is made of the system under scrutiny.

sinking fund. (fin) A fund into which sums are paid (usually) at annual intervals to provide for meeting, a future commitment such as the repayment of a loan or the replacement of machinery or of some other asset and to cover DEPRECIATION.

site. (n) The place where some project (e.g. building or plant) is situated, or to be situated. (v) To erect or set down the building or plant which is the subject of a project. Note: in contracts, some points to cover include: inspection of site, safety of personnel [and public], security, stores, payment and control of site labour. *See* TERMS AND CONDITIONS OF CONTRACT. CIPS.

skewness. (stats) The degree to which a FREQUENCY CURVE is asymmetric. This is an important characteristic in many frequency distributions associated with purchasing and supply.

skip. A container which may be open or lidded for collecting/transporting waste.

slow-moving. Supplies, such as stocks which may have a slow turn-over rate or which are seldom called for. *See* STOCK, TURN *and* STOCK THROUGHPUT.

social audit. An audit of the social balance that results from activities (e.g. purchases) by an enterprise. It may be associated with VALUE ANALYSIS and COST BENEFIT ANALYSIS.

software. (IT) Programs, routines and procedures that can be loaded up for use on a computer system.

software escrow. (IT) An arrangement whereby the source code to a piece of software is held by a third party. This reassures the supplier that no unauthorized individual has access, and protects the buyer in the event of the supplier becoming bankrupt or insolvent.

sortation systems. Systems designed to divert materials or packages to their appropriate storage or despatch location. Usually based on ramps or roller conveyors making use of divertor gates and bar coded labels.

source documents. Those (such as PURCHASE ORDERS, REQUISITIONS, 'GRNS', etc) which can be used to record physical and financial movements/ commitments, etc.

sourcing. A term coined by supplies staff to cover their activities in locating satisfactory and economical sources of supply of goods and services. *See also* SUPPLIES, SOURCING OF SUPPLIES.

sourcing of supplies. *See* SUPPLIES, SOURCING OF SUPPLIES.

spares stock. *See* STOCK, SPARES.

spares, strategic spares. Those which are vital for the functioning of plant or equipment. (May be of relatively low price and quantity in classification 'C' of 'ABC ANALYSIS' but require priority treatment in the stock control system to ensure continued availability).

specific duties. Customs duties which are levied on weight or other measure of quantity instead of on value. *See* AD VALOREM.

specific goods. *See* GOODS, SPECIFIC GOODS.

specific performance. *See* PERFORMANCE, SPECIFIC.

specification. A statement of the attributes of a product, process or service. These attributes may be performance or conformance requirements, depending upon the use to which the specification is put.

specification, conformance. A specification which tells the recipient exactly what is wanted. They must supply goods or services which conform. Alternatives or variations are nor allowed.

specification, functional specification. (BS) 1. Document that describes in detail the characteristics of a product with regard to its intended capabilities. 2. The description of any object, material or process in sufficient detail to enable its manufacture, or procurement, to be identically produced, reproduced or procured. 3. A detailed statement of a set of requirements to be satisfied by a product, material or process, indicating, whenever appropriate, the procedure by means of which it may be determined whether the requirements given are satisfied. 4.

Open specification: one which does not fully specify a need but which leaves a latitude for the suppliers) to provide variants or alternatives.

specification, over-specification. Specification for dimensions, quality or other description of supplies or services beyond that needed for the satisfactory performance of the supplies or services.

specimen. (BS) A representative single item or a measured quantity of material. Note: the term is often used in the formation of a SAMPLE.

speculator. A person who tries to predict future prices, buying when it is felt that the price will rise, and selling when it is felt that the price will fall.

spend. Jargon for 'expenditure' or 'spent'.

spontaneous combustion. The self-ignition of a substance without the application of an external source of ignition. Of particular relevance in the bulk storage of powders, coal, hay, straw, etc.

spot cash. *See* PAYMENT CASH, SPOT.

spot goods. Goods actually available and ready for delivery.

spot price. *See* PRICE, SPOT.

spot sale. Goods which were in stock and have been sold for immediate delivery.

spreadsheet. An electronic device using a computer program. It comprises the well known matrix tabulation layout prepared electronically. Vertical columns relate to headings such as periods (months, years, etc.) or alternative quotations, distribution networks, routes, projects, etc. Horizontal lines define the PARAMETERS which affect the data which appears in the vertical columns opposite each parameter, such as costing details of quotations, costs of different routes in distribution, etc.

stage payments. *See* PAYMENTS, STAGE PAYMENTS.

standard. 1. The establishment of a unit of measurement, or reference instrument or component for use in the calibration of other instruments. 2. A standard may be a specification or practice adopted formally (See definition 3, below) or informally by established usage, for example 'A COURSE OF DEALING', or other informal but regularly used commercial or technical practice.* 3. 'A standard, in the sense of ISO/IEC/CEN/CENELEC A specification established by consensus and approved by a recognised body, and that provides common and repeated use, rules, guidelines or characteristics for activities or their results, aimed at the achievement of the optimum degree of order in a given context.'** (Notes: *Those engaged in buying, selling and trading, particularly overseas, should be alert to the possible problems which may arise when they encounter practices, conditions, etc. with which they are unfamiliar. ** A standard may be a code of practice, a guide, method, specification, etc. A standard may become binding only if it is made mandatory by legislation, if a party is contracted to work to it or once a claim for compliance with it has been made).

standard costs. *See* COSTS, STANDARD.

standard deviation. A measure of the VARIANCE of individual ITEMS of DATA from the MEAN of all the items of data. It can be calculated by taking the square root of the sum of the squares of all the deviations from the mean divided by their frequency. The result can then be manipulated mathematically in further statistical calculations. It is a very important tool in purchasing and supply. Provided that

its basis is a NORMAL FREQUENCY curve its mathematical properties enable it to be used for planning stock control levels, etc.

standard price. *See* PRICE, STANDARD.

standard, European standards. (EU) Such standards, designated by the prefix or suffix 'EN' carry the obligation on the members of CEN and CENELEC to implement them at national level by giving them the status of national standards and by withdrawing any conflicting national standards. The technical content of an 'EN' is identical in each country.

standard, harmonization documents. (EU) A harmonization document constitutes a CEN/ CENELEC standard. It carries the same obligations to withdraw any conflicting national standards. But, the public announcement of its number and title is otherwise sufficient. Harmonization documents are established if transposition into national standards is unnecessary if (for example) a CEN or CENELEC member has already adopted an 180 or IEC being endorsed in Europe, or impracticable, and particularly if agreement is subject to the acceptance of national deviations.

standardization. 1. The activity of establishing, with regard to actual or potential problems, provision of specifications or procedures for common and repeated use. 2. The adoption of standards. *See also* VARIETY REDUCTION.

standards, 'conformity'. (EU) 'Conformity' in the single market implies to producers, suppliers, purchasers and users that a product (or service) does in fact conform to a STANDARD or SPECIFICATION, which in some cases may be a legal requirement. Both kinds of requirement, purely commercial or legal, are met by ASSESSMENT OF CONFORMITY and the granting of a CERTIFICATE OF CONFORMITY. [*See* QUALITY]

standing order (purchase). *See also* ORDERS AND CONTRACTS A-Z.

standing order(s). Rules governing conduct, procedures, etc., usually for a public authority or similar body. *See* ORDERS & CONTRACTS A-Z, STANDING ORDER.

standing order, banker's standing order. Instructions to a bank by a depositor to pay a stated sum at set agreed intervals to a stated payee.

statute barred. A transaction, contract, or other act which is forbidden by statute.

statute law. *See* LAW, STATUTE LAW.

stillage. A workshop or storage platform on legs, transportable by stillage truck.

stochastic. (stats) The statistical situation in which targets are set, based upon estimates which are themselves based upon variable data, e.g. RE-ORDER LEVEL based upon varying demand as distinct from a 'deterministic' system where all the data can be determined precisely. The word is frequently used as a synonym for a target or guess.

stock. (BS) All the tangible material assets of a company other than the fixed assets. Comprises all the finished or saleable products, all the items to be incorporated into the finished products, and all the items to be consumed in the process of manufacturing the product or in carrying out the business.

stock account, One of the control accounts kept to reconcile the various accounts which flow into the main stock accounts, which finally contribute to the balance sheet.

stock audit. A physical count made by an agency external to stores to ensure veracity of records against physical stock. *See also* AUDIT and STOCK-TAKING.

stock check, periodic check. (BS) A stock check which involves the physical check of all stock at one time and which is performed periodically, e.g. annually by annual stock take.

stock check, physical stock check. (BS) A check on stock by direct measurement or scrutiny together with the subsequent comparison with and reconciliation to the stock records. Synonymous with: 'physical stock count', 'stock audit'. May be continuous or periodic.

stock control. (BS) The system whereby the levels of supplies in stock are regulated to maintain quantities required without STOCK EXCESS or STOCK DEFICIENCIES.

stock control, audit of stock. An accounting check on the accuracy of stock-control records for INVENTORY or accounting purposes. Involves reconciling the stores accounts, vouchers, printouts, etc. with stock control records. Sometimes used (incorrectly) as a synonym for STOCKTAKING which may or may not be carried out at the same time.

stock control, base stock control. A system of stock control, whereby in a sequence (usually) of major projects (e.g. ships), PROVISIONING stock for each next unit is undertaken at a suitable time in advance of its commencement to ensure a smooth and accurate stock level of supplies at the starting date. (Application of NETWORK ANALYSIS is appropriate).

stock control, bin card control. The recording of stock movements on record cards attached to or located at the location of stock. Formerly the most popular method of stock control prior to the introduction of centralised control. Now largely abandoned in favour of the latter thus avoiding clerical work at the storage points (bins). Still used for special applications, such as valuable goods requiring frequent checks at the bin (e.g. jewellery) or strategic spares under ONE-FOR-ONE control, etc.

stock control, continuous control. Stock control in which the stock balance is continuously updated promptly, e.g. by on-line computer at each transaction. If valuation of the stock is simultaneously recorded, the term 'perpetual inventory' (used by the Americans for all stock control) can be correctly applied.

stock control, coverage analysis. A control technique which aims to maximize the use of capital invested in stock. This is done by making a quantitative assessment of likely throughput of the various stock lines and adjusting intakes to minimise investment (inventory) whilst assuring continuity of supply for production/process.

stock control, cyclical timing. The control of stock by review of stock levels at predetermined time intervals. *See also* STOCK CONTROL, RE-ORDER LEVEL CONTROL METHOD AND STOCK, CYCLE STOCK..

stock control, imprest. A method of controlling stock without the necessity of records. It is usually based upon a predetermine maximum stock level. This is checked at regular intervals and made up to the maximum level required.

stock control, 'one-for-one'. A system of stock control where one of the following methods is applied: 1. a new item is only issued upon the return of the. old one, e.g. protective clothing, small tools, etc.; 2. directly an item is taken from stock a new one is ordered, e.g. spare parts for plant, etc.

stock control, max-min method. *See* STOCK CONTROL, RE-ORDER LEVEL METHOD.

stock control, pre- (or forward) allocation method. (BS) Known forward requirements are pre-allocated on the stock records and a 'cover' known as 'forward balance' is maintained. *See* STOCK, RESERVED STOCK.

stock control, 'reserve package' method. Quantities of stock (e.g. stationery) are made up into suitable size packages and when the 'reserve package' (so labelled) is removed and used last. The label is then detached and sent to the central stores, or to purchasing, for replenishment.

stock control, re-order level control method. A method of stock control in which the level is maintained by setting a re-order level. Directly this is reached a replenishment is put in hand. *See also* REORDER LEVEL.

stock control, three bin system. As 'two bin' system described below but with the provision of a third bin for SAFETY STOCK.

stock control, two bin system. A system of visual stock control by means of two bins (or two levels) so arranged that when one bin is empty (or the lower level is reached) a replenishment is called for from main store, or ordered by purchasing. The term is sometimes used to describe control by RE-ORDER LEVEL - the level of the second bin (or second level) is determined in the same manner.

stock control, visual control. General term for a number of methods of controlling stock by visual examination of levels, in some cases avoiding the necessity of any clerical work. *See* IMPREST; 'ONE-FOR-ONE'; OPEN ACCESS BINS; STORES, OPEN ACCESS; RESERVE PACKAGE; TWO-BIN SYSTEM, etc.

stock cover. 1. The sum of stock physically on hand, less any reserved stock. 2. The length of time that a given supply or level of stock will satisfy a given production or process demand at a given rate of consumption for production or process.

stock deficiency. Situations where demands upon stock result in an actual failure to supply and make a production stoppage imminent.

stock evaluation. The evaluation of stock for the preparation of the financial accounts. *See* STOCK VALUATION.

stock handling cost. *See* COSTS, STOCK HANDLING COSTS.

stock holding costs. *See* COSTS, STOCK HOLDING COSTS.

stock levels. The quantities of stock carried, normally controlled by stock control systems.

stock level, balance level (physical). Physical balance: actual quantities of supplies in stock as determined by count, measurement, stock check, etc.

stock level, excess stock level, indication of. A level set in stock control records which will alert those responsible for the maintenance of stock levels when excess stock is indicated. Also indicated as 'maximum stock level'.

stock level, exhaust stock or exhaust bin level. Stock completely exhausted including safety stock.

stock level, forward stock balance level. Stock balance based on PHYSICAL BALANCE and 'dues in'. It equals physical balance + (dues in - any forward allocation.)

stock level, free stock balance level. Physical stock balance minus forward allocations.

stock level, maximum level. The planned highest level of stock, above which is considered to be in excess and is normally flagged for management attention. *See also* STOCK LEVEL, EXCESS STOCK LEVEL above.

stock level, minimum level. A level below which stock quantity should not be permitted to fall. Sometimes used as a synonym for **RE-ORDER LEVEL** but may not always be identical with that level.

stock level, opening stock level. Stock level at the commencement of a particular period. Usually taken at beginning of financial year or budgetary period or, in the case of a project, may be at the time work starts on the project.

stock level, progressing. The level at which **PROGRESSING** action should take place to ensure delivery is on target. May be earlier than that given by a STOCK WARNING LEVEL so as to leave time for provisioning if the reply is unsatisfactory. *See also* PLANNING AND PROGRESSING.

stock level, re-order level. *See* STOCK CONTROL, RE-ORDER LEVEL CONTROL.

stock level, stock-out level. *See* STOCK CONTROL, RE-ORDER LEVEL CONTROL.

stock level, stock-out level. Stockout level is that at which **ACTIVE (OR CYCLE) STOCK** is exhausted and **SAFETY STOCK** is called upon. Sometimes referred to as **MINIMUM STOCK**

LEVEL but this can be ambiguous and should not be used as a synonym for STOCK OUT.

stock level, warning level. A level intermediate between RE-ORDER LEVEL and STOCK-OUT LEVEL which although seldom expressed in formal terms can be very important in high priority stock. It is the point after which it will be too late to take alternative action to avoid a stockout if replenishment orders outstanding arrive late or if there is a sudden surge in demand.

stock life. Stock life should be measured from the instant of INTAKE to that of arrival at the WORK-CENTRE or other point of use. Supplies management must ensure that stock-life never exceeds SHELF-LIFE. Note: batch life should not be used as a synonym for stock-life since it is a production term which implies the length of time a batch of material will last during the production work-cycle. *See also* BATCH LIFE.

stock optimization. Reduction in total STOCK HOLDING COST by looking at raw materials, materials stock, work in progress and finished goods to ensure that any stocks are held at the appropriate point in the sequence of conversion or production. As a general rule it is preferred to carry stocks of pre process or partly processed materials rather than finished goods, thereby postponing value adding activity and avoiding the costs associated with tying up high values of stock.

stock order. *See* ORDERS & CONTRACTS - STOCK ORDER.

stock record, perpetual / continuous. (CIMA) The recording as they occur of receipts, issues and calculations of resulting balances of individual stock items in quantitative measure, and, (if including price) comprising an INVENTORY.

stock record. A record of the quantity of stock of a single item, often containing a history of recent transactions and information for controlling the replenishment of stock.

stock relief. An allowance against taxable profits given by the Inland Revenue, to offset increase in closing value due to inflation of stocks of saleable goods.

stock requisition. *See* REQUISITION, STOCK REQUISITION.

stock rotation. (BS) A procedure which attempts to ensure that supplies do not remain in stock longer than their SHELFLIFE. *See* FIFO.

stock throughput ('turnover', 'usage'). The total volume or value of a commodity (or all commodities) of stock passing through stores during a given period (usually 12 months). It should include all issues, plus wastage, loss, deterioration, spillage, etc., but allowing for returns to stock from work-centres, etc.

stock turn. The complete cycle of use of a quantity or batch of stock, from receipt to exhaustion of the quantity or batch. An important statistic of physical stock control since it involves shelf-life and stock life. Not to be confused with rate of turnover. *See* STOCK-TURNS, RATE OF.

stock turns, rate of stock turns. (BS) The rate of consumption of stock. Calculated by dividing the annual (or other chosen period) total THROUGHPUT by the average level of stock.

stock utilization ratio. An important ratio affecting profitability of supplies management. It is particularly relevant in class 'A' supplies.

$$SUR = \frac{Tp}{So + In}$$

Where: SUR is stock utilisation ratio.

Tp is total throughput in period.

So is opening stock including safety stock at commencement of the period.

In is intake during period.

stock valuation. (BS) The total value of stock, usually measured in monetary terms.

stock valuation, average price (avco). (BS) A price which is calculated by dividing the total cost of materials in stock (from which the material to be priced could be drawn) by the total quantity of materials in that stock. (For sales and estimating purposes 'first in price' may lead to an 'other than current market price' and thus to an error in a sales ESTIMATE or QUOTATION.)

stock valuation, first in, first out (FIFO). (historical cost. *See* COSTS, HISTORICAL COSTS,) The price for the material first taken into the stock from which the material to be priced could have been drawn. *See also* FIRST-IN, FIRST-OUT, PHYSICAL CONTROL.

stock valuation, last in, first out. he price paid for the material last taken into the stock from which the material to be priced could have been drawn.

stock valuation, replacement price. (CIMA) The price at which material could be purchased, identical to that which is being replaced or revalued. *See also* PRICE, REPLACEMENT PRICE.

stock valuation, standard price. (BS) A predetermined price fixed on the basis of a specification of all factors affecting that price. Where supplies departments are involved, the standard price may be (in the first place) provided by, or agreed with, the purchasing depart-

ment based on their experience and statistical analysis of price trends and also estimates from suppliers.

stock verification. The procedure whereby stocks are verified against records and for serviceability, obsolescence and methods of storage.

stock, accommodation. Stock provided by a supplier to a purchaser. The latter usually holds it in his stores. He may pay for it as it is used, or 'part on delivery' and the balance as it is used, or other arrangement.

stock, accounting/accountancy. CIMA Includes current assets at the end of an accounting period. Includes: raw materials, work in progress, finished goods, and goods in transit or on consignment (i.e. to a customer).

stock, allocated stock. *See* STOCK, PRE-ALLOCATED STOCK and STOCK RESERVED, STOCK or PHYSICALLY ALLOCATED STOCK.

stock, buffer. (BS) A proportion of work-in-progress stock held because of varying production rates, not necessarily planned and usually held on the shop floor. Note: it is not a synonym for SAFETY STOCK and should no longer be used in the context of stock control. For this, the term 'safety stock' should be used. *See also* STOCK, UNCOUPLING EFFECT OF STOCK.

stock, consignment. Stock (supplies) provided 'on consignment' in commercial trading and to be paid for as used or sold. *See also* STOCK, SALE OR RETURN and STOCK, ALLOCATION STOCK and STOCK, ACCOMMODATION STOCK.

stock, consumable. (BS) That portion of INDIRECT STOCK which consists of items which do not form part of the saleable product and are not normally used in the manufacturing process [e.g. stationery, oil, etc.].

stock, costs of holding. *See* COSTS, STOCK HOLDING COSTS OF.

stock, costs of investment. *See also*, STOCK, INVESTMENT, COSTS OF.

stock, cycle stock ('active stock'. 'live stock', 'working stock'.) (BS) That portion of stock available (or planned to be available) for normal demands, excluding 'excess stock' and 'safety stock'. So called because it tends to move in cycles in phase with the demands of production or sales,

stock, 'dead stock'. Stock which never turns over or does so slowly that is unprofitable to carry it.

stock, direct. (BS) That which is incorporated directly into an ENDPRODUCT.

stock, dues-in. Supplies which are due to arrive in stock either from purchase orders or production orders IN HOUSE, or from a branch stores or depot. Note: stock records must be adjusted to allow for quantities to be received from outstanding purchase or production orders. Usually shown in a special column.

stock, dues-out (allocated). Quantities, usually shown in a special column, on stock control record indicating known future demands which must be met. These are often associated with a 'forward allocation system'.

stock, excess. A situation where stock exceeds maximum permitted stock. Warrants immediate investigation of DEMAND rate, INTAKE rate, size of purchase order QUANTITIES, PROGRESSING action, etc. *See also* SURPLUS STOCK.

stock, fast moving. Stock (or direct supplies) for which there is a frequent or continuous demand. Usually needs special consideration in respect of physical MATERIALS MANAGEMENT such as location in stores, special

packaging, and administrative materials management in respect of ordering and stock control, etc.

stock, finished-goods, parts, products. (BS) Stock which is available for supply to an external consumer, including items which have been supplied but not invoiced, but excluding items which have been invoiced to the external consumer. Note: A product which may be both INTERMEDIATE STOCK and FINISHED GOODS STOCK is considered as INTERMEDIATE STOCK until such time as a quantity is physically reserved for external consumption. The quantity reserved then becomes FINISHED GOODS STOCK.

stock, free issue. 1. Stock received from a customer for use in producing goods against his purchase order. 2. Stock of low value made freely available. *See* STORE, OPEN ACCESS STORE.

stock, free. Stock which is uncommitted and available for use, i.e. after allowing for allocations and reservations.

stock, idle. Stock which fails to move through lack of demand. e.g. SAFETY STOCK which only moves occasionally . to meet an emergency. *See also* STOCK, DEAD STOCK.

stock, indirect. (BS) Stock which is not incorporated in an end product but comprises SUPPORTING GOODS, e.g. stationery, tools lubricants, etc. Note: stock which is incorporated in the end-product but is of indefinite quantity is sometimes regarded as indirect stock, e.g. paint, solder, etc.

stock, intermediate. (BS) That portion of WORK IN PROGRESS STOCK which consists of completed parts subassemblies and assemblies which are held available in stores.

153

stock, pre-allocated. *See* STOCK CONTROL, PRE (OR FORWARD) ALLOCATION CONTROL. *also* STOCK, RESERVED STOCK.

stock, policy. Stocks held for investment or speculation. (Buying or manufacture may be more advantageous now than later because of expected price arises).

stock, pricing of. The method of pricing of stock financial purposes requiring policy decision and must be consistent in method on all matters such as inclusion or exclusion of discounts, carriage, packing, insurance.

stock, 'promotion'. Stock of finished goods provided for a specific sales promotion where demand is expected to exceed capacity during the life of the promotion.

stock, purchased parts. (BS) Stock which is held in the same state as when purchased and has not yet been issued is held in 'from stores', i.e. in purchased parts store.

stock, raw material. (BS) Stock which is not part of WORK IN PROGRESS, i.e. is held in the raw materials store.

stock, reserved. (Also known as allocated assigned, earmarked or appropriated). Material committed to specific orders, usually but not necessarily, physically separated from other stock. Where physically set aside it is usually segregated in a RESERVATION STORE or reservation area. *See also* STOCK CONTROL, PRE (OR FORWARD) ALLOCATION CONTROL.

stock, safety. (BS) A proportion of stock planned to be held to protect against unforeseen circumstances (increased usage, lengthened lead times, etc.) and normally held in store.

stock, seasonal stocks. (BS) Stock to enable production or purchasing to be carried out at a more constant rate throughout the year when customer demand (or supply) is seasonal.

stock, service level (or factor or ratio). (BS) 'A measure of the achievement of success in satisfying demand for stock during a predetermined period'. Usually expressed as the percentage of requests met on submission.

stock, slow moving. Stock which is only issued occasionally or continually but in very small quantities. It may need special attention for obsolescence, excess build-up, exceeding SHELF LIFE, provisioning for emergency use, etc.

stock, spares. (BS) 'Items which are held available for MAINTENANCE purposes or for the replacement of defective parts, or for supply to customers.

stock, surplus. Stock in excess of requirements.

stock, transport. (BS) Stock held because of the time taken to transport goods. Often a significant cost in wholesale/retail distribution costs.

stock, uncoupling effect of. The degree of freedom provided by stockholding to a consuming department or other user to cover variations in demand or supply. It is a direct function of stock levels, intake and consumption rates. *See also* STOCK, BUFFER STOCK *and also* STOCK, BUFFER STOCK and STOCK, SAFETY. *Also* HOMEOSTASIS.

stock, usage rate of. (BS) The rate of consumption of stock. The use of the data requires it shall be related to some time scale, viz. production period, accounting period, weekly, monthly, annual periods, etc.

stock, warehouse stock. (BS) The portion of finished goods held at a warehouse.

stock, work-in-progress (WIP). Stock upon which work has been performed or has been made ready for work to be started, but which is not available for supply to an external consumer. Note: it is important when subdividing WORK-IN-PROGRESS that adequate description is made, e.g. shop work in progress, sub-contracted work in progress.

stock, working *See* STOCK,CYCLE STOCK.

stock-keeping unit. The measure by which the quantity of stock is recorded on the stock record, e.g. each, metre, kilogram.

stock-out or exhaust stock. (BS) The occurrence of a zero stock balance, not necessarily reflecting a shortage if safety stock or other is advisable.

stock-taking. (CIMA) Checking of stocks and verification of stock records against physical quantities held in store and also those at WORK-IN-PROGRESS stage and FINISHED GOODS on hand. Stock-taking may be 1. continuous; 2. cyclical (i.e. at regular intervals - as at the end of the financial year, or; 3. random. It may be over the entire stock or a section at a time. *See also* STOCK CONTROL CONTINUOUS, and STOCK-CONTROL, AUDIT OF.

stock-wastage. *See* WASTAGE, DAMAGE AND LOSS.

stockist. A MIDDLEMAN who agrees to maintain an agreed level of specified manufacturer's goods in return for special trading terms.

stockyard. An outdoor compound (or other enclosure) usually with a prepared surface with access roads, for storage of materials which do not require protection from the weather or are improved by weathering.

stop list (or 'black list'). A register 1. of suppliers who are not acceptable to the purchaser; 2. of particular supplies which are not to be purchased or used because they are not acceptable for technical reasons. *See* VENDOR RATINGS.

stoppage in transitu. (law) The right of an unpaid seller to stop delivery being taken of the goods, if, after shipment but before arrival at the buyer's works, he discovers the customer is insolvent.

storage. Within the context of this dictionary, the term storage is taken to include the housing of supplies of all kinds, and also the physical handling associated with their stowage, retrieval from storage and their distribution.

storage costs. *See* COSTS, STORAGE.

storage stacks and stacking. The stowage in stacks, of supplies usually on pallets by means of lift trucks. Stacks may be handled from aisles or 'block stacked' in bulk without aisles in situations where first-in, first-out (FIFO) practice is not needed.

storage, life. *See* STOCK-LIFE and SHELF LIFE.

storage, utilization factors. The utilization factors for storage can be apportioned as follows: 1. building utilization factor: this factor is obtained by measuring the volume of space actually occupied by storage equipment - racks, shelves, etc. and expressing this as a percentage of the total volume of stores which could be used. 2. storage equipment utilization factor: this should be assessed as indicated under UTILIZATION FACTOR. In this case the factor is calculated on the volume actually used as a percentage of total usable capacity; 3. value to volume factor: this factor expresses the relative value of stock in terms of value per unit volume occupied and may be used when considering items of considerable value and the costs of security, etc.

store or stores. (n) A place equipped and suitably maintained for the housing of supplies and for keeping them in a condition suitable for use when they are required. The varieties of store are as numerous as the industrial and commercial activities which require them. Some of the principal types of store are given, not in alphabetic sequence below in order of importance. *See also* WAREHOUSE/ STORE, WAREHOUSE BONDED/STORE. (v) To keep for future use.

store, allocation. A store set aside for housing supplies which have been PRE-ALLOCATED to specific jobs. Enhanced security and other steps may be needed to ensure that such pre-allocated stocks are not taken for jobs other than those intended. Such stock is IDLE STOCK and may thus attract added costs. The term BONDED STORE is sometimes used (incorrectly) to describe an 'allocation' or 'reservation' store. The use of this term should strictly speaking be reserved for stores subject to one described here under WAREHOUSE (OR STORE) BONDED WAREHOUSE.

store, bonded. *See* WAREHOUSE BONDED WAREHOUSE.

store, central. 1. One from which are supplied all the main needs of a single perimeter enterprise. 2. One supplying a group of industrial units which are geographically separated.

store, concentration store. Stores at geographically dispersed plants of a large enterprise (or GROUP) whereby each store concentrates upon the main requirements of its plant and serves the others with the supplies in which it specialises.

store, departmental. A store specialising in supplies for main materials peculiar to the department it serves. In this case

SUPPORTING GOODS may be provided from a CENTRAL STORE 2. A large retail establishment with several departments.

store, finished goods. A store (usually located near the despatch area) where the ENDPRODUCTS of an enterprise are housed. Such a store may be specially equipped and secure to protect goods which may have a final finish and possibly pre-packed for prompt delivery as spares or for distribution for the domestic market. Security may also be necessary if ATTRACTIVE finished goods are stored.

store, free issue supplies. A store for housing FREE-ISSUE SUPPLIES. Because the enterprise managing this store is BAILEE for the free-issue goods it is important the stores be SECURE and suitably equipped and maintained in such a way as to preserve these supplies in (at least) the condition they were in when received.

store, general. Store for GOODS needed throughout an enterprise. Most of the supplies will be Class C and UNIT CONTAINERS may be appropriate. Many of the items carried may be ATTRACTIVE.

store, group. Store serving a group of enterprises which may or may not be in the same PRODUCT GROUP. The actual operation may vary therefore in the supplies held and in the distribution and control systems. *See* CENTRAL STORES and CONCENTRATION STORES.

store, maintenance. *See* STORE, PLANT ENGINEER'S STORE.

store, open access and open access bin. Stores and bins where the normal rules of restricted access are relaxed in favour of operatives helping themselves to supplies as and when required. In some cases omitting any clerical control. Open access bins may be located within stores or at workcentres.

store, packaging. One set aside for packaging materials. Some of these may be ATTRACTIVE and many are subject to the need for humidity control. This store is (usually) within or adjacent to the package or despatch bay.

store, pattern. One, reserved and equipped for housing patterns. Whether part of a main store, or separate, humidity control is essential for wooden patterns and special binning may be needed owing to their (often) awkward shapes. Close control of issues and intakes and pattern number records are very important.

store, piece parts. A store for PIECE PARTS whether BOUGHT or made IN HOUSE are used in most assembly type industries. Provision of UNIT CONTAINERS, PRE-ASSEMBLY or KITTING are often profitable activities.

store, plant engineer's. A special store for plant maintenance and similar requirements usually situated within or adjacent to the plant engineer's department for housing strategic and fast-moving spares and consumables used in plant maintenance.

store, processed materials. An important store in process plants (usually) closely integrated with the process and process control and also with laboratory and batch testing.

store, production. A store specialising in supplies required specifically for production.

store, quarantine. A stores for housing supplies which are awaiting inspection, rectification, return to suppliers or other action. Such stores must be specially SECURE so as to avoid any possibility of their contents circulating or from entering the production or process system without authority. Sometimes referred to (incorrectly) as bonded stores. *See* WAREHOUSE, BONDED.

store, raw material. A main store housing a major part of the enterprise's assets. Usually storage is in bulk. Special binning, racking, hoppers, silos, etc. may be warranted with their associated handling and control equipment.

store, reservation. A store in which supplies are held which have been physically RESERVED for a future known (or anticipated) demand. *See also* STOCK PRE-ALLOCATED STOCK.

store, salvage. A very necessary area for the reception, sorting and despatch of ARISINGS for disposal as WASTE or sale or RE-CYCLING as SCRAP. Should be outside the production area and made secure if arisings include valuable materials e.g. copper cable. Part of the CONSERVATION SYSTEM.

store, secure. One where more than normal security is provided for supplies held against unauthorized access or removal. They may be kept there for special reasons such as value, hazards, property of a customer, etc. The term bonded store is not a synonym for secure store and should only be so used if a bond has been entered into. *See* WAREHOUSE AND STORE, BONDED.

store, site stores. Stores set up by contractors and construction firms for servicing their teams on site. Security and safety at unattended site stores must be carefully worked out.

store, sub-store (satellite store). A general term applicable to many types of stores which are subordinate to another which supplies it, e.g. an OPEN ACCESS STORE at a work centre supplied from a main store.

storekeeping. (BS) Those procedures and means whereby goods are received, identified, stored, issued, accounted for and replenished in accordance with defined levels of service and with due regard for the statutory requirements for health and safety.

storeperson. A employee working within a store whose activities are chiefly confined to manual operations.

stores. Stock, items held in store. Note: the term STOCK is widely preferred.

stores catalogue. A list of all items held in stock on a regular basis. It must be compatible with the COMMODITY CATALOGUE, where such exists, and use the terminology of the VOCABULARY. The stores catalogue may be incorporated into the COMMODITY CATALOGUE.

stores control account. The control account in which the totals of transactions shown on stock records are entered.

stores ledger. (CIMA) A subsidiary ledger containing an account for each separately identifiable class of material handled by the stores organization. It is controlled by the STORES CONTROL ACCOUNT in the principal ledger. It is sometimes referred to as the RAW MATERIALS LEDGER.

stores manager. The person who controls and administers the whole of the store's operation and function.

stores reports. *See* REPORTS.

stores requisition. *See* REQUISITION STORES, REQUISITION.

stores vocabulary. *See* VOCABULARY..

stores, main store. *See* STORE, CENTRAL STORE.

stores, management functions. (BS) Main functions in stores are: receiving supplies; identifying supplies; storage of supplies; issuing of supplies; accounting for supplies; replenishment of supplies.

stores, service factors in stores. *See* STOCK, SERVICE LIFE.

stores, wastage in. A significant contributor to costs enumerated under STOCK, COSTS OF HOLDING. Allowance may be needed when provisioning if wastage cannot be reduced or eliminated.

straddle carrier. A mobile handling device for the movement and stacking of freight containers (usually of the ISO type fitted with twistlocks for use with the standardized carrier equipment) which suspends the container between the 'Goliath' type wheeled legs upon which the vehicle travels. In common use, world-wide at dockside and transport distribution centres. *See also* HANDLING, STRADDLE HANDLING and *also* TRUCK, STRADDLE TRUCK.

strategic gap analysis. *See* GAP ANALYSIS, STRATEGIC GAP ANALYSIS.

strategic spares. *See* SPARES, STRATEGIC SPARES.

stuffing. A colloquialism for the loading of freight containers. The term is 'non-preferred' by some authorities owing to its implication of possible overloading and bad loading of transport containers. The term LOADING is preferred.

sub-assembly. *See* ASSEMBLY.

subcontracts. *See* ORDERS & CONTRACTS A-Z.

subject to being unsold. A clause frequently inserted in quotations for SPOT GOODS and in this case the would-be buyer may purchase the goods provided that they have not been sold elsewhere in the mean-time.

subjectivity. Emotional or prejudiced considerations which proceed from, or relate to, the mind of a person and not the basic facts or nature of the subject under consideration. Although inimical to value analysis or value engineering, in some areas 'subjective aspects' are important.

subsidiarity. (EU) The principle of devolving powers to the lowest appropriate level of government so as to take decisions as near as

subsidization. The terms applied to a variety of forms of direct or. indirect financial assistance which governments may give to exporters.

substance. Any kind of matter, in any form (e.g. solid, liquid or gas etc.) which has clearly recognisable characteristic properties, and, composition independent of its origin.

substance, immiscible substances. Substances (usually refers to liquids) which cannot readily be mixed e.g. oil and water.

substance, noxious substance. (HS) One which is nauseous and may, or may not be harmful, but may give rise to industrial disputes working conditions.

substances hazardous to health, control of. (HS) Statutory regulation, enforced 1988 onwards requiring that wherever there is a potential for exposure to HAZARDOUS SUBSTANCES during work, a suitable and sufficient ASSESSMENT OF RISKS is made, and the necessary precautions are to be completed before the work is carried out.

substances, hazardous substances. (HS)

Those which have potential to cause HAZARDS and which may, in transit, storage, handling, etc. present a danger to other goods, property or persons. [In purchasing and supply due regard must be paid (particularly under EC DIRECTIVES and corresponding enactments within the United Kingdom) to scientific MATERIALS MANAGEMENT with full documentation, labelling, safety instructions for storage, handling, packaging and transportation. *See also* VICE, INHERENT VICE.

substances, package of dangerous/ hazardous. (HS) Criteria for packing and packaging dangerous substances: 1. flammable solids; 2. spontaneously combustible substances; 3. substances which, on contact with water, emit flammable gas; 4. organic peroxides.

suitability for purpose. (law) *See* QUALITY, MERCHANTABLE.

supplier. A general term used by supplies staff for all kinds of providers of goods and services purchased or procured by them.

supplier appraisal Assessment of a potential supplier's capability of controlling quality (delivery, quantity, price, and all other factors to be embodied in a contract). Appraisal is carried out before placing orders.

supplier approved list. List of approved suppliers. May also include a blacklist of non-approved suppliers with any comments kept under strict security.

supplier assessment. *See* VENDOR APPRAISAL.

supplier association. A group of suppliers to a single customer organized, with the customers assistance, to share ideas and information on working more efficiently.

supplier base. The range of suppliers that an organization maintains trading relations with. VENDOR BASE

supplier development. The provision of advice, finance, technology or other forms of assistance by a buyer to a supplier to enable the supplier to offer a product or service which meets the buyer's needs, or to interface with the buying organization in a mutually appropriate way.

supplier evaluation. Assessment of a supplier's control of quality and other factors under consideration carried out prior to placing orders.

supplier rating. An index of the actual performance of a supplier.

supplier, approved. A supplier or vendor who meets a client organization's standards and who has been placed on record as having done so.

supplier, first tier. A direct supplier.

supplier, Nth tier. A supplier to a supplier in the nth tier.

supplier, second tier. A supplier to a first tier direct supplier.

supplies. All the materials, goods and services used in an enterprise, regardless of whether they are purchased outside, transferred from another branch of the company or manufactured IN HOUSE.

supplies officer (or supply officer). An officer, usually of executive status responsible for obtaining and management of supplies.

supplies research. Research into all the supplies needed by an enterprise, particularly those used in production and processing, raw materials, parts, etc, as regards: specification, quality, quantity, transport inwards, packaging,

dispensing, storage, handling, etc.

supplies throughput. The measure of total supplies obtained and/ or used in a given period expressed in money, quantity, volume or other measure for various categories of supplies or for total of all supplies. The term 'throughput' is preferred to 'turnover' in this context, but *see also* SUPPLIES, TURNOVER RATE and RATIO.

supplies, classification of. Classification (classes) of supplies in most enterprises fall into three main classes. *See* ABC CLASSIFICATION. 'A' main requirements; raw materials, etc. 'B' secondary requirements; some raw materials, EMBODIMENT GOODS, plant equipment and spares. 'C' minor needs; supporting goods and consumables.

supplies, consumable. (BS) All supplies consumed in an enterprise which are classified as INDIRECT and which do not form part of a saleable product and are not normally used in the manufacturing process, e.g. stationery.

supplies, free-issue. Supplies provided by a purchaser to the supplier for use in the manufacture or assembly of the product he has ordered.

supplies, rate of turnover of. (BS) The rate at which supplies are consumed per unit time, e.g. per annum, per production period, etc. *See also* SUPPLIES TURNOVER RATIO.

supplies, sourcing of (multiple sources). The selection of more than one source of supply. A primary source may be given the task of a major proportion of demand, say 80%, and a secondary source the lesser quantity as back up or to maintain a competitive edge.

supplies, sourcing of. The investigation and selection of sources of supply which meet the criteria of quality, price, delivery and other requirements of the enterprise needing them.

supplies, sourcing of (single source). The restriction of intake of supplies to a single source. Usually restricted to cases where there is no alternative source, or where single source trading benefits outweigh risks of loss of supply through shortage or financial benefits outweigh those of competition in the market.

supplies/supply cycle. 1. Internal: that including the entire field of supplies from intake to despatch (excluding the actual production phase) and covering in particular PROVISIONING, PURCHASING, MATERIALS MAN-AGEMENT, RESEARCH, etc. 2. External: the supply cycle between trading enterprises. 3. Economic (national) cycle: trade in supplies from EXTRACTIVE INDUSTRIES, to DOMESTIC CONSUMER, through MARKETS, PROCESS PLANTS, MANUFACTURING and serviced by WAREHOUSES, transportation and the (national) INFRASTRUCTURE. 4. Global: trade in supplies between independent states.

supplies/supply management. All aspects of administration and management of the entire SUPPLIES/ SUPPLY CYCLE, including formulation of and/or the carrying out of company policy on supplies. *See also* MATERIALS MANAGE-MENT.

supply. 1. The amount of an item of goods that will come onto the market over a given range of prices. 2. Within the context of the Chartered Institute of Purchasing and supply the following meanings apply: (v) the provisioning, administration, service, stock control, storage, handling and distribution and all associated operations connected with supplies, services and materials management. (n) all goods, materials

and services which come into the possession of an enterprise as the result Of contracts for purchase, hire or procurement by other processes and for which the enterprise has responsibility.

supply and demand, law of or principle of. An empirical rule relating supply and demand whereby if price falls demand may increase, or if supply increases price may fall, with (in theory) price equilibrium at the point where supply and demand break-even. The basis of much economic theory.

supply chain. The chain of operations and centres through which supplies move from the source of supply to the final customer or point of use.

supply chain management. The manage-ment of materials and services whilst 'upstream' in the hands of suppliers (or their suppliers), and 'downstream' whilst in distribution or the possession of customers.

Supply of Goods (Implied Terms) Act 1973. Act which implies a number of terms into contracts for hire purchase relating to the goods (very similar to those found in ss.12-15 Sale of Goods Act 1979 on satisfactory quality, fitness for purpose etc).

Supply of Goods and Services Act 1982. Act amending the law with respect to the terms to be implied in certain contracts for the transfer of the property in goods, in certain contracts for the hire of goods and in certain contracts for the supply of a service.

supply, essentiality. A term sometimes used in supply terminology to describe the degree to which the availability of' an item of supply (such as a plant spare) is essential to the successful operation of the plant. (We suggest the use of the more usual words, e.g. 'important', 'critical', 'vital' according to the degree of urgency).

supply, inelastic. A situation where a large change in available supply only induces a small change in demand. *See also* DEMAND, INELASTIC DEMAND.

supply, lean. The approach to supply employed where LEAN PRODUCTION takes place. The use or consumption of materials or parts brings new materials into existence, thereby avoiding stocks or unnecessary work. Suppliers are expected to provide defect free materials at the right time to meet customer requirements, and to employ lean supply ideas themselves.

supply, planning of. *See* PLANNING.

supporting goods. Goods (supplies) used directly to support production or process but not directly accountable to specific end-products, etc. Usually Class C, and CONSUMABLE and EXPEND-ABLE.

surplus stock. *See* STOCK, SURPLUS STOCK.

suspense. A state of insecurity and uncertainty, hence, a decision whether to cancel an order or eliminate a stock item, or in the case of an account, to make an entry in a suspense account until the proper determination of the entry can be decided.

synergy. A biological and medical term currently used in management and kindred subject areas. In those contexts, its meaning should be used to imply 'the working together of two or more forces (etc) to produce an effect greater than the sum of their individual efforts.' Can have serious implications in health and safety and accident research and prevention. The combined effects of two or more forces (or chemicals) may produce results far exceeding their individual capacities for action, damage, danger or hazard. *See also* FACTORIAL.

systems contracts. Sometimes known as stockless purchasing. Systems whereby users can call off materials directly from the supplier. *See* ORDERS, VARIETIES.

T

T form procedure. (EU) Transit documents which indicate to customs officers the status of goods in the Community but also permit sealed container goods to cross the Community frontiers without inspection.

tachographs. Devices which record upon removable discs (usually card) the speeds, movements, mileage, standing times, etc. of the vehicles to which they are fitted. Obligatory on goods vehicles over 3½ tonnes under European Community Regulations.

take-over, in contracts. The stage in a contract (usually buildings, plant, etc.) at which, when final test and COMMISSIONING are completed, the subject of the contract is handed over to the purchaser.

tally. (v) To check that goods being unloaded from a ship correspond to the documentation under which they were shipped. The person who makes the check is a tally clerk.

tare. Allowance made for case, crate, or other container in which goods are packed. There are five sorts of tare. 1. Real, the actual measured weight. 2. Customary, the amount normally allowed in the CUSTOM OF THE TRADE. 3. Average, the mean or average weight of containers used. 4. Estimated, where it is not practicable to weigh the containers used. 5. Super, where packages are beyond a certain weight set as a limit by the carrier, for example; the excess weight is termed super tare. Used in transportation for the unladen weight of a vehicle, or railway truck, etc. and where certified and shown on the vehicle can be used as a basis for charging in conjunction with a certified weighbridge ticket.

target price. *See* PRICE, TARGET PRICE.

tariff. 1. Tax imposed by a country on imports so as to restrict or otherwise control the level of importation. *See also* DUTIES. 2. Rate of charges for a supply or service, e.g. gas, electricity, etc.

tariff, block. A method of charging for services, such as energy, whereby the price varies for different 'blocks' of usage, e.g. a higher price up to a certain quantity and a (usually) lower price thereafter.

tariff, two part. A method charging for service where (for example) a 'standing charge' may be made representing the interest on capital investment in providing the supply. The price per unit of supply may then be by a BLOCK TARIFF, single fixed rate charge per unit, or other means.

technology transfer. The practice of organizations passing technical knowledge to those with whom they deal. For example to facilitate more efficient supply.

tender and tendering. Offers from tenderers without collusion, usually in sealed envelopes, delivered by a time and date specified in the invitation to tender, for the supply of goods or services. Such tenders are opened only at the time and date specified by a tender panel of qualified persons who record the necessary details. Late tenders are not considered.

tender bonds. *See* BONDS, TENDER

tender negotiation, pre-ender negotiations. Discussions with, and questions to, proposed contractors clarifying what is expected of their best offer in their final sealed tender.

tender negotiations, post-tender negotiations. A tender procedure whereby tenders are met individually or together to discuss details of offers which may affect the purchaser's final selection of the best bid. *See* below, TENDERS, NEGOTIATED PROCEDURES.

tender, invitation to tender. An invitation to prospective suppliers (may be on an 'approved list') to submit tenders for, the supply of goods or services. The procedures are intended to safeguard the expenditure ʾ(particularly) of public moneys and on large projects and items. Community Regulations and Directives apply over this field.

tender, negotiated procedures. (EU) National procedures whereby contracting authorities consult suppliers of their choice and negotiate the terms of the contract with one or several of them.

tender, open. One where the original enquiry has been open and free for all to enter and make offers, as distinct from a closed or restricted list of those invited to tender. (EU) The use of OPEN TENDERS called for by the Commission. Generally a notice inviting tenderers should be advertised in the Official journal of the Communities, where the likely value of the contract is over a certain amount. Technical specifications must not mention 'goods of a specific make or source, or of a particular process which may have the effect of favouring or eliminating certain undertakings'.

tender, post-tender negotiations. Negotiations after receipt and opening of tenders and before the letting of contract(s) with the supplier(s) who submit the lowest acceptable tenders.

The purpose is to obtain an improvement of price, delivery or other factor. It is a rule that this shall not put other tenderers at a disadvantage or adversely affect their confidence or trust in the competitive tendering system.

tender, restricted procedures. (EU). All who apply to tender must be given an equal opportunity to qualify. The contracting entity must generally complete qualification within six months but may then invite selected tenderers.

tender, single offer. One for a single project. The unqualified acceptance of such an offer constitutes a contract.

tender, standing order. One for the supply of goods and services 'as required'. The tenderer is obliged to supply as orders (i.e. demands) are received but he cannot insist that orders shall be given to him. *See also* ORDERS AND CONTRACTS section.

tenderer. A party who submits a tender to another party at the invitation of the latter to carry out work, supply goods or service, etc.

tendering, compulsory competitive. An approach to purchasing whereby organizations (usually public sector) are compelled to seek TENDERS from more than one SUPPLIER.

terminal market. *See* MARKET, FUTURES MARKET. A synonym for futures market. Called a terminal market because dealings are specified in terms of periods of time in the future.

terms of shipment. *See* INCOTERMS.

terms of trade. A term used to indicate the current situation of a country in respect of its international trade. For a good situation input prices should be low in relation to exports so that imports can be financed.

terms, conditions, warranties. Terms in the context of purchasing and supply management comprise the substantive components of a contract which create contractual obligations the breach of which may lead to action. Terms are, broadly speaking, of two kinds. 1. 'Conditions'. These are essential terms which go to the heart of a contract. The breach of a 'condition' entitles the injured party to treat the contract as at an end. e.g. failure to meet a delivery date if this was stated as a 'condition of the contract'. 2. 'Warranty', a subordinate term in a contract. *See* WARRANTY.

terms, express. (law) Express terms are clear statements communicated by the parties to a contract and by which they intend to be bound.

terms, implied. (law) Implied terms are those which have been implied by 1. statutory provisions or 2. the manifest INTENTIONS of the parties. They come into existence whether or not they are mentioned by the buyer or seller.

terotechnology. (BS) A combination of management, financial, engineering, building and other practices applied to physical assets in pursuit of economic LIFE CYCLE COSTS. Its practice is concerned with the specification and design for RELIABILITY and MAINTAINABILITY of machinery, equipment, buildings and structures, with their installation, COMMISSIONING, operation, MAINTENANCE, modification, and replacement, and with FEEDBACK of information on design, performance and costs.

test. *See* QUALITY CONTROL, TESTS.

testing, 'witness testing'. Certain pre-agreed tests to be witnessed by the representative of the purchaser. Such tests usually include performance tests to simulate or exceed normal working conditions.

third country. A country other than a member state of the European Union. *See also* INTER-STATE and INTRA-STATE.

third party. A party other than the principals involved in any proceedings. For example, a 'third party' inspector may be appointed by an importer to check goods prior to shipment.

three-bin system of stock control. *See* STOCK CONTROL, THREE BIN.

threshold. (EU) Contracts below the threshold value do not need to be open to competition under the EU procurement regime. These thresholds are adjusted from time to time.

through transit concept. The system whereby goods are packed in unit loads, e.g. palletized or containerized in such a manner that they can travel from supplier to user point with minimum (or nil) disturbance en route.

through-transport. Concept of moving cargo on a door-to-door basis in trucks, containers or other units, without unloading (or transfer of load) en route.

throughput. 1. The amount of goods and/or materials which pass through a plant and usually expressed in physical units. May be used as a measure of productive efficiency. 2. Applies also to materials and supplies passing through stores, etc. The term preferred to TURNOVER which has important accountancy implications.

tie-in sales. A practice of some suppliers to tie the sale of one product to the sale of another. *See also* FULL-LINE FORCING and NEGOTIATION.

tied sales conditions. Conditions by which a seller seeks to enforce the commitment of his customer only to use his materials, services, etc, by introducing CONDITIONS into the contract which have this effect. (e.g. A typical example is to introduce a clause which revokes a guarantee if materials or services are employed by the purchaser other than from that supplier). *See also* NEGOTIATION.

tilt. A cover of fabric or similar material over a frame which is secured to the bed of a vehicle. For TIR compliance it must be capable of being sealed and be free from tears or repairs except those which comply with TIR regulations.

time charter. The hire of a vessel for a contracted period of time, with or without specified routes and destinations which may also be specified in the CHARTER PARTY.

time cycle. The period of time occupied by a series of events, e.g. production periods, seasonal demands, etc. which will continue to recur in similar overall periods. For example, 'long horizon' (say) 5 years, 'medium horizon' (say) I year, and 'short horizon' (say) 3 months. *See also* PLANNING AND PROGRESSING.

time is of the essence. An expression commonly used in contracts where it is essential that the good or service is delivered or provided by the date specified. Inserted where delay could result in significant consequential loss to the buyer.

time to market. The time taken to convert an idea into a product or service available for sale to customers.

time utility. (econ) The value associated with having a product at the time needed, rather than later.

time window. The difference in lead times between the shortest lead time a supplier can offer and the longest lead time he can guarantee for delivery.

time, periods of time. The time intervals in industry and commerce may be expressed in: 1. chronological time; hours and minutes or days, weeks, months, years; 2. accountancy/budgetary periods; 3. production periods. (Important measurements for PROGRESS CHASING, PLANNING PRODUCTION CONTROL, etc.) For numbering of weeks *see* BS 4760/ISO/R2015.

title deed. A document establishing the right of ownership.

title, (ownership of goods). The legal entitlement to goods or property of any kind by their possessor. Also, documentary evidence of the right of ownership, e.g. a receipt for payment for the goods. UK law tends to support the owner of goods against all comers including buyers, hence caveat emptor.

title, retention of. The establishment of legitimate rights under which a supplier may exercise rights over goods he has sold by clauses in the contract of sale. May be in 'small print' on his acknowledgement. Such as: 1. property in the goods shall not pass until payment in full has been made; 2, the seller reserves interest in the goods or the proceeds of any sale if the buyer sells them on before payment has been made in full. Leading case, *Romalpa* 1976.

tolerance, specification tolerance. (BS) The permitted variation in a process or a characteristic of an item. Note: the relationship between the process variability and specification tolerance is termed 'relative precision'.

tonnage. The freight-carrying capacity of a vessel expressed in 'ocean tons'. *See* TONNAGE, DEAD-WEIGHT TONNAGE.

tonnage, deadweight tonnage. The total load-carrying capacity of a vessel expressed in tons weight calculated at 100 cubic feet per ton. ('Registered tonnage' is usually much less than 'dead weight' tonnage because few cargoes stow at less than 100 cubic feet to the ton, e.g. iron ore about 20 ft' per ton).

tonnage, deadweight tonnage (registered). The weight of cargo a vessel can (is registered to) carry and which will take its level in the water to the maximum LOAD LINE.

tonnage, gross registered tonnage (GRT). The cubic capacity of a vessel taking one ton as being equal to 100 cubic feet. *See* DEAD WEIGHT TONNAGE.

tonnage, net registered tonnage (NRT). The measure used for port/ canal dues, etc. It is calculated as GROSS REGISTERED TONNAGE less the non-earning portions of the vessel (engine room, crew space, etc). Usually about 55-65% of GRT.

tort. A civil wrong (not being a breach of contract or trust) in respect of which there lies an action for damages.

total distribution costs (TDC). Costs incurred from the end of a production line to consumers (or industrial users).

total productive maintenance. There are many competing definitions. The approach is defined by N. Rich in his book of the same title as 'A Company-wide approach to the management and operation of all the factory assets, both human and equipment, in such a manner as to achieve the optimisation of the conversion process and the generation of customer "value" over the economic working lifetime of assets employed.'

Total Quality Management. An integrated and organisation-wide approach to quality management. Pioneered by Joseph Juran.

tote. A box-type container designed for the storage and movement of (usually) small parts. Often used for work in progress.

tote pan A small container used for storage usually comprising an open to box capable of self-stacking. *See* CONTAINERS.

totology. The technology of optimizing the overall performance of a manufacturing company or sector by minimizing the number of products, component parts, manufacturing processes and materials consistent with satisfying reasonable present and foreseeable requirements. BS PD6470. *See also* VARIETY REDUCTION.

traceability. Systems designed to ensure that the origin and manufacturing history of parts or materials can be discovered.

tractive force, effort. The force/effort which a locomotive or tractor unit can exert at its drawbar for pulling (or pushing) vehicles to which it is coupled. The limiting value is given by the weight on the wheels of the tractor unit and the coefficient of friction between the wheels and the rails, or the roadway.

tractive resistance ('coefficient of traction'). The frictional resistance per unit of weight being moved, e.g. the resistance encountered when moving cases, or plant by sliding along a surface in the absence of mechanical aids such as a roller, trolley, conveyor or other means.

trade association. An association of traders or producers to cooperate on questions affecting their interests.

Trade Descriptions Act 1968. Act prohibiting misdescriptions of goods, services, accommodation and facilities provided in the course of trade; to prohibit false or misleading indications as to the price of goods; to confer power to require information or instructions relating to goods to be marked on or to accompany the goods or to be included in advertisements.

trade discount. *See* DISCOUNT, TRADE.

trade gap. The amount by which the value of visible imports exceeds the value of visible exports. (In this context, 'visibles' = goods and 'invisibles' = services, financial, technical and others).

trade mark. *See* BRAND NAME.

Trade Marks Act 1994. Act reforming trade mark law to harmonize UK position with other members of European Union; to make provision on the new Community trade mark and to give effect to the Madrid Protocol relating to International Registration of Marks; to provide grounds for refusal of registration and rights where infringement occurs; to provide rules relating to licences and the duration and renewal of registration; to provide for collective marks and certification marks.

trade pack. The packaging normally provided by a supplier for the shipping of his goods. The purchaser must be aware of this if exportation is required. *See* TRADE, PACK EXPORT.

trade pack (export trade pack). The packaging normally provided by a supplier for shipment overseas. May need careful checking dependent upon

the destination and storage at the final location.

trade, balance of trade. (econ) The difference, usually expressed in financial terms, between exports and imports of a country.

trade, intra-Community. Trade conducted between members of the Community.

trade, restraint of. *See* RESTRAINT OF TRADE.

Trade, Technical Barriers to Trade Agreement. An agreement under the WTO that sets disciplines for product regulations and standards irrespective of the domestic policy purpose which they serve.

trading down (to trade down). Trading down, or 'down market', by selling low priced goods and relying on high turnover to secure profit, or in order to penetrate an existing market.

trading up. The converse of TRADING DOWN. The object may be to gain entry into an area of the market where higher quality prevails.

tramp vessel. (mar) One which carries cargo between any destinations, to no fixed schedule.

transactional relationship. A straightforward relationship between buyer and seller whereby the two parties do not get closely involved with each other, but simply exchange goods or services for payment.

transfer costs. *See* COSTS, TRANSFER COSTS.

transfer note. *See* MATERIALS TRANSFER NOTE.

Transfer of Undertakings (Protection of Employment) Regulations 1981. Regulations which implemented the Acquired Rights Directive (E.U.

Council Directive No 77/187) to achieve harmonization of UK law with law of other member states on safeguarding employee rights in the event of transfer of undertakings or activities within undertakings. Infringements of the regulations allow for claims for unfair dismissal or redundancy by affected employees. The regulations also require consultation in appropriate circumstances with representatives of affected employees.

transferable credit. See CREDIT, DOCUMEN-TARY.

transire. A permit granted by customs for the removal of goods.

transit documentation (simplified). (EU) A system of transit documentation for intra-Community use. Procedures are: 1. movement certificates and 2. full 'T' FORM procedures.

transit shed. A place approved by the Commissioners at a seaport or airport for the deposit of imported goods which have not yet been reported to customs, entered, or cleared from customs charge.

transit time. Time taken, actual or estimated for transit of goods from, the time actually loaded on board to the time of arrival at destination. Purchaser must ascertain if time includes loading and unloading time.

transmission charges. (energy) The charge made for using the electricity distribution system.

transnational corporations. Term for multinational corporations, usually understood to mean those private corporations with direct investments and production facilities abroad. It does not formally mean those companies whose overseas operations are confined exclusively to sales.

transparency. (EU) A fundamental principle of Community policy. It implies 'accessibility of information, responsiveness, realistic time scale for consultation and freedom from built-in bias'.

transport, bi-modal. The utilization of more than one means of transport for shipments, e.g. use of ISO CONTAINERS on swap-bodies from road and rail for a transit.

transport capacity per ton-mile (or metric units per kilometre). The unit of costing transportation, viz. cost of operating the means of transport number of freight ton-miles transported.

Transport International per Chemin de Fer. The international railways customs procedures similar to TIR for road haulage.

Transport Internationaux per Route. The international road carnet system which enables goods in sealed, approved vehicles or containers to cross frontiers without inspection by customs, so long as the seals are unbroken and the tilts, if employed, are undamaged.

transport IT form procedure. (EU) Simplified Community procedure by a document which indicates to CUSTOMS Officers the status in the Community of the goods being transported. Provided the seals are unbroken the consignment can then proceed across frontiers without inspection.

transport log book. A book in which are recorded the arrivals and departures of vehicles at an undertaking, giving date and time of arrival and departure, vehicle registration number, name of haulier and other details as required by the undertaking.

transport payload. That position of a load which contributes to revenue for the enterprise.

transport, operating ratio. A ratio used in the transportation industry to assess the operating costs of the service. Operating costs are expressed as a percentage of receipts. The higher the percentage the lower the PROFITABILITY; over 100 percent indicates a loss.

transportation. General term for carriage and distribution of supplies. It is a significant factor in the COSTS OF ACQUISITION and distribution.

travelling requisition. *See* REQUISITION, TRAVELLING.

treat, invitation to treat. A preliminary stage in any transaction which may lead to a firm contract, e.g. a seller who sends a mail-shot, catalogue or price list, a quotation or estimate, or who places a price tag on goods is merely inviting the prospective purchaser to place an order, negotiate, or make an offer.

Treaty on European Union. (EU). Known also as the Maastricht treaty, came into effect in November 1993. Essentially it extended the areas of competence embraced by the EU into such fields as justice, security and defence. It also increased the powers of the European Parliament.

trend. The general tendency of data to move in a particular direction revealed by statistical analysis, e.g. a rising or a falling trend.

trend, forecasting of. If growth (or decay) is at a steady rate or constant then a forecast of the trend may be calculated by EXPONENTIAL SMOOTHING.

trespass of goods. The unlawful interference with goods in the possession of another person, either by damaging them or by the mere moving of them.

tret. An allowance made for waste and evaporation on certain goods.

triad peaks. (energy) A method of calculating electricity transmission charges. The term is a reference to the three times of peak demand during a given year.

tribology. The science of interaction between moving surfaces which are in relative motion to one another, and the results of friction, lubrication and wear. An area for consideration when carrying out VALUE ENGINEERING.

trucks, straddle. Lift trucks, (manual or powered) which handle loads between the points of support, i.e. between the wheels or rollers upon which the truck travels.

truss (n). Material formed into a loose unit for handling or transport, etc. without pressure, banding or other restraint. *See* BALE.

turning radius. The distance between the centre of turn of a vehicle such as a fork lift truck and the furthest point of the truck or other vehicle and its load. Similar calculations apply to all transport vehicles and also to their clearance above ground on slopes and curves.

turnover. (CIMA) Amounts derived from the provision of goods and services falling within an enterprise's ordinary activities after deduction of trade discounts, value added tax and any other taxes based on the amounts so derived'. (Companies Act). This would normally be invoiced sales less returns and allowances.

turnover, stock turnover. *See* STOCK THROUGHPUT and STOCK TURNOVER.

two bin. *See* STOCK CONTROL, TWO BIN SYSTEM.

type approval. *See* QUALITY CONTROL, TYPE APPROVAL.

type tests. *See* QUALITY CONTROL, TYPE TESTS.

U

uberrimae fidei. Latin term translating as 'in the utmost good faith'. Used in contracts such as insurance, where one party relies upon the other to disclose material facts.

ullage. Customs term, 'what a vessel wants of being full', i.e. gap above the top level of the liquid or other contents.

ultra vires. Action, etc. which is beyond the legal power or authority of a body such as a corporation, etc. or a person such as a purchasing officer, or for example a sales agent.

unascertained goods. *See* GOODS, UNASCERTAINED GOODS.

uncoupling effect of stock. *See* STOCK, UNCOUPLING EFFECT OF STOCK.

undertaking. Any industrial or commercial ENTERPRISE. The latter is the preferred term.

undue influence. An improper exercise of 'power' possessed by one party to a contract over the mind of the other party. *See* NEGOTIATION.

unenforceable contracts. *See* CONTRACT, UNENFORCEABLE CONTRACT.

Unfair Contract Terms Act 1977. Act imposing further limits on the extent to which civil liability for breach of contract, or for negligence or other breach of duty, can be avoided by means of contract terms and otherwise ñ essentially by means of exclusion clauses or notices. The Act only relates to exclusion of liability, not other forms of 'unfair' term.

Unfair Terms in Consumer Contracts Regulations 1999. Regulations which govern unfair terms in contracts concluded between a seller or supplier and a consumer. The regulations contain guidance on what is to be regarded as an unfair term based on the principle of good faith and the creation of an imbalance in the partiesí rights and obligations to the detriment of the consumer. An unfair term will not be binding on the consumer. The Regulations, unlike the Unfair Contract Terms Act, relate to 'unfair' terms in the wider sense.

Uniform Customs Practices. Standard rules for DOCUMENTARY LETTERS OF CREDIT developed by the INTERNATIONAL CHAMBER OF COMMERCE and adopted world-wide.

Uniform Laws on International Sales Act 1967. Act giving effect to the Hague Convention on Uniform Law on the International Sale of Goods (1964). Latter was intended to harmonize rules relating to formation of contract for sale of goods and general provisions which apply where parties belong to different Contracting States. Can be excluded expressly or by implication.

unit load. A quantity of goods grouped together to form a single unit of dimensions and physical characteristics that optimise the costs of handling and transport throughout the distribution cycle. Applies particularly to the THROUGH TRANSIT CONCEPT.

unit load device (ULD). Container or pallet designed to fit into the structure of an aircraft.

unit of issue. (BS) The smallest measure of an item of stock that may be issued from a store. Normally it is the same as the stock-keeping unit.

United Nations Numbers. *See* COMMODITY NUMBERS.

unitization. The planning of suitable quantities of goods to form unit loads for transport and/or handling, and/or storage, and/ or use in process or at WORKCENTRES.

units of account. *See* ACCOUNT, UNITS OF.

units of measurement. *See* MEASUREMENT.

universal product code (UPC). A code widely adopted for bar coding

unliquidated damages. *See* DAMAGES, UNLIQUIDATED DAMAGES.

update. To modify an existing file or record so as to bring its contents up to date.

upstream management. Management of suppliers and supplies of materials and services, including, where appropriate, supplier's suppliers and so on.

Uruguay round. The objectives of GATT have been pursued by a series of of extended discussions known as rounds. This round was concluded in 1993 and brought the World Trade Organization into existence.

usage (also off-take and sales). (BS) In the case of supplies the quantities actually used. May not be the same as DEMAND owing to rejects and other causes such as damage or loss.

usage rate. The rate of consumption of supplies e.g. stock, i.e. the quantity, or other measure, consumed (used) per unit time.

usance (time or term) draft. SITPRO. A draft (BILL OF EXCHANGE) which is payable at a fixed or determinable future date.

use-by date. Date marked on goods indicating the date beyond which they must not be used

utilization factor. (UF) Ratio of machine (or other plant and equipment running time) to: total machine or other plant and equipment available time.

Utilities Directive. (EU) The Directive which relates to the provision of such public services as water, gas, electricity and transport services. It came into force in 1994 and was subsequently updated by an amending directive in 1999.

utility, marginal utility. (CIMA) The amount of additional utility that can be gained by the addition of one unit of product.

V

valuable goods. *See* GOODS, VALUABLE GOODS.

valuation of stock. *See* STOCK, VALUATION OF.

value. (com) Intrinsic worth. It is determined by the lowest overall cost at which a satisfactory supply of goods or services can be reliably provided. *See also* ACCRETION.

value added tax (VAT). A multi-stage tax paid by each trader on the value which is added (*See* VALUE ADDED) to any goods or services. Thus tax liability is spread over every stage through which a product or service passes before it reaches the consumer. The tax at the final sale to the consumer represents the total collected.

value added. (CIMA) The increase in realisable value resulting from an alteration in form, location or availability of a product or service, excluding the cost of purchased materials and services. Note: unlike conversion cost, 'value added' includes profit.

value adding. Any activity which helps an organization towards its objectives in relation to its customers.

value analysis. (BS) A systematic inter-disciplinary examination of design and other factors affecting the cost of a product or service in order to devise a means of achieving the specified purpose most economically at the required standard of quality and reliability. (In the case of plant an assessment is required of the LIFE CYCLE and COSTS IN USE in relation to the purchase PRICE.)

value chain. The sequence of events through which a raw material is converted into a product for ultimate use or consumption. Value is added at various points in the sequence. *See* SUPPLY CHAIN.

value engineering. An activity involving the design of value into a product at the design stage. Supplies staff should be involved because there are many points to which supplies and materials management may contribute, *See also* VALUE ANALYSIS.

value for money. An attempt to maximize benefits from a purchase while minimizing amount expended. *See also* COST BENEFIT.

value-in-use. The worth of an asset in terms of objectives which can be expressed in cash terms. In addition, where practicable, value should take account of subjective attributes such as social or environmental aspects which may only be evaluated by COST BENEFIT ANALYSIS, estimates or WEIGHTINGS.

value, best. Introduced on a progressive basis from 1997 onwards as a tool for purchasing goods and services in local government. Implicit is the acknowledgement that value, not simply price, should be the key determinant in the purchasing process.

value, Brussels definition of. This specifies that customs duty be taken on the value of the goods which corresponds to the value in open market in the country of destination. This may be defined as 'FOB Port of Shipment' or 'CIF landed' at port of arrival.

value, cost. The cost of producing item.

value, esteem. The subjective value given to an item by reason of its own prestige or other characteristic which makes it more desirable than others when compared with them.

value, face. The value (price) stated or given in documents, price tags, etc. as distinct from other value measurements such as INTRINSIC VALUE, VALUE IN USE, etc. Where the face value is said to be a 'price reduction' the previous price from which the reduction was made should be shown. *See also* VALUE, MARKET VALUE, etc.

value, gross present. The present 'value' of the sum of the initial cost of a project or plant plus the interest foregone on the capital spent, during its expected LIFE CYCLE. Estimates of maintenance and repair costs, etc. may also be estimated. *See also* VIABILITY.

value, intrinsic. The value contained in the substance from which an article is produced as distinct from its stated value or price tag. *See* VALUE, FACE VALUE.

value, market. The sum that an asset would be sold for in a free, OPEN MARKET.

value, net present. (NPV). A very important concept in purchasing and supply when giving consideration to a major purchase or project. The NPV of a purchase or project is the difference between the net present cost of the purchase or project and all the future revenues from the purchase or project discounted back to the present time. Various allowances may be needed, such as the value of the purchase or project at the end of its useful life, or in the case of nuclear equipment the possible costs of decommissioning.

value, residual. Value of plant at the end of its useful life, and the value of an ITEM which has served its purpose (e.g. recovered solvent) but retains some value.

value, use or utility value. The value of the function performed or primary function.

value stream. *See* VALUE CHAIN.

value/volume ratio. The ratio of value of an item of supply in relation to its volume. Can be a useful measure and check on storage costs, and purchase price.

variable (n) (BS) Term used in quality control to indicate a characteristic which needs to be measured, e.g. dimension, volume etc. BS 4778 'A characteristic that is appraised in terms of values on a continuous scale'.

variable cost. *See* COST, VARIABLE.

variance. An expression of how ITEMS of a POPULATION vary from the MEAN of all the ITEMS in the POPULATION.

variance accounting. (CIMA) A technique whereby planned activities of an enterprise are qualified in budgets, STANDARD COSTS, standard selling prices, and standard profit margins and the difference between these and the actual results are accounted for.

variance analysis. (CIMA) An analysis of variances arising in a cost system and analysed into their constituent parts.

variation order. *See* ORDERS & CONTRACTS, VARIATION ORDER.

variety reduction. The process of reducing the number of types, sizes, grades, etc. of a product manufactured, purchased, or stocked. *See also* STANDARDIZATION.

vehicle scheduling. A plan whereby vehicles are allocated to specific tasks, generally on a timed basis and indicating the task on which each vehicle is deployed at a given time.

vendor. Strictly: a person who sells, particularly one who hawks his goods in public, but, term sometimes adopted in purchasing and supply for all who sell whether manufacturer or commercial undertakings, etc.

vendor appraisal. Assessment of a potential supplier's capability of controlling quality (delivery, quantity, price and all other factors to be embodied in a contract). Appraisal is carried out before placing orders.

vendor approved list. (BS) List of approved suppliers. May also include a blacklist of non-approved suppliers with any comments kept under strict security.

vendor base. The range of suppliers an organization maintains trading relations with. *See* SUPPLIER BASE.

vendor evaluation. ('Supplier evaluation'.) Assessment of a supplier's control of quality and other factors under consideration carried out prior to placing orders.

vendor rating. *See* SUPPLIER RATING.

vendor, approved. *See* SUPPLIER, APPROVED.

very narrow aisle. (VNA). A storehouse arrangement whereby specialised equipment operates in narrow gangways to maximize storage space.

viability. A viable idea, proposal, scheme, plan, etc. which is sound, workable and would be economic if translated into actuality. For a project, purchase or scheme to be viable the total of all outgoings through the lifecycle must not exceed present values at the time of purchase, etc. *See* NET PRESENT VALUE and CASH FLOW, DISCOUNTED CASH FLOW.

vice, inherent. Goods which by their nature are liable to deteriorate and/or cause damage to other goods with which they may come into contact are said to have 'inherent vice.' A carrier may not be liable for them if their nature makes them an exceptional risk unless this fact has been made known to him in advance.

Vienna Convention (1964). In 1964 two Conventions were adopted on the international sale of goods and the formation of international sale contracts. Both Conventions were adopted by HMG/UK wef August 1972.

vocabulary, stores. A list compiled of all the supplies contained under stock control in a storehouse and stockyard. The stores (or commodity) vocabulary should contain the unique name for each commodity with cross references from other names or nomenclatures, etc. *See* COMMODITY CATALOGUE and STORES CATALOGUE and CODING. *See* **BS 5729 Pt. 5 (0.4(b))**.

void. This term as applied to a contract refers to one that is 'destitute of all legal effect', and neither party can then enforce it.

voidable. When applied to a contract, it implies that although the contract is capable of being carried out it has some defect which would enable either party to stop its execution. *See also* ENFORCEABLE CONTRACTS.

volume cargo. Cargo which has low weight per unit volume and therefore occupies more cargo space than heavier goods.

Von Thunen's belts. A series of concentric rings around a city determining the appropriate location for various kinds of agricultural activity, taking transportation costs into account. Can also apply to location of stores and storage distribution points.

vote head. An identification of finance allocated within a budget for specific tasks and against which all financial transactions are recorded for control purposes. *See also* SUB HEAD.

voucher. (CIMA) A document serving as evidence for a claimed transaction which records for example a stores or financial transaction, and supports an accounting entry.

voyage charter. Under a voyage charter the charterer usually pays for an agreed rate per ton for a full and complete cargo. If the ship is not filled he pays for DEAD FREIGHT.

W

waiting time. (BS) The period of time for which an operator is available for production but is prevented from working by a shortage of material, or tooling, machine breakdown, etc. *See also* IDLE TIME *and* DOWN TIME.

warehouse. A place where goods (wares) are stored and on which storage charges will be imposed.

warehouse (or store), bonded. One in which dutiable goods are stored and upon which the warehouse (or stores) owner has entered into a bond with HM Customs. Goods are stored subject to the inspection and control of the excise officer until duties have been paid and the goods released.

warehouse stock. *See* STOCK, WAREHOUSE STOCK.

warehouse, automated. One in which the stacking, stowage and retrieval of supplies are effected by handling equipment programmed to transport, place and withdraw supplies automatically.

warranty in contract. An agreement with reference to goods which are the subject of a contract of sale, but collateral to the main purpose of the contract, the breach of which gives rise to a claim for damages but not the repudiation of the contract. Sale of Goods Act 1979. *See also* CONTRACT, CONDITIONS OF CONTRACT.

warranty period. The period (usually 12 months) following completion of work (e.g. construction) or COMMISSIONING (e.g. of plant) in a contract. During this time the contractor is responsible for the repair and rectification of any defects in the work. Also referred to as the 'guarantee period'.

See also RETENTION MONEY *and* MAINTENANCE PERIOD *and* TERMS AND CONDITIONS OF CONTRACT IPS.

warranty, implied. (law) A warranty which the purchaser may assume to apply to a contract without necessity for it to be written into the agreement. e.g. 'that the goods shall be suitable for use'.

Warsaw Convention (1929). The original Convention, which still applies in modified form, controlling the carriage of goods by air.

wastage, damage and loss. Contingencies which must be allowed for in provisioning and which may occur at various stages of the SUPPLIES CYCLE, viz. in transit, loading and unloading, in stores and at issue from stores, etc. Avoidance of wastage, damage and loss is a matter for MATERIALS MANAGEMENT but allowances may be needed in purchasing and stock levels to allow for these.

waste. (CIMA) 1. Discarded substances having no value, unreclaimable for SALVAGE or RECYCLING. 2. Rag, old clothing and similar materials provided for cleaning hands and machinery, etc. *See also* SCRAP and, ARISINGS. 2. Activities which add cost but not value.

waste management. The control of the generation and disposal of waste to meet economic and environmental constraints.

waste, controlled. *See* SUBSTANCES CONTROLLED.

waste, disposal of. Disposal of waste of CONTROLLED SUBSTANCES is covered by Section 33 of the Environmental Protection Act, 1990.

wasting assets. *See* ASSETS, WASTING ASSETS.

waybill. A document by railways, airlines and other hauliers on which is recorded the list of goods and articles which are being carried on that particular journey from point to point.

waybill, air waybill. (SITPRO) A form of waybill introduced by Warsaw Convention. It is used for air shipments instead of the normal BILL OF LADING used for sea transits. This is because the speed of transit shipment may have been completed before a normal bill of lading could be prepared. It is evidence of the contract between the shipper and the carrier. It serves as: 1. receipt of goods for shipment; 2. despatch note listing any special instructions by the shipper; 3. invoice evidencing freight charges; 4. insurance - if insurance certificate - if insured through the airline; 5. document for import, export, and transit requirements by Customs; 6. delivery receipt.

waybill, sea waybill. (SITPRO) A non-negotiable alternative to the bill of lading. It provides for delivery to a named consignee without presentation of the documents at destination. It thus helps to solve the problem caused by arrival of documents at the destination after the arrival of the goods. It is particularly useful when trading on open account or between multinational and associated companies or between long established trading partners. It can be used with documentary credits if the letter of credit specifically authorizes its acceptance.

Web. *See* WORLD WIDE WEB.

Web page. An image from the WORLD WIDE WEB that appears as a single continuous image on a computer display.

Web site. A series of linked WEB PAGES published by a single organization.

weight, dead weight. Heavy goods paying freight by weight.

weighting (W). A mathematical and statistical method for ascribing value to an item of data in proportion to its importance or 'weight' by the use of a WEIGHTING FACTOR. *See also* WEIGHTING, STATISTICAL WEIGHTING.

weighting factor (WF). (BS) A factor by which the results of statistical calculations can take account of the relative importance, frequency, etc. of events and data in the range of data being analysed, etc.

weighting, statistical. The technique of applying WEIGHTING FACTORS for presentation of statistical information. This weighting emphasises and reflects the importance of the various ITEMS in the data being studied, analysed or reported.

wharf. A bank or quay where vessels may tie up to be loaded or unloaded.

wharfage. The change made to vessel for using a wharf.

wharfinger. The person in charge of a wharf. He acts as bailee for the goods and is under the same discipline as a warehouseman for this purpose.

where-used-list. (prod) A list of all assemblies that use a particular part or assembly.

wholesaler. An enterprise which makes its profits through buying supplies in bulk at TRADE PRICES and sells and distributes them to retail, business and industrial enterprises on trade terms. Originally a wholesaler was so designed as a middleman who sold 'whole pieces' of materials and goods to retail customers via shop-keepers.

winding up, a business. The termination of trading by a business by its LIQUIDA-TION. 1. Compulsory liquidation as the result of a Court Order. 2. Voluntary liquidation by: (i) an ordinary resolution because it has achieved its objectives; (ii) a special resolution for other reasons; (iii) an extraordinary resolution if it cannot continue trading by reason of its liabilities.

WIP. *See* WORK IN PROGRESS.

without engagement. A phrase intended by a supplier as an EXCLUSION CLAUSE by which he may escape commitments implied in his offer or other document. (Should be resisted when negotiating any contract).

without prejudice. (law) A term used in correspondence or in making offers which renders such correspondence (or offers) incapable of being used as evidence and thus devoid of all legal force.

without recourse. A term used on bills of exchange, coupons, warrants etc when they are sold to a third party. The buyers have no recourse whatever upon the seller should the documents not be honoured when they are due.

work cycle. *See* PRODUCTION: WORK CYCLE.

work in progress (work in process). Stock (or other supplies) upon which work has been performed or which has been made ready for work to be started, but which is not available to differentiate between 'shop' WIP and sub-contract WIP, etc. *See* CURRENT ASSETS.

work measurement. (BS) The application of techniques designed to establish the time for a qualified worker to carry out a specified task/job at a defined level of performance.

work measurement. (BS) Defines the objectives and establishes procedures for work measurement. Outlines the benefits to be gained by the use of work measurement in the field of operations management.

work requisition. (BS) A document requesting work to be carried out.

work specification. (BS) A document describing the way in which work is to be carried out. It may define the materials, tools, time, standards.

work station. (BS) the smallest set of resources or the purpose of planning and control that form a productive unit at a particular location.

work study. (BS) A management service based on those techniques (particularly METHOD STUDY and WORK MEASUREMENT) which are used in the examination of human work in all its contexts, and which lead to the systematic investigation of all the resources and factors which affect the efficiency and economy of the situation being reviewed, in order to affect improvement. *See* BS 3138 for glossary of terms used in work study and organization and method. *See also* BS 3375. BS 3138: 1979 Glossary of terms used in work study and organization methods (0 & M), defining terms and symbols, with sections on organization study, method study, work measurement and work performance control. Diagram to illustrate the problem solving techniques used in work study. Examples of the construction of standard time for operator and machine controlled work. *See also* BS 3375.

Workplace Directive. Regulation which requires employers and others in control of workplaces to comply with health and safety requirements including welfare. These include:

maintenance of equipment and devices, ventilation, temperature, lighting, cleanliness, space, workstations, falling objects, glazing, windows, seating, traffic routes, doors and gates, sanitary conveniences, drinking water, accommodation for clothing, washing facilities, eating and rest arrangements in facilities for non-smokers.

works order. (BS) A written instruction detailing work to be carried out.

works order. (prod) *See* ORDER, PRODUCTION.

works, clerk of. *See* CLERK OF WORKS.

World Trade Organisation (WTO). The legal and institutional foundation for the liberalization of world trade. Set up in 1994 during the Uruguay round (the final round) of GATT, which the WTO succeeded.

World Wide Web. Often referred to as the WEB. A graphical information retrieval system that operates on the INTERNET.

writ. (law) A legal document by which the person named is summoned to attend a certain place at a time stated at a written instruction from a law court or other legal authority, or alternatively to perform some act (or to abstain from doing something) in accordance with the terms contained in the writ.

write down. (fin) Authorized financial adjustment to reduce the value of stock or plant as a result of obsolescence or/partial deterioration.

write off. Authorized financial adjustment to support the removal of an item of stock or plant from the financial accounts as a result of loss, damage or deterioration.

written communications. *See* COMMUNICATIONS, WRITTEN.

Z

z chart, *See* OGIVE.

ACRONYMS

This list of acronyms includes those that the authors believe will be most frequently encountered by the purchasing and supply student or practitioner.

A complete list of business acronyms has not been attempted; for those unable to find what they are seeking here, the authors commend the *Penguin Dictionary of Acronyms,* and the *Glossary of Computing Terms* (BCS). There are, of course, other publications on the subject.

Where the acronym and its associated expansion appear in bold type, further clarification can be found in the main body of the dictionary.

Our inclusion of an acronym should not be taken to indicate approval by the authors or the Chartered Institute of Purchasing and Supply. Indeed some of the expressions, such as 'ASAP' are best avoided. Nevertheless, such terms are in use, hence their inclusion.

Users of this book are invited to submit for consideration acronyms that they feel should be added, together with an authoritative definition to the authors c/o the publisher.

ABC	Activity Based Costing
AGV	Automatically Guided Vehicle
ANSI	American National Standards Institution
APICS	American Production and Inventory Control Society
APR	Annual Percentage Rate
AQL	**Acceptable Quality Level**
ASAP	As Soon As Possible
ASEAN	Association of South East Asian Nations
AUPO	Association of University Purchasing Officers
AVCO	Average Costing
BD	Brought Down
B/D	Bank, or Banker's Draft
B/L	**Bill of Lading**
B2B	Business to business (E Commerce
B2C	Business to consumer (E Commerce)
BACS	Bankers Automated Clearing System
BCS	British Computer Society
BEAMA	British Electrical and Allied Manufacturers Association
BiE	Business in the Environment
BIS	Bank for International Settlements
BOM	**Bill of Materials**
BPIC	British Production and Inventory Control Society
BSA	Business Software Association
BTN	**Brussels Tariff Nomenclature**
CAD	**Computer-Aided Design**
CADR	Centre for Alternative Dispute Resolution
CAE	Computer Aided Engineering
CAM	Computer-Aided Manufacture
CAP	Common Agricultural Policy
CAPS	Center for Advanced Purchasing Studies
CBI	Confederation of British Industry
CCT	**Compulsory Competitive Tendering**
CCTA	Central Computer and Telecoms Agency

CD ROM	**Compact Disk Read Only Memory**
CDRW	**Compact Disk ReWritable**
CEN	European Committee on Standardization
CET	Common External Tariff
CFR	**Cost and Freight (Incoterm)**
CF	Carried Forward
CHAPS	Clearing House Automated Payments System
CIF	**Cost, Insurance and Freight (Incoterm)**
CIM	Computer-Integrated Manufacture
CIP	**Carriage and Insurance Paid (Incoterm)**
CIMA	**Chartered Institute of Management Accountants**
CIPFA	Chartered Institute of Public Finance and Accountancy
CIPS	**The Chartered Institute of Purchasing and Supply**
CKD	Completely Knocked Down
CLAN	Centre Led Action Network
C/O	Care Of
COD	Cash On Delivery
COSHH	**Control of Substances Hazardous to Health**
COSLA	Convention of Scottish Local Authorities
CPA	**Contract Price Adjustment**
CPA	**Critical Path Analysis**
CPC	Central Product Classification
CPT	**Carriage Paid To (Incoterm)**
CRINE	Cost Reduction in the New Era
CRM	Customer Relationship Management
CSSA	Computing Services and Software Association
CTO	Combined Transport Operations
CUP	Central Unit on Purchasing (now OGC)
CVCP	Committee of Vice-Chancellors and Principals
CWO	**Cash With Order**
DAF	**Delivered at Frontier (Incoterm)**
DCA	**Differential Cost Analysis**
DDP	**Delivered Duty Paid (Incoterm)**
DDU	**Delivered Duty Unpaid (Incoterm)**
DEQ	**Delivered Ex Quay (Incoterm)**
DES	**Delivered Ex Ship (Incoterm)**
CXT	Common Ext. Tariff
DETR	Department of the Environment Transport and the Regions
DOC	Department of Commerce (US)
DPA	Defence Procurement Agency
DRP	**Distribution Resource Planning**
DTI	Department of Trade and Industry
E	Electronic (as in E-Commerce)
E and OE	Errors and Omissions Excepted
EAN	European Article Numbering
ECB	**European Central Bank**
ECOWAS	Economic Community of West African States
ECR	Efficient Customer Response
ECU	**European Currency Unit**
EDI	**Electronic Data Interchange**
EEMA	European Electronic Messaging Assn
EFT	**Electronic Funds Transfer**
EFTA	European Free Trade Association
EMF	**European Monetary Fund**

EMU	Economic and Monetary Union
EPA	Environmental Protection Agency
EPOS	**Electronic Point of Sale**
EXW	**Ex Works (Incoterm)**
ERM	**Exchange Rate Mechanism**
ERP	**Enterprise Resource Planning**
ESI	**Early Supplier Involvement**
ESPO	Eastern Shires Purchasing Organization
ETA	Estimated Time of Arrival
ETD	Estimated Time of Departure
EURIM	European Informatics Market
FAS	**Free Alongside Ship (Incoterm)**
FAST	Federation Against Software Theft
FCA	**Free Carrier (Incoterm)**
FIFO	First In, First Out
FLT	Fork-Lift Truck
FMEA	**Failure Mode and Effect Analysis**
FMS	**Flexible Manufacturing System**
FMS	Flexible Manufacturing System
FOB	**Free On Board (Incoterm)**
FOC	Free of Charge
FOREX	Foreign Exchange
FT	**Freight Tonne**
FTP	File Transfer Protocol
GATT	**General Agreement on Tariffs and Trade**
GDP	**Gross Domestic Product**
GM	Genetically Modified
GNP	Gross National Product
GRN	**Goods Received Note**
GRT	**Gross Registered Tonnage**
HAS	Healthcare Supplies Association :
HASWA	**Health and Safety at Work Act**
HAZCHEM	Hazardous Chemicals
HRM	Human Resources Management
HSE	Health and Safety Executive
HTML	Hypertext Mark up Language
HTTP	Hypertext Transfer Protocol
IBC	**Intermediate Bulk Containers**
ICC	International Chamber of Commerce
ICE	Institution of Civil Engineers
ICM	Institute of Credit Management
IdeA	Improvement and Development Association
ILO	International Labour Organization
ILT	Institute of Logistics and Transport
IMF	International Monetary Fund
INCOTERM	International Chamber of Commerce Team
IMF	International Monetary Fund
IOD	Institute of Directors
IOM	Institute of Management
loTL	Institute of Transport and Logistics
IPR	Intellectual Property Rights
IPSERA	International Purchasing and Supply Education Research Association
ISDN	Integrated Services Digital Network
ISO	**International Standards Organization**

ITT	Invitation to Tender
JPPSG	Joint Procurement Policy and Strategy Group
KM	Knowledge Management
KPI	Key Performance Indicators
KWh	Kilowatt Hours
LAFTA	Latin American Free Trade Association
LGN	Local Government Network
LIFO	Last In First Out
LME	London Metal Exchange
LRMC	Long Run Marginal Costs
MEAT	Most Economically Advantageous Tender
MFN	Most Favoured Nation
MIS	Management Information System
MMC	**Monopolies and Mergers Commission**
MNC	Multinational Corporation
MRO	**Maintenance Repair and Operating**
MRP	**Materials Requirements Planning**
MRPII	**Manufacturing Resource Planning**
NACCB	National Accreditation Council for Certification Bodies
NAFTA	North American Free Trade Association
NAICS	North American Industrial Classification System
NAICS	North American Industry Classification System
NAPM	National Association of Purchasing Management
NCC	National Computing Centre
NEC	National Exhibition Centre
NEC	Not Elsewhere Classified
NETA	New Electricity Trading Agreement
NHMC	National Materials Handling Centre
NIGP	National Institute of Governmental Purchasing
NOS	Not Otherwise Specified
NPV	**Net Present Value**
NRT	**Net Registered Tonnage**
NSV	National Supply Vocabulary
NTB	**Non-Tariff Barrier**
NYMEX	New York Mercantile Exchange
NYSE	New York Stock Exchange
O&M	**Organization and Method**
OECD	Organization for Economic Cooperation and Development
OEM	Original Equipment Manufacture
OFGEM	Office of Gas and Electricity markets (incorporated OFFER and OFGAS)
OFT	**Office of Fair Trading**
OFTEL	Office of Telecommunications
OFWAT	Office of Water Services
OGC	**Office of Government Commerce**
OJEC	**Official Journal of the European Communities**
OPEC	**Organization of the Petroleum Exporting Countries**
OPT	**Optimized Production Technology**
OR	**Operational, or Operations Reasearch**
ORM	Operating Resource Management
OSI	Open Systems Integration
PERT	**Programme Evaluation and Review Technique**
PFI	**Private Finance Initiative**
PIN	**Prior Indicative Notice**

PPM	Parts Per Million
PPP	Public/Private partnerships
QFD	Quality Function Deployment
R and D	Research and Development
RAT	Reverse Auction Tendering
REC	Regional Electricity Company
RFQ	Request for Quotation
ROCE	**Return on Capital Employed**
ROI	Return on Investment
ROM	Read Only Memory
RORO	**Roll On, Roll Off**
SAE	Society of Automotive Engineers
ROSPA	Royal Society for the Prevention of Accidents
SCM	Supply Chain Management
SCRIA	Supply Chain Relationships in Aerospace
SDR	Special Drawing Rights
SET	Secure Electronic Transactions
SIC	Standard Industrial Classification
SIMAP	Systeme d'Information pour les Marches Publics
SITC	Standard International Tariff Classification
SITPRO	**Simplification of Trade Procedures**
SKU	Stock-Keeping Unit
SLA	**Service Level Agreement**
SME	Small/Medium-sized Enterprise
SOLACE	Society of Local Authority Chief Executives
SOPO	Society of Purchasing Officers in Local Government
SPC	Statistical Process Control
SWL	**Safe Working Load**
TARIC	Integrated Tariff System
TDC	**Total Distribution Cost**
TED	Tenders Electronic Daily
TIF	Transport Internationaux par Chemin de Fer
TIR	Transports Internationaux par Route
TM	Trade Mark
TUPE	**Transfer of Undertaking (Protection of Employment)**
TQM	Total Quality Management
ULW	**Unladen Weight**
UPC	Universal Product Code
USC	United States Code
VAN	Value Added Network
VAT	**Value Added Tax**
VDU	Visual Display Unit
VNA	**Very Narrow Aisle**
VRA	Voluntary Restraint Agreement
WAP	Wireless Application Protocol
WEEE	Waste Electrical and Electronic Equipment
WIP	**Work in Progress**
WIPO	World Intellectual Property Organization
WTO	**World Trade Organization**
WWW	World Wide Web
XML	Extensible Markup Language
YPO	Yorkshire Purchasing Organisation